OHIO

By Christopher Walsh

"Keep cool baby, and run those
fat tackles to death."
—WOODY HAYES

TRIUMPH
BOOKS

Table of Contents

Introduction

In 1968, Ohio State was in the midst of a 50–14 rout of rival Michigan, when Woody Hayes decided to go for a completely unnecessary two-point conversion. The play failed, so naturally reporters asked him why he went for two after the game.

"Because they wouldn't let me go for three!" he responded.

Yeah, there's no love lost between the two football powers, especially on the Ohio State side. With Michigan dominating both the series and the conference for years, Columbus was known for a stretch as "the graveyard for coaches," with 18 of them coming and going during a 60-year span.

Of course, those days are long gone, but not forgotten. There are still urinals throughout Columbus with a blue "M" painted on them, and some people still won't mention Michigan by name, rather as "that school up north."

Have you heard the story about the time Hayes supposedly threatened to push his car across the state border rather than buy gasoline in Michigan?

"They brainwash you into hating those suckers, and then you really believe it," Ohio State linebacker Steve Tovar once said, and he never even played for Hayes.

For example, in 1974 Hayes was among those to greet President Gerald Ford, a former Michigan lineman, at the Columbus airport. In the next day's newspaper the photo caption was: "Woody Hayes and Friend."

However, there's no truth to the rumor that football caused the 1835–36 border dispute known as the Toledo War because otherwise it almost certainly wouldn't have been bloodless. The football rivalry actually didn't begin until 1897.

It also took something extreme like the Snow Bowl in 1950 for Hayes to get involved.

With Columbus in the midst of a blizzard, Ohio State was given the option of canceling the Michigan game, which would have given the Buckeyes the Big Ten title by default and a trip to the Rose Bowl, but refused. The teams combined for 45 punts, sometimes even on first down. Without recording a single first down, the Wolverines scored on two blocked punts for a 9–3 victory to win the game and conference title. Coach Wes Fesler subsequently resigned, leading to Hayes being hired.

With Hayes winning 12 of the next 18 contests, Michigan countered by hiring his former assisant, Bo Schembechler. Thus began the unbelievably intense "Ten-Year War" between the programs.

It took until 2006 for the teams to meet undefeated and ranked No. 1 and 2, and it occurred the day after Schembechler died. With Troy Smith completing 71 percent of his passes for 316 yards and four touchdowns, Ohio State pulled out a dramatic 42–39 victory and the quarterback essentially locked up the Heisman Trophy.

That, more than anything, is what the rivarly is all about. Since 1935, Ohio State and Michigan have decided the Big Ten title between themselves on 23 different occasions, and have affected the determination of the conference title an additional 24 times.

But it took Hayes to make the rivarly what it is today. ■

SEASON PREVIEW

Perception can be a funny thing in college football, which Ohio State knows as well as any other program in the country.

Take the 2008 Buckeyes, for example. Ohio State crushed Michigan, managed to claim a share of the Big Ten title, and went to a Bowl Championship Series game for the fourth straight year.

But was the season considered a major success? Um, well…

It was. However, the program's consistency has put it on such an exceptional level that its postseason losses have caused both it and the conference to be labeled as "overachievers" of late. In the eyes of the football world, Ohio State has yet to recover from its 41–14 pounding by Florida for the 2006 national championship, and has essentially lost all subsequent showcase meetings, including the 2007 title game against LSU, 38–24.

Was the 2002 national championship, decided in overtime against Miami, really that long ago? How about the Fiesta Bowl victory against Notre Dame at the end of the 2005 season?

"We won one and we lost one badly," cornerback Malcolm Jenkins said before last season's Fiesta Bowl against Texas. "This would be a nice way to redeem ourselves."

He added: "It's a win-win situation for us. If we lose, everyone probably thinks we're going to lose anyway. If we win, it'll show we've made some strides since our last loss." Of course, the Buckeyes didn't win.

Ohio State's fifth trip to Phoenix for a bowl game in seven years only contributed to the image problem, thanks to the 24–21 defeat. It was the Buckeyes' third major disappointment of the season, joining the narrow 13–6 loss to Penn State and the 35–3 pounding to then-No. 1 Southern California—Ohio State's worst showing since 1994.

To some fans, not even the crushing 42–7 victory against the rival Wolverines was enough because it was expected. In Rich Rodriguez's first year at Michigan, the winning streak grew to five, and it had never been so easy.

"Coach Jim Tressel always preaches that every yard versus Michigan is worth two yards," running back Chris "Beanie" Wells said after the win. "It is an honor and blessing to be a part of a team that has made history. It is an unreal feeling and amazing to be a part of something so great."

But Jenkins and Wells are both gone, and those remaining are left to struggle with perception and image, in addition to all the opposing players and coaches who will be trying to stop them.

In 2009, Ohio State will again have an early test against potential Rose Bowl opponent Southern California, and many expect the Big Ten title to be decided against Penn State. If so, the Buckeyes figure to be in the national title picture again even if they lose, though critics will again wonder if Ohio State can finally get over the hump.

That's the perception. The reality is that in many ways it's a terrific problem to have and only comes with being at the top.

Offense

Offense

While most of the buzz surrounding Ohio State's game against Troy in 2008 dealt with true freshman Terrelle Pryor making his first start at quarterback, few noticed that the person lined up in front of him was also making his starting debut as well.

"At first I was a little nervous, but after the first couple plays you realize that you're playing football and it's what you do every day in practice," freshman center Mike Brewster said. "It's a learning experience and I'm getting better.

"To play center as a freshman is hard. I'm still learning a lot, but it's good to have Jim Cordle next to me. I really appreciate him being there. It's great anytime you have a veteran to learn from."

Cordle called Brewster's performance that day "solid," and both figure to be leaned upon heavily this season, along with right tackle Bryant Browning. They're the only returning starting linemen playing on a unit that's coming off an inconsistent season.

With coaches making the decision that they could no longer afford not to have Pryor as a pivotal contributor to the offense, the playing time came at the expense of Todd Boeckman, who the year before had led the Buckeyes to both the Big Ten champion-ship and national title game appearance.

Although Pryor set a school freshman record with four touchdown passes against Troy, coaches essentially tore the playbook up and went with a run-first offense to try to keep the turnovers and mistakes to a minimum. Even with running back Chris "Beanie" Wells missing three games due to a foot injury, he still reached 1,000 rushing yards.

"It felt really comfortable," Pryor said after defeating Minnesota. "Coming into the game, we really wanted to take it down the field on the first drive and were really happy to do that. I want to keep it going and I know I have to keep proving myself.

"Coach (Jim) Tressel is a smart coach because he kept putting fresh players in. It will help everyone gain experience, especially playing in a Big Ten game. Tressel knows what he is doing."

Pryor grew more confident with each start, and Ohio State scored at least 30 points in four of its last five regular-season games, including three with more than 42.

Those are the kinds of numbers Ohio State fans may want to get more familiar with, although a lot of the offensive success will depend on the revamped offensive line. Mike Adams and J.B. Shugarts are both coming off injury-plagued freshman seasons, and Michigan transfer Justin Boren should be ready to contribute.

Another key will be finding more playmakers to help Pryor (who actually made a start at wide receiver)—like DeVier Posey and Lamaar Thomas—in addition to finding a new starting running back.

Defense

Defense

If there's been one staple to Ohio State football for the past decade or so, it's how the Buckeyes play defense.

Defensive coordinator Jim Heacock, who has been with the program since 1996, likes to have four defensive tackles to rotate, and defensive ends who can slide over into the heart of the line for obvious passing situations.

The unit's philosophy is to usually play a soft zone, focus on the run, and not give up big plays. Ideally, the Buckeyes keep everything in front of them, with the linebackers and defensive backs cleaning everything up and making a ton of tackles.

In 2008, opponents completed more than 55 percent of their passes, which was fine with Ohio State because the longest pass play yielded during the regular season was 49 yards and opponents averaged less than 10 yards per completion. Consequently, no opponent scored more than 21 points.

It's also why two years ago, when Heacock's unit kept opponents from reching a first down on nearly half of their possessions, he was presented with the Broyles Award as the nation's top assistant coach.

"I read and hear a lot about our inside guys and not getting many (sacks), but if you look over the years, inside guys aren't going to get as many as outside guys. That's a fact. Whether we want to believe it or not, that's the truth," Heacock told cleveland.

Season Preview

com last year. "For these guys, because they heard so much negativity about their sack production, you can look back over the years and look back at the Ryan Picketts of the world, how many sacks did he have when he played? (He had eight in 37 career games.) And he was a first-round draft choice. And you go on and on.

"In our defensive scheme, we really try to control the line of scrimmage and let our linebackers run. We ask our defensive line to do a good job of keeping people off the linebackers and let them run, and that's what we've been good at. Sometimes that doesn't equate to a great pass rush."

Although the defense lost Lott Trophy winner James Laurinaitis and Thorpe Award winner Malcolm Jenkins, the unit as a whole should be a typical Ohio State defense, which is a compliment. Overall, the returning players made 93 starts last season.

Austin Spitler has been the backup at middle linebacker for three years and will be joined by players like Ross Homan, Brian Rolle, and Etienne Sabino. Although depth will be a concern in the secondary, Chimdi Chekwa looks ready to step in for Jenkins.

On the line, end Thaddeus Gibson will be one to watch, Lawrence Wilson will be coming off knee surgery after starting seven games in 2008, and Nathan Williams had a strong showing in the Fiesta Bowl after being arrested for shoplifting during Christmas break.

Player to Watch: Terrelle Pryor

It's hard to say which was more impressive: the debut as a starter or the Big Ten coming-out party.

The debut was at home against Troy when, coming off a demoralizing loss at No. 1 Southern California, freshman quarterback Terrelle Pryor gave Ohio State fans something to be really excited about. He set a new freshman record with four touchdown passes, and wowed them with his long strides in tallying 66 rushing yards on 14 carries.

"I thought I messed up a lot," Pryor said about his performance. "When we sit down in the film room, I'm going to get yelled at but that's a good thing. We all need to keep improving going into the Big Ten schedule."

Two weeks later, Pryor led two fourth-quarter scoring drives to snap Wisconsin's 16-game home winning streak.

"All the hype, and all the people saying, 'you're great' this is the time to show it," said Pryor, who completed 13 of 19 passes for 144 yards and also ran an option-keeper 11 yards for the crucial touchdown with 1:08 remaining.

"I told him, 'It's a man's world right now,' and he's taking a step into manhood right now," running back Chris "Beanie" Wells said. "He said he was ready."

Michigan found out the hard way too, when the most highly sought-after prospect in the recruiting class of 2008—who selected the Buckeyes over the

Terrelle Pryor showed tantalizing glimpses of greatness as a freshman. The sky's the limit heading into his sophomore year after he earned valuable playing experience in 2008.

Wolverines and others—didn't do much statistically but had two touchdown passes to help lead a 42–7 rout.

"We tried to make sure he didn't leave the pocket," Michigan senior defensive end Tim Jamison said. "Of course he's a great athlete, but he makes big plays when he gets out of the pocket."

Said Pryor, "It made me think about my very first game here at Ohio State. I was so hyped up for that game and even more for this one. We all expect to be perfect and to make big plays against this team."

But there were some bumps in the road as well.

Against Troy the Buckeyes were actually outgained 315 to 309.

Against Penn State, Navorro Bowman recovered Pryor's fumble at the Ohio State 38, leading to the game's only touchdown. Pryor led the Buckeyes into Nittany Lions territory in the final minute, only to see his last pass into the end zone intercepted by Lydell Sargeant.

He also completed just five passes in the Fiesta Bowl, a 24–21 loss to Texas.

But coaches had Pryor focus on limiting his mistakes, and in 165 pass attempts he had just four interceptions.

The rookie finished the season with 1,311 passing yards and 12 touchdowns, and ran for 853 yards and six touchdowns, which had his own coaches gushing and the opposition deeply concerned about the next couple of years.

"He will be a guy that's in a Heisman race, and it may be sooner than we think because he is a leader," Texas coach Mack Brown said. ■

As a threat to pass and run, Terrelle Pryor inadvertently strikes a pose strangely familiar to a certain trophy given to the best player in college football.

After a nice recruiting class, Jim Tressel and the Buckeyes should be reloaded and ready to roll through 2009.

2009 National Signing Day Class

C.J. Barnett, DB, 6-0, 180, Dayton, Ohio/Northmont

Dorian Bell, LB, 6-1, 220, Monroeville, Penn./Gateway

Adam Bellamy, DT, 6-4, 280, Aurora, Ohio/Aurora

Jaamal Berry, RB, 5-11, 195, Pinecrest, Fla./Miami Palmetto

Zach Boren, LB, 6-1, 255, Pickerington, Ohio/Pickerington Central

Corey Brown, DB/WR, 6-1, 185, Monroeville, Penn./Gateway

Duron Carter, WR, 6-2, 190, Fort Lauderdale, Fla./St. Thomas Aquinas

Dominic Clarke, DB, 5-11, 180, Frederick, Md./Tuscarora

Melvin Fellows, DE, 6-5, 235, Garfield Heights, Ohio/Garfield Heights

Chris Fields, WR, 6-1, 185, Painesville, Ohio/Painesville Harvey

Reid Fragel, TE, 6-7, 260, Grosse Pointe Farms, Mich./Grosse Pointe South

Kenny Guiton, QB, 6-3, 180, Houston, Texas/Eisenhowser

Jordan Hall, RB, 5-10, 190, Jeannette, Penn./Jeannette

Marcus Hall, OL, 6-5, 300, Cleveland, Ohio/Glenville

Adam Homan, RB/LB, 6-4, 235, Coldwater, Ohio/Coldwater

Carlos Hyde, RB, 6-1, 230, Naples, Fla./Naples

James Jackson, WR, 5-11, 175, Grand Ledge, Mich./ Grand Ledge

Storm Klein, LB, 6-3, 225, Newark, Ohio/Licking Valley

Corey Linsley, OL, 6-4, 275, Youngstown, Ohio/Boardman

Sam Longo, OL, 6-6, 280, Spring Valley, Ohio/Bellbrook

Jack Mewhort, OL, 6-7, 290, Toledo, Ohio/St. John's

Jonathan Newsome, DE, 6-3, 290, Cleveland, Ohio/Glenville

John Simon, DT, 6-3, 265, Youngstown, Ohio/Cardinal Mooney

Jordan Whiting, LB, 6-1, 235, Louisville, Ky./Trinity

Jamie Wood, DB, 6-2, 190, Pickerington, Ohio/Pickerington Central

The Ohio State University

Location: Columbus, Ohio

Founded: 1870

Enrollment: 53,715 (Columbus campus, 40,212 undergrads), 61,568 (all campuses)

Nickname: Buckeyes

Colors: Scarlet and gray

Mascot: Brutus Buckeye

Stadium: Ohio Stadium (101, 568)

Tickets: 1-800-GO BUCKS

Website: http://www.ohiostatebuckeyes.com

National Championships (6): 1942, 1954, 1957, 1961, 1968, 2002

The "Other" Title: The Official NCAA Football Records Book also recognizes Ohio State as producing a national championship in 1970.

Big Ten Championships (33): 1916, 1917, 1920, 1935, 1939, 1942, 1944, 1949, 1954, 1955, 1957, 1961, 1968, 1969, 1970, 1972, 1973, 1974, 1975, 1976, 1977, 1979, 1981, 1986, 1993, 1994, 1996, 1998, 2002, 2005, 2006, 2007, 2008

Bowl Appearances: 40 (18–22)

First Season: 1890

O

2008 SEASON REVIEW

Brian Hartline, one of the stars of 2008's Big Ten champions, caps off a memorable regular season with this fourth-quarter touchdown against Michigan. The Wolverines were hapless all year, never more so than in the 42-7 drubbing laid on them by the Buckeyes.

2008 Season Review
10–3, Big Ten champions (tied)

Aug. 30	Youngstown State	Columbus	W	43–0
Sept. 6	Ohio	Columbus	W	26–14
Sept. 13	at Southern California	Los Angeles	L	35–3
Sept. 20	Troy	Columbus	W	28–10
Sept. 27	Minnesota	Columbus	W	34–21
Oct. 4	at Wisconsin	Madison	W	20–17
Oct. 11	Purdue	Columbus	W	16–3
Oct. 18	at Michigan State	East Lansing	W	45–7
Oct. 25	Penn State	Columbus	L	13–6
Nov. 8	at Northwestern	Evanston	W	45–10
Nov. 15	at Illinois	Champaign	W	30–20
Nov. 22	Michigan	Columbus	W	42–7
Jan. 5	Texas	Fiesta Bowl	L	24–21

Coach: Jim Tressel 359–181

Captains: James Laurinaitis, Malcolm Jenkins, Todd Boeckman, Brian Robiskie.

Ranking (AP): Preseason No. 2; Postseason No. 11.

All-American: James Laurinaitis, LB; Malcolm Jenkins, CB.

All-Big Ten: Alex Boone, T; James Laurinaitis, LB; Malcolm Jenkins, CB.

Leaders: Rushing—Chris Wells (1,197 yards, 207 carries); Passing—Terrelle Pryor (100 of 165 for 1,311 yards); Receiving—Brian Robiskie (42 catches, 535 yards).

Linebacker James Laurinaitis was Big Ten defensive player of the year, and Terrelle Pryor was the conference freshman of the year. ... Pryor, considered the nation's top recruit, picked Ohio State over Michigan and others. The 6-foot-6 quarterback became the first true freshman to start for the Buckeyes since Art Schlichter in 1978 and had four touchdown passes against Troy. ... Running back Chris "Beanie" Wells had 134 rushing yards, including a 59-yard touchdown, in Ohio State's fifth-straight victory against rival Michigan, resulting in the series' most lopsided score since 1968. ... Penn State won in Columbus for the first time since joining the Big Ten (0–7). ... The loss to No. 1 Southern California was Ohio State's worst defeat since 1994 and its worst non-conference loss since 1989, also to the Trojans.

Game 1: No. 2 Ohio State 43, Youngstown State 0

COLUMBUS | Despite losing running back Chris "Beanie" Wells in the third quarter to a foot injury, Ohio State cruised to its 30th consecutive season opening victory.

Coming off a sophomore season in which he rushed for 1,609 yards and 15 touchdowns, Wells was thought to be a serious challenger for the Heisman Trophy, especially playing on a team with 18 returning starters.

True freshman quarterback Terrelle Pryor rushed for 52 yards in his debut, including an 18-yard touchdown.

Ryan Pretorius, the 29-year-old senior from South Africa, kicked four field goals and Aaron Pettrey later kicked a 54-yard field goal, the fourth longest at 86-year-old Ohio Stadium.

	1st Qtr	2nd Qtr	3rd Qtr	4th Qtr	Final
YOUNGSTOWN ST	0	0	0	0	**0**
OHIO ST (2)	13	13	7	10	**43**

SCORING PLAYS

OHIO ST–TD, C Wells 44 YD RUN (R Pretorius KICK) 2:54 1st Qtr

OHIO ST–FG, R Pretorius 28 YD 7:06 1st Qtr

OHIO ST–FG, R Pretorius 32 YD 14:52 1st Qtr

OHIO ST–FG, R Pretorius 26 YD 2:09 2nd Qtr

OHIO ST–FG, R Pretorius 51 YD 9:44 2nd Qtr

OHIO ST–TD, B Robiskie 32 YD PASS FROM T Boeckman (R Pretorius KICK) 13:44 2nd Qtr

OHIO ST–TD, D Posey 26 YD PASS FROM T Boeckman (R Pretorius KICK) 12:59 3rd Qtr

OHIO ST–TD, T Pryor 19 YD RUN (R Pretorius KICK)
2:12 4th Qtr

OHIO ST–FG, A Pettrey 54 YD 9:52 4th Qtr

GAME STATISTICS

	YOUNGSTOWN ST	OHIO ST (2)
First Downs	5	24
Yards Rushing	-11	251
Yards Passing	85	244
Sacks – Yards Lost	1–8	2–24
Passing Efficiency	12–18–0	21–31–0
Punts	9–42.7	0–0
Fumbles–Lost	1–1	1–1
Penalties–Yards	3–15	6–48
Time of Possession	23:54	36:06

INDIVIDUAL STATISTICS – RUSHING
YOUNGSTOWN ST–Dana Brown 5–11, Jabari Scott 5–4, Kamryn Keys 2–0, Brandon Summers 4–MINUS 1, Ferlando Williams 3–MINUS 2, Da'Michael Horne 1–MINUS 5, Todd Rowan 1–MINUS 18. OHIO ST–Chris Wells 13–111, Terrelle Pryor 9–52, Maurice Wells 5–32, Brandon Saine 5–20, Daniel Herron 5–17, Todd Boeckman 4–10, Joe Bauserman 2–9.

INDIVIDUAL STATISTICS – PASSING
YOUNGSTOWN ST–Todd Rowan 8–13–46– 0, Brandon Summers 3–4–24– 0, Paul Corsaro 1–1–15– 0. OHIO ST–Todd Boeckman 14–19–187– 0. Terrelle Pryor 4–6–35– 0. Joe Bauserman 3–6–22– 0.

INDIVIDUAL STATISTICS – RECEIVING
YOUNGSTOWN ST–Dominique Barnes 3–33, Ferlando Williams 2–16, Donald Jones 1–15, Derrick Bush 2–9, Dana Brown 1–7, Patrick Bellish 1–3, Aaron Pitts 2–2. OHIO ST–Brian Hartline 2–59, DeVier Posey 4–47, Brian Robiskie 3–41, Ray Small 3–35, Rory Nicol 1–14, Maurice Wells 1–10, Chris Wells 3–10, Jake Ballard 1–9, Lamaar Thomas 1–9, Brandon Smith 1–6, Dane Sanzenbacher 1–4.

ATTENDANCE: 105,011

Game 2: No. 3 Ohio State 26, Ohio 14

COLUMBUS | Ohio State trailed entering the fourth quarter but rallied to avoid its first loss to a school from the state of Ohio since 1921 (Oberlin).

"It was a pathetic performance," Ohio State wide receiver Brian Hartline said in regard to the Buckeyes being 33-point favorites. "OU should've won the game. I don't know how we came out with it."

Brandon Saine's 2-yard run on the third play of the fourth quarter gave Ohio State the lead, and Ray Small's 69-yard punt return for a touchdown put the game away.

Ohio made five turnovers, and without running back Chris "Beanie" Wells the Buckeyes still managed 162 yards rushing.

	1st Qtr	2nd Qtr	3rd Qtr	4th Qtr	Final
OHIO	0	7	7	0	**14**
OHIO ST (3)	3	3	6	14	**26**

SCORING PLAYS

OHIO ST–FG, R Pretorius 27 YD 12:00 1st Qtr

OHIO–TD, D Harden 15 YD RUN (B Way KICK) 8:04 2nd Qtr

OHIO ST–FG, R Pretorius 38 YD 9:58 2nd Qtr

OHIO –TD C Meyers 0 YD FUMBLE RECOVERY (B Way KICK) 9:00 3rd Qtr

OHIO ST–TD D Herron 1 YD RUN (kick failed) 2:51 3rd Qtr

OHIO ST–TD B Saine 2 YD RUN (R Pretorius KICK) 14:00 4th Qtr

OHIO ST–TD R Small 69 YD PUNT RETURN (R Pretorius KICK) 5:57 4th Qtr

GAME STATISTICS

	OHIO	OHIO ST (3)
First Downs	15	17
Yards Rushing	145	162
Yards Passing	109	110
Sacks – Yards Lost	3–6	1–1
Passing Efficiency	12–34–4	16–28–0
Punts	6–38.3	5–40.0
Fumbles–Lost	2–1	1–1
Penalties–Yards	2–9	1–5
Time of Possession	28:45	31:15

2008 Review

INDIVIDUAL STATISTICS – RUSHING
OHIO–Donte Harden 11–63, Boo Jackson 7–55, Chris Garrett 7–22, Theo Scott 3–10, LaVon Brazill 1–MINUS 1, – Team 2–MINUS 4. OHIO ST–Daniel Herron 12–50, Maurice Wells 9–48, Terrelle Pryor 5–37, Todd Boeckman 8–26, Brandon Saine 5–15, – Team 1–MINUS 14.

INDIVIDUAL STATISTICS – PASSING
OHIO–Boo Jackson 9–25–86– 3, Theo Scott 3–9–23– 1. OHIO ST–Todd Boeckman 16–26–110– 0. Terrelle Pryor 0–2–0– 0.

INDIVIDUAL STATISTICS – RECEIVING
OHIO–Taylor Price 2–34, Andrew Mooney 2–21, LaVon Brazill 2–17, Steven Goulet 1–14, Riley Dunlop 1–13, Donte Harden 1–8, Chris Garrett 3–2. OHIO ST–Dane Sanzenbacher 4–32, Ray Small 5–27, Jake Ballard 1–25, Brian Hartline 2–14, Brian Robiskie 3–8, Maurice Wells 1–4.

ATTENDANCE: 105,002

Game 3: No. 1 Southern California 35, No. 5 Ohio State 3

LOS ANGELES | Mark Sanchez had four touchdown passes and Joe McKnight tallied 105 rushing yards on 12 carries to dominate the highly anticipated showdown.

A holding penalty nullified a touchdown in the second quarter, and Rey Maualuga intercepted Todd Boeckman, returning it 48 yards for a touchdown to give the Trojans a decisive 21-3 lead with 2:49 left in the first half. Ohio State gained only 30 yards in the second half.

"We played as well as we could, with or without Beanie (Wells)," Ohio State coach Jim Tressel said. "We played against a great team tonight. We were never able to take control on offense or defense. We must now roll up our sleeves and realize we can't play like this and win."

It was Ohio State's worst loss since 1994 and its worst nonconference loss since 1989, also at Southern California. It was the first time the Buckeyes were held without a touchdown since 1996 against Michigan.

	1st Qtr	2nd Qtr	3rd Qtr	4th Qtr	Final
OHIO ST (5)	3	0	0	0	3
USC (1)	7	14	14	0	35

SCORING PLAYS

OHIO ST–FG, R Pretorius 29 YD 11:54 1st Qtr

USC–TD, S Havili 35 YD PASS FROM M Sanchez (D Buehler KICK) 14:27 1st Qtr

USC–TD, B Ayles 1 YD PASS FROM M Sanchez (D Buehler KICK) 4:00 2nd Qtr

USC–TD, R Maualuga 48 YD INTERCEPTION RETURN (D Buehler KICK) 12:11 2nd Qtr

USC–TD, D Williams 24 YD PASS FROM M Sanchez (D Buehler KICK) 8:58 3rd Qtr

OHIO STATE FOOTBALL

USC–TD, D Williams 17 YD PASS FROM M Sanchez (D Buehler KICK) 13:27 3rd Qtr

GAME STATISTICS

	OHIO ST (5)	USC (1)
First Downs	15	21
Yards Rushing	34–71	32–164
Yards Passing	136	184
Sacks – Yards Lost	5–36	1–11
Passing Efficiency	21–30–2	18–30–1
Punts	7–41.9	5–35.2
Fumbles–Lost	1–1	1–0
Penalties–Yards	10–78	8–76
Time of Possession	32:03	27:57

INDIVIDUAL STATISTICS – RUSHING
OHIO ST–Daniel Herron 11–51, Terrelle Pryor 11–40, Brandon Saine 2–10, – Team 1–MINUS 1, Maurice Wells 1–MINUS 2, Todd Boeckman 8–MINUS 27. USC–Joe McKnight 12–105, Stafon Johnson 4–23, C.J. Gable 4–18, Allen Bradford 5–16, Stanley Havili 2–9, Marc Tyler 1–2, Garrett Green 2–1, Mark Sanchez 2–MINUS 10.

INDIVIDUAL STATISTICS – PASSING
OHIO ST–Todd Boeckman 14–21–84– 2, Terrelle Pryor 7–9–52– 0. USC–Mark Sanchez 17–28–172– 1. Aaron Corp 1–2–12– 0.

INDIVIDUAL STATISTICS – RECEIVING
OHIO ST–Ray Small 6–30, Dane Sanzenbacher 3–29, Brian Robiskie 4–23, Daniel Herron 3–23, Brian Hartline 3–19, Maurice Wells 1–7, Brandon Saine 1–5. USC–Stanley Havili 5–49, Damian Williams 3–49, Patrick Turner 4–43, Allen Bradford 2–29, C.J. Gable 3–13, Blake Ayles 1–1.

ATTENDANCE: 93,607

Game 4: No. 13 Ohio State 28, Troy 10

COLUMBUS | With a third straight trip to the BCS Championship Game seemingly out of reach, Coach Jim Tressell turned the offense over to true freshman quarterback Terrelle Pryor days before he took his first collegiate class.

The 6-foot-6 standout completed 10 of 16 passes for 139 yards with one interception and an Ohio State-freshman-record four touchdowns. He also ran 14 times for 66 yards.

"Coming off the loss to USC, I think we took a half step forward," Pryor said.

Pryor was the first true freshman to start for the Buckeyes since Art Schlichter in 1978.

When senior Todd Boeckman took two snaps and was booed, defensive lineman Lawrence Wilson told reporters: "Hey, we're just kids. We're not professionals. There's no way that adults should treat us that way."

	1st Qtr	2nd Qtr	3rd Qtr	4th Qtr	Final
TROY	0	10	0	0	**10**
OHIO ST (13)	7	7	0	14	**28**

SCORING PLAYS

OHIO ST–TD, R Nicol 13 YD PASS FROM T Pryor (R Pretorius KICK) 4:46 1st Qtr

TROY–FG, S Glusman 22 YD 1:25 2nd Qtr

OHIO ST–TD, B Hartline 39 YD PASS FROM T Pryor (R Pretorius KICK) 5:52 2nd Qtr

TROY–TD, J Jernigan 45 YD PASS FROM J Hampton (S Glusman KICK) 13:11 2nd Qtr

OHIO ST–TD, B Robiskie 38 YD PASS FROM T Pryor (R

Pretorius KICK) 1:32 4th Qtr

OHIO ST–TD, B Hartline 16 YD PASS FROM T Pryor (R Pretorius KICK) 10:14 4th Qtr

GAME STATISTICS

	TROY	OHIO ST (13)
First Downs	15	17
Yards Rushing	23–97	42–170
Yards Passing	218	139
Sacks – Yards Lost	2–11	1–16
Passing Efficiency	30–43–2	10–17–1
Punts	8–38.8	7–46.6
Fumbles–Lost	1–0	0–0
Penalties–Yards	8–80	6–46
Time of Possession	29:50	30:10

INDIVIDUAL STATISTICS – RUSHING
TROY–DuJuan Harris 11–54, Jamie Hampton 10–35, Xavier Moreland 1–5, Jerrel Jernigan 1–3. OHIO ST–Daniel Herron 20–94, Terrelle Pryor 14–66, Maurice Wells 2–9, Brandon Saine 4–9, Ray Small 1–MINUS 1, Brian Hartline 1–MINUS 7.

INDIVIDUAL STATISTICS – PASSING
TROY–Jamie Hampton 30–43–218– 2. OHIO ST–Terrelle Pryor 10–16–139– 1. Todd Boeckman 0–1–0– 0.

INDIVIDUAL STATISTICS – RECEIVING
TROY–Jerrel Jernigan 8–66, Kennard Burton 5–42, Andrew Davis 2–35, DuJuan Harris 8–29, Mykeal Terry 3–19, Zack Marcum 2–16, Frederick Turner 2–11. OHIO ST–Brian Hartline 2–55, Brian Robiskie 2–41, Brandon Smith 2–20, Brandon Saine 1–12, Rory Nicol 2–10, Daniel Herron 1–1.

ATTENDANCE: 102,989

Game 5: No. 14 Ohio State 34, Minnesota 21

COLUMBUS | With Chris "Beanie" Wells returning from a foot injury, the Buckeyes rushed for a season-best 279 yards on 37 attempts. He finished with 106 rushing yards on 14 carries, while freshman quarterback Terrelle Pryor ran for two scores and threw for another despite splitting time with senior Todd Boeckman.

Pryor ran for 97 yards on eight carries, with 33- and 1-yard touchdowns, as Ohio State attempted just 22 passes.

Ohio State won its sixth straight game against Minnesota and handed the Golden Gophers their first loss of the season.

"He has all the talent in the world," Minnesota quarterback Adam Weber said of Pryor. "It's all about how far he wants to go. It's pretty amazing to see a true freshman like that come in and do that."

	1st Qtr	2nd Qtr	3rd Qtr	4th Qtr	Final
MINNESOTA	3	0	3	15	**21**
OHIO ST (14)	7	13	7	7	**34**

SCORING PLAYS

OHIO ST–TD, T Pryor 33 YD RUN (R Pretorius KICK) 2:13 1st Qtr

MINNESOTA–FG, J Monroe 34 YD 7:59 1st Qtr

OHIO ST–FG, R Pretorius 22 YD 5:15 2nd Qtr

OHIO ST–FG, R Pretorius 44 YD 10:50 2nd Qtr

OHIO ST–TD, B Robiskie 8 YD PASS FROM T Pryor (R Pretorius KICK) 14:27 2nd Qtr

MINNESOTA–FG, J Monroe 28 YD 4:20 3rd Qtr

OHIO ST–TD, T Pryor 1 YD RUN (R Pretorius KICK) 7:23 3rd Qtr

OHIO STATE FOOTBALL

OHIO ST–TD, B Robiskie 31 YD PASS FROM T Boeckman (R Pretorius KICK) 0:05 4th Qtr

MINNESOTA–TD, R Spry 3 YD RUN (J Monroe KICK) 6:36 4th Qtr

MINNESOTA–TD, D McKnight 22 YD PASS FROM A Weber (M Maciejowski PASS TO E Decker FOR TWO–POINT CONVERSION) 13:47 4th Qtr

GAME STATISTICS

	MINNESOTA	OHIO ST (14)
First Downs	18	21
Yards Rushing	28–81	37–279
Yards Passing	187	135
Sacks – Yards Lost	1–5	2–8
Passing Efficiency	23–36–1	13–22–0
Punts	4–42.5	2–54.5
Fumbles–Lost	3–2	1–1
Penalties–Yards	8–54	10–90
Time of Possession	30:10	29:50

INDIVIDUAL STATISTICS – RUSHING
MINNESOTA–DeLeon Eskridge 18–76, Eric Decker 1–6, Shady Salamon 2–4, Ralph Spry 1–3, Adam Weber 6–MINUS 8. OHIO ST–Chris Wells 14–106, Terrelle Pryor 8–97, Daniel Herron 10–50, Brandon Saine 3–11, Todd Boeckman 1–8, Joe Bauserman 1–7.

INDIVIDUAL STATISTICS – PASSING
MINNESOTA–Adam Weber 23–36–187– 1. OHIO ST–Terrelle Pryor 8–13–70– 0. Todd Boeckman 5–9–65– 0.

INDIVIDUAL STATISTICS – RECEIVING
MINNESOTA–DeLeon Eskridge 8–55, Eric Decker 5–52, Jack Simmons 3–36, Da'Jon McKnight 1–22, Ben Kuznia 4–16, Ralph Spry 1–4, Brodrick Smith 1–2. OHIO ST–Brian Robiskie 8–90, Brian Hartline 1–22, DeVier Posey 1–11, Rory Nicol 1–8, Lamaar Thomas 2–4.

ATTENDANCE: 105,175

Game 6: No. 14 Ohio State 20, No. 18 Wisconsin 17

MADISON | Ohio State's double-threat backfield proved to be too much for Wisconsin as Terrelle Pryor ran for an 11-yard touchdown with 1:08 remaining and Chris "Beanie" Wells had 167 rushing yards.

"Guys really don't know who to key on, me or Terrelle," Wells said. "I like that about our offense, having two guys out there who can really run the ball."

Malcolm Jenkins ended Wisconsin's attempt to answer Pryor's score by intercepting an Allan Evridge pass with just under a minute remaining. It was Bret Bielema's first home loss, and snapped the Badgers' 16-game home win streak dating back to November 12, 2005, against Iowa.

"Just didn't see Jenkins," said Evridge, who finished 13 of 25 for 147 yards and also lost a fumble.

	1st Qtr	2nd Qtr	3rd Qtr	4th Qtr	Final
OHIO ST (14)	7	0	3	10	**20**
WISCONSIN (18)	0	10	0	7	**17**

SCORING PLAYS

OHIO ST–TD, C Wells 33 YD RUN (R Pretorius KICK)
3:11 1st Qtr

WISCONSIN–TD, M Turner 9 YD PASS FROM A Evridge
(P Welch KICK) 10:25 2nd Qtr

WISCONSIN–FG, P Welch 20 YD 14:59 2nd Qtr

OHIO ST–FG, R Pretorius 21 YD 7:17 3rd Qtr

OHIO ST–FG, R Pretorius 34 YD 4:08 4th Qtr

WISCONSIN–TD, P Hill 2 YD RUN (P Welch KICK) 8:29
4th Qtr

OHIO ST–TD, T Pryor 11 YD RUN (R Pretorius KICK)
13:52 4th Qtr

GAME STATISTICS

	OHIO ST (14)	WISCONSIN (18)
First Downs	17	19
Yards Rushing	40–183	39–179
Yards Passing	144	147
Sacks – Yards Lost	4–24	2–11
Passing Efficiency	13–19–1	13–25–1
Punts	4–48.8	6–42
Fumbles–Lost	4–1	1–1
Penalties–Yards	5–30	3–19
Time of Possession	30:32	29:28

INDIVIDUAL STATISTICS - RUSHING
OHIO ST–Chris Wells 22-168, Terrelle Pryor 15-20, Maurice Wells 1-0, – Team 2–MINUS 5. WISCONSIN–John Clay 10-69, P.J. Hill 16-63, David Gilreath 5-36, Bill Rentmeester 3-15, Zach Brown 1-0, Allan Evridge 4–MINUS 4.

INDIVIDUAL STATISTICS - PASSING
OHIO ST–Terrelle Pryor 13-19-144- 1. WISCONSIN–Allan Evridge 13-25-147- 1.

INDIVIDUAL STATISTICS - RECEIVING
OHIO ST–Brian Hartline 3-57, Dane Sanzenbacher 2-40, Ray Small 2-20, Brian Robiskie 2-10, Brandon Smith 1-9, DeVier Posey 1-5, Daniel Herron 1-3, Chris Wells 1-0. WISCONSIN–Travis Beckum 6-60, Kyle Jefferson 2-42, David Gilreath 3-28, Mickey Turner 1-9, Isaac Anderson 1-8.

ATTENDANCE: 81,608

2008 Review

Game 7: No. 12 Ohio State 16, Purdue 3

COLUMBUS | Although the offense didn't score a touchdown, it didn't need to as Ohio State defeated Purdue for the 12th time in their last 14 meetings.

Even though Curtis Painter threw for 228 yards to become just the fourth Big Ten quarterback to reach 10,000 career passing yards, Purdue didn't get inside the Ohio State 30-yard line until the final 30 seconds.

"The offense came up and said, 'We owe you,'" Ohio State linebacker James Laurinaitis said.

Malcolm Jenkins blocked a punt and Etienne Sabino returned it 20 yards for the only touchdown.

	1st Qtr	2nd Qtr	3rd Qtr	4th Qtr	Final
PURDUE	0	0	3	0	**3**
OHIO ST (12)	10	3	0	3	**16**

SCORING PLAYS

OHIO ST–TD, E Sabino 19 YD BLOCKED PUNT RETURN (R Pretorius KICK) 3:19 1st Qtr

OHIO ST–FG, R Pretorius 24 YD 14:03 1st Qtr

OHIO ST–FG, A Pettrey 49 YD 10:06 2nd Qtr

PURDUE–FG, C Wiggs 53 YD 3:57 3rd Qtr

OHIO ST–FG, R Pretorius 22 YD 0:30 4th Qtr

GAME STATISTICS

	PURDUE	OHIO ST (12)
First Downs	18	14
Yards Rushing	26–70	42–125
Yards Passing	228	97

OHIO STATE FOOTBALL

Sacks – Yards Lost	2–16	3–19
Passing Efficiency	23–51–1	10–14–0
Punts	6–31.7	6–35.2
Fumbles–Lost	1–1	0–0
Penalties–Yards	4–34	2–10
Time of Possession	27:20	32:40

INDIVIDUAL STATISTICS – RUSHING
PURDUE–Kory Sheets 20–67, Ralph Bolden 1–3, Curtis Painter 5–0. OHIO ST–Chris Wells 22–94, Terrelle Pryor 14–27, Maurice Wells 5–5, – Team 1–MINUS 1.

INDIVIDUAL STATISTICS – PASSING
PURDUE–Curtis Painter 23–51–228– 1. OHIO ST–Terrelle Pryor 10–14–97– 0.

INDIVIDUAL STATISTICS – RECEIVING
PURDUE–Greg Orton 6–73, Desmond Tardy 5–55, Keith Smith 2–42, Brandon Whittington 5–37, Kory Sheets 4–13, Jeff Lindsay 1–8. OHIO ST–DeVier Posey 2–28, Brian Robiskie 2–19, Maurice Wells 1–18, Lamaar Thomas 1–16, Jake Ballard 1–8, Brian Hartline 1–5, Chris Wells 2–3.

ATTENDANCE: 105,378

76

Yards the Purdue offense outgained the Buckeyes by in their 2008 matchup. Nearly all of the yardage came on their own end of the field, as the Boilermakers failed to cross the OSU 30-yard line until there was less than a minute to play.

Game 8: No. 12 Ohio State 45, No. 20 Michigan State 7

COLUMBUS | Freshman Terrelle Pryor passed for 116 yards and a touchdown and ran for 72 yards and another score, while running back Chris "Beanie" Wells had 140 rushing yards and two touchdowns as Ohio State outgained Michigan State on the ground 216 to 52.

The Buckeyes defense limited Javon Ringer to a season-low 67 yards and kept him out of the end zone. Meanwhile, Ohio State scored a season-high 45 points and defeated the Spartans for the 12th time in 14 meetings.

The Spartans had three fumbles and two interceptions after losing the ball just six times in their first seven games.

"Pryor played an excellent game and Wells was dominant," said Michigan State coach Mark Dantonio, a former Ohio State assistant. "They came together today and had zero turnovers."

	1st Qtr	2nd Qtr	3rd Qtr	4th Qtr	Final
OHIO ST (12)	21	7	0	17	**45**
MICHIGAN ST (20)	0	0	7	0	**7**

SCORING PLAYS

OHIO ST–TD, T Pryor 18 YD RUN (R Pretorius KICK)
6:35 1st Qtr

OHIO ST–TD, B Robiskie 7 YD PASS FROM T Pryor (R Pretorius KICK) 10:27 1st Qtr

OHIO ST–TD, C Wells 1 YD RUN (R Pretorius KICK)
12:16 1st Qtr

OHIO ST–TD, C Wells 12 YD RUN (R Pretorius KICK)
8:26 2nd Qtr

MICHIGAN ST–TD, C Gantt 3 YD PASS FROM K Cousins
(B Swenson KICK) 4:09 3rd Qtr

OHIO STATE FOOTBALL

OHIO ST–TD, T Gibson 69 YD FUMBLE RETURN (R Pretorius KICK) 0:19 4th Qtr

OHIO ST–FG, A Pettrey 40 YD 9:33 4th Qtr

OHIO ST–TD, J Hines 48 YD FUMBLE RETURN (A Pettrey KICK) 14:45 4th Qtr

GAME STATISTICS

	OHIO ST (12)	MICHIGAN ST (20)
First Downs	18	14
Yards Rushing	52–216	21–52
Yards Passing	116	188
Sacks – Yards Lost	2–13	3–23
Passing Efficiency	7–11–0	23–39–2
Punts	5–41.8	6–45.7
Fumbles–Lost	3–0	3–3
Penalties–Yards	5–45	2–15
Time of Possession	35:17	24:43

INDIVIDUAL STATISTICS - RUSHING
OHIO ST–Chris Wells 31–140, Terrelle Pryor 12–72, Maurice Wells 5–7, Brandon Saine 4–MINUS 3. MICHIGAN ST–Javon Ringer 16–67, Keyshawn Martin 1–10, Blair White 1–MINUS 2, Kirk Cousins 1–MINUS 8, Brian Hoyer 2–MINUS 15.

INDIVIDUAL STATISTICS - PASSING
OHIO ST–Terrelle Pryor 7–11–116– 0. MICHIGAN ST–Kirk Cousins 18–25–161– 1. Brian Hoyer 5–13–27– 1. Keyshawn Martin 0–1–0– 0.

INDIVIDUAL STATISTICS - RECEIVING
OHIO ST–Brian Hartline 1–56, Brandon Smith 3–37, DeVier Posey 1–13, Brian Robiskie 2–10. MICHIGAN ST–Mark Dell 4–53, Blair White 6–47, Charlie Gantt 3–32, B.J. Cunningham 2–23, Javon Ringer 6–19, Keyshawn Martin 1–14, A.J. Jimmerson 1–0.

ATTENDANCE: 77,360

Game 9: No. 3 Penn State 13, No. 10 Ohio State 6

COLUMBUS | Pat Devlin came off the bench for injured starting quarterback Daryll Clark in the fourth quarter and led two scoring drives for Penn State, which won in Columbus for the first time since joining the Big Ten in 1993 (0–7). The Nittany Lions' last win at Ohio State before that was 1978.

Buckeyes freshman quarterback Terrelle Pryor lost his first game as a starter (5–1), and Ohio State dropped just its third Big Ten game since 2005.

"One turnover was the ballgame," Penn State coach Joe Paterno said. "We played the game we had to play."

That turnover was by Pryor, due to defensive back Mark Rubin using his left hand to knock the ball away as the freshman quarterback carried on a third-and-1 early in the fourth quarter.

"I can't explain this," Pryor told reporters after the game. "I just didn't hold the ball. I saw the end zone. It was there and the ball just fell out. I thought I was on my way to a touchdown but I just lost the ball. As soon as I fumbled it, I knew they would score."

	1st Qtr	2nd Qtr	3rd Qtr	4th Qtr	Final
PENN ST (3)	0	3	0	10	**13**
OHIO ST (10)	0	3	3	0	**6**

SCORING PLAYS

PENN ST–FG, K Kelly 31 YD 13:27 2nd Qtr

OHIO ST–FG, A Pettrey 41 YD 15:00 2nd Qtr

OHIO ST–FG, A Pettrey 36 YD 11:41 3rd Qtr

PENN ST–TD, P Devlin 1 YD RUN (K Kelly KICK) 8:35 4th Qtr

PENN ST–FG, K Kelly 35 YD 13:53 4th Qtr

GAME STATISTICS

	PENN ST (3)	OHIO ST (10)
First Downs	18	14
Yards Rushing	37–160	31–61
Yards Passing	121	226
Sacks – Yards Lost	1–3	1–9
Passing Efficiency	12–20–0	16–28–1
Punts	4–43.5	5–38.6
Fumbles–Lost	0–0	1–1
Penalties–Yards	0–0	4–48
Time of Possession	31:26	28:34

INDIVIDUAL STATISTICS – RUSHING
PENN ST–Evan Royster 19–77, Daryll Clark 8–39, Stephfon Green 3–23, Derrick Williams 3–17, Pat Devlin 3–3, Dan Lawlor 1–1. OHIO ST–Chris Wells 22–55, Terrelle Pryor 9–6.

INDIVIDUAL STATISTICS – PASSING
PENN ST–Daryll Clark 12–20–121– 0. OHIO ST–Terrelle Pryor 16–25–226– 1. – Team 0–3–0– 0.

INDIVIDUAL STATISTICS – RECEIVING
PENN ST–Graham Zug 1–49, Evan Royster 3–20, Brett Brackett 1–18, Derrick Williams 3–13, Deon Butler 2–11, Mickey Shuler 1–6, Jordan Norwood 1–4. OHIO ST–Dane Sanzenbacher 6–82, Brian Robiskie 4–56, Ray Small 2–37, Brandon Saine 1–20, Brian Hartline 1–15, Chris Wells 1–13, Maurice Wells 1–3.

ATTENDANCE: 105,711

Game 10: No. 12 Ohio State 45, Northwestern 10

EVANSTON | Freshman Terrelle Pryor rebounded from the Penn State loss by throwing three touchdown passes, while running back Chris "Beanie" Wells had 140 rushing yards and two touchdowns.

Pryor completed 9 of 14 passes for 197 yards, and had more touchdown passes (three) than the previous five weeks combined (two). It was Wells' 14th career 100-yard game, the fifth most in school history.

Northwestern was the fourth consecutive opponent held to fewer than 300 yards, and Ohio State scored on a fake punt in the fourth quarter and again with 7 seconds left. "I've got nothing to say about that," Northwestern coach Pat Fitzgerald said when asked if Ohio State ran up the score. "We need to go out and play better for us to win, and we didn't do that."

	1st Qtr	2nd Qtr	3rd Qtr	4th Qtr	Final
OHIO ST (12)	7	17	7	14	**45**
NORTHWESTERN	7	0	3	0	**10**

SCORING PLAYS

OHIO ST–TD, C Wells 2 YD RUN (R Pretorius KICK) 4:12 1st Qtr

NORTHWESTERN–TD, M Kafka 1 YD RUN (A Villarreal KICK) 10:17 1st Qtr

OHIO ST–TD, C Wells 55 YD RUN (R Pretorius KICK) 0:57 2nd Qtr

OHIO ST–FG, R Pretorius 33 YD 4:56 2nd Qtr

OHIO ST–TD, B Robiskie 15 YD PASS FROM T Pryor (R Pretorius KICK) 13:34 2nd Qtr

NORTHWESTERN–FG, A Villarreal 25 YD 3:57 3rd Qtr

OHIO ST–TD, R Nicol 6 YD PASS FROM T Pryor (R Pretorius KICK) 14:26 3rd Qtr

OHIO ST–TD, B Robiskie 34 YD PASS FROM T Pryor (R Pretorius KICK) 7:24 4th Qtr

OHIO ST–TD, D Herron 16 YD RUN (R Pretorius KICK) 14:53 4th Qtr

GAME STATISTICS

	OHIO ST (12)	NORTHWESTERN
First Downs	23	20
Yards Rushing	45–244	43–117
Yards Passing	197	177
Sacks – Yards Lost	1–5	4–39
Passing Efficiency	9–16–0	18–27–1
Punts	3–35.7	4–32.3
Fumbles–Lost	0–0	3–2
Penalties–Yards	6–62	7–85
Time of Possession	30:57	29:03

INDIVIDUAL STATISTICS – RUSHING
OHIO ST–Chris Wells 28–140, Daniel Herron 6–38, Terrelle Pryor 6–33, Maurice Wells 4–24, A.J. Trapasso 1–9. NORTHWESTERN–Mike Kafka 29–83, Stephen Simmons 14–34.

INDIVIDUAL STATISTICS – PASSING
OHIO ST–Terrelle Pryor 9–14–197– 0, Todd Boeckman 0–2–0– 0. NORTHWESTERN–Mike Kafka 18–27–177– 1.

INDIVIDUAL STATISTICS – RECEIVING
OHIO ST–Brian Hartline 2–90, Brian Robiskie 3–58, Rory Nicol 2–28, Dane Sanzenbacher 1–14, Lawrence Wilson 1–7. NORTHWESTERN–Eric Peterman 6–78, Ross Lane 4–32, Rasheed Ward 2–30, Andrew Brewer 3–21, Josh Rooks 1–12, Jeremy Ebert 2–4.

ATTENDANCE: 47,130

2008 Review

Game 11: No. 10 Ohio State 30, Illinois 20

CHAMPAIGN | Terrelle Pryor and Beanie Wells became the first Buckeyes to have 100-yard rushing performances in the same game since Troy Smith and Antonio Pittman against Iowa in 2005.

Pryor had 110 yards in his first career 100-yard game, while Wells had 143.

"We knew we would have a lot better chance of winning running the ball," Coach Jim Tressel said. "You could pass it but you couldn't try to make a living doing it."

Although Illinois had 455 yards of offense, Ohio State was able to get revenge for the 2007 upset loss thanks to the Illini making two turnovers and a number of mistakes on special teams, including Malcolm Jenkins' blocked punt for a safety.

	1st Qtr	2nd Qtr	3rd Qtr	4th Qtr	Final
OHIO ST (10)	9	14	0	7	30
ILLINOIS	7	6	0	7	20

SCORING PLAYS

OHIO ST–TD, T Pryor 1 YD RUN (R Pretorius KICK) 6:12 1st Qtr

ILLINOIS–TD, J Cumberland 7 YD PASS FROM J Williams (M Eller KICK) 9:30 1st Qtr

OHIO ST–SAFETY, 13:50 1st Qtr

OHIO ST–TD, C Wells 3 YD RUN (R Pretorius KICK) 0:45 2nd Qtr

OHIO ST–TD, D Sanzenbacher 20 YD PASS FROM T Pryor (R Pretorius KICK) 8:30 2nd Qtr

ILLINOIS–FG, M Eller 28 YD 12:20 2nd Qtr

ILLINOIS–FG, M Eller 44 YD 15:00 2nd Qtr

OHIO ST–TD, D Herron 14 YD RUN (R Pretorius KICK)
3:05 4th Qtr

ILLINOIS–TD, C Duvalt 24 YD PASS FROM J Williams (M Eller KICK) 14:18 4th Qtr

GAME STATISTICS

	OHIO ST (10)	ILLINOIS
First Downs	16	25
Yards Rushing	52–305	35–214
Yards Passing	49	241
Sacks – Yards Lost	0–0	2–12
Passing Efficiency	6–10–0	20–34–1
Punts	5–39.6	5–30.6
Fumbles–Lost	2–1	4–1
Penalties–Yards	4–18	4–40
Time of Possession	33:50	26:10

2008 Review

INDIVIDUAL STATISTICS – RUSHING
OHIO ST–Chris Wells 24–143, Terrelle Pryor 13–110, Daniel Herron 12–29, Brian Hartline 2–24, – Team 1– MINUS 1. ILLINOIS–Daniel Dufrene 8–79, Juice Williams 9–48, Jason Ford 8–43, Jeff Cumberland 1–23, Eddie McGee 9–21.

INDIVIDUAL STATISTICS – PASSING
OHIO ST–Terrelle Pryor 6–10–49– 0. ILLINOIS–Juice Williams 17–26–192– 1. Eddie McGee 3–7–49– 0. – Team 0–1–0– 0.

INDIVIDUAL STATISTICS – RECEIVING
OHIO ST–Dane Sanzenbacher 2–22, Brian Hartline 1–16, Brian Robiskie 2–9, Daniel Herron 1–2. ILLINOIS–Arrelious Benn 3–65, Daniel Dufrene 5–42, A.J. Jenkins 2–32, Chris Duvalt 1–24, Jeff Cumberland 3–22, Eddie McGee 2–22, Jason Ford 2–21, Michael Hoomanawanui 2–13.

ATTENDANCE: 62,870

Game 12: No. 10 Ohio State 42, Michigan 7

COLUMBUS | Running back Chris "Beanie" Wells had 134 rushing yards, including a 59-yard touchdown, as Ohio State enjoyed not only its fifth-straight victory against rival Michigan, but the series' most lopsided result since 1968 — when Woody Hayes went for a late two-point conversion because he "couldn't go for three!"

Freshman Terrelle Pryor threw two touchdown passes, Brian Hartline caught two scoring passes, and Dan Herron found the end zone twice as well. Wells left the game in the second half after aggravating a right hamstring injury sustained against Illinois.

Michigan tallied just 198 total yards and punted 12 times. After the Buckeyes' first three possessions ended in an interception and two three-and-outs, Wells took off for his tone-setting touchdown to begin the rout.

"The turning point was when they punted us down to the 9 and then two plays later we scored," Coach Jim Tressel said. "That was huge. A big run by Beanie, and then a big run by 'Boom' Herron. That really made a difference."

Ohio State needed a victory and a Penn State loss to Michigan State to clinch at least a spot in the Rose Bowl, but the Nittany Lions won, 49-18.

	1st Qtr	2nd Qtr	3rd Qtr	4th Qtr	Final
MICHIGAN	0	7	0	0	7
OHIO ST (10)	7	7	14	14	42

SCORING PLAYS

OHIO ST–TD, C Wells 59 YD RUN (R Pretorius KICK) 11:03 1st Qtr

OHIO ST–TD, B Hartline 53 YD PASS FROM T Pryor (R Pretorius KICK) 1:50 2nd Qtr

MICHIGAN–TD, B Minor 1 YD RUN (K Lopata KICK) 12:09 2nd Qtr

OHIO STATE FOOTBALL

OHIO ST–TD, D Herron 49 YD RUN (R Pretorius KICK)
3:56 3rd Qtr

OHIO ST–TD, B Robiskie 8 YD PASS FROM T Pryor (R
Pretorius KICK) 11:06 3rd Qtr

OHIO ST–TD, D Herron 2 YD RUN (R Pretorius KICK)
0:08 4th Qtr

OHIO ST–TD, B Hartline 18 YD PASS FROM T Boeckman
(R Pretorius KICK) 1:44 4th Qtr

GAME STATISTICS

	MICHIGAN	OHIO ST (10)
First Downs	11	13
Yards Rushing	41–111	43–232
Yards Passing	87	184
Sacks – Yards Lost	3–22	3–25
Passing Efficiency	8–25–0	8–16–1
Punts	12–36.5	7–34.7
Fumbles–Lost	2–2	0–0
Penalties–Yards	3–15	2–20
Time of Possession	29:25	30:35

INDIVIDUAL STATISTICS – RUSHING
MICHIGAN–Brandon Minor 14-67, Michael Shaw 12-41, Martavious Odoms 1-8, Carlos Brown 3-3, Justin Feagin 3-2, Nick Sheridan 8-MINUS 10. OHIO ST–Chris Wells 15-134, Daniel Herron 8-80, Marcus Williams 2-11, Maurice Wells 6-8, Joe Gantz 1-3, Brandon Saine 3-3, Terrelle Pryor 8-MINUS 7.

INDIVIDUAL STATISTICS – PASSING
MICHIGAN–Nick Sheridan 8-24-87- 0, - Team 0-1-0-0. OHIO ST–Terrelle Pryor 5-13-120- 1. Todd Boeckman 3-3-64- 0.

INDIVIDUAL STATISTICS – RECEIVING
MICHIGAN–Martavious Odoms 5-37, Darryl Stonum 1-33, LaTerryal Savoy 1-14, Carlos Brown 1-3. OHIO ST–Brian Hartline 2-71, Brian Robiskie 2-54, Dane Sanzenbacher 2-49, Jake Ballard 1-10, Maurice Wells 1-0.

ATTENDANCE: 105,564

Fiesta Bowl: No. 3 Texas 24, No. 10 Ohio State 21

GLENDALE | Texas quarterback Colt McCoy hit Quan Cosby for a 26-yard touchdown with 16 seconds to play to cap a dramatic 11-play, 78-yard drive that took only 1:42, as Ohio State lost its third straight Bowl Championship Series game.

"That's the problem in tight ballgames like this," Ohio State Coach Jim Tressel said. "Two outstanding teams, sometimes you finish it, the game ends when you are the one ahead, and sometimes the game ends when you're not."

Running back Chris "Beanie" Wells had 106 rushing yards on 16 carries in his final collegiate game, but missed most of the second half due to a concussion.

Senior Todd Boeckman completed 5 of 11 passes for 110 yards and a touchdown, while freshman Terrelle Pryor was 5 of 14 for 66 yards, and also ran for 78 yards on 15 carries.

"He will be a guy that's in a Heisman race, and it may be sooner than we think because he is a leader," Texas coach Mack Brown said.

	1st Qtr	2nd Qtr	3rd Qtr	4th Qtr	Final
OHIO ST (10)	3	3	0	15	**21**
TEXAS (3)	0	3	14	7	**24**

SCORING PLAYS

OHIO ST–FG, A Pettrey 51 YD 7:32 1st Qtr

TEXAS–FG, H Lawrence 27 YD 3:15 2nd Qtr

OHIO ST–FG, R Pretorius 30 YD 9:21 2nd Qtr

TEXAS–TD, C McCoy 14 YD RUN (H Lawrence KICK) 6:31 3rd Qtr

TEXAS–TD, Q Cosby 7 YD PASS FROM C McCoy (H Lawrence KICK) 13:56 3rd Qtr

OHIO STATE FOOTBALL

OHIO ST–FG, A Pettrey 44 YD 1:38 4th Qtr

OHIO ST–TD, T Pryor 5 YD PASS FROM T Boeckman
7:34 4th Qtr

OHIO ST–TD, D Herron 15 YD RUN 12:55 4th Qtr

TEXAS–TD, Q Cosby 26 YD PASS FROM C McCoy (H
Lawrence KICK) 14:44 4th Qtr

GAME STATISTICS

	OHIO ST (10)	TEXAS (3)
First Downs	21	33
Yards Rushing	39–203	28–72
Yards Passing	176	414
Sacks – Yards Lost	3–26	3–27
Passing Efficiency	10–25–0	41–59–1
Punts	4–40.3	5–46.8
Fumbles–Lost	1–0	2–0
Penalties–Yards	7–67	8–83
Time of Possession	30:13	29:47

INDIVIDUAL STATISTICS – RUSHING
OHIO ST–Chris Wells 16–106, Terrelle Pryor 15–78,
Daniel Herron 5–30, Maurice Wells 1–MINUS 2, Todd
Boeckman 2–MINUS 9. TEXAS–Chris Ogbonnaya 11–42,
Foswhitt Whittaker 6–23, Colt McCoy 7–3, Rashad Bo-
bino 1–2, Cody Johnson 3–2.

INDIVIDUAL STATISTICS – PASSING
OHIO ST–Todd Boeckman 5–11–110– 0, Terrelle Pryor
5–14–66– 0. TEXAS–Colt McCoy 41–59–414– 1.

INDIVIDUAL STATISTICS – RECEIVING
OHIO ST–Brian Robiskie 5–116, Jake Ballard 1–21, Chris
Wells 1–21, DeVier Posey 2–13, Terrelle Pryor 1–5.
TEXAS–Quan Cosby 14–171, Jordan Shipley 10–78,
Brandon Collins 7–60, Chris Ogbonnaya 4–56, James
Kirkendoll 5–41, Peter Ullman 1–8.

ATTENDANCE: 72,047

A little trickery worked to perfection on this play, as quarterback Terrelle Pryor showed off his athleticism in hauling in this Todd Boeckman pass. Blake Gideon came close, but he was unable to prevent Pryor from hanging on and truly igniting the Buckeyes.

FINAL STATISTICS

TEAM STATISTICS	OSU	OPP
SCORING	359	181
Points Per Game	27.6	13.9
FIRST DOWNS	230	232
Rushing	133	96
Passing	82	117
Penalty	15	19
RUSHING YARDAGE	2502	1433
Yards Gained Rushing	2880	1781
Yards Lost Rushing	378	348
Rushing Attempts	540	406
Average Per Rush	4.6	3.5
Average Per Game	192.5	110.2
TDs Rushing	21	7
PASSING YARDAGE	1953	2386
Att-Comp-Int	267–160–6	440–253–15
Average Per Pass	7.3	5.4
Average Per Catch	12.2	9.4
Average Per Game	150.2	183.5
TDs Passing	17	12
TOTAL OFFENSE	4455	3819
Total Plays	807	846
Average Per Play	5.5	4.5
Average Per Game	342.7	293.8
KICK RETURNS: #–Yards	33–633	58–1015
PUNT RETURNS: #–Yards	35–455	16–66
INT RETURNS: #–Yards	15–105	6–82
KICK RETURN AVERAGE	19.2	17.5
PUNT RETURN AVERAGE	13.0	4.1
INT RETURN AVERAGE	7.0	13.7
FUMBLES–LOST	15–7	24–14
PENALTIES–Yards	68–567	60–507
Average Per Game	43.6	39.0
PUNTS–Yards	60–2445	80–3114

Daniel Herron uses his speed to escape the grasp of Texas' Earl Thomas and score a touchdown in the fourth quarter of the Fiesta Bowl. The score helped put the Buckeyes ahead, but it was not enough.

OHIO STATE FOOTBALL

Average Per Punt	40.8	38.9
Net Punt Average	38.0	32.0
TIME OF POSSESSION/Game	31:42	28:18
3RD-DOWN Conversions	74/172	66/187
3RD-Down Pct	43%	35%
4TH-DOWN Conversions	4/9	11/18
4TH-Down Pct	44%	61%
SACKS BY–Yards	28–223	29–195
MISC YARDS	0	0
TOUCHDOWNS SCORED	42	21
FIELD GOALS–ATTEMPTS	22–27	11–14
ONSIDE KICKS	0–0	0–4
RED ZONE SCORES	78–82, 95%	46–58, 79%
RED ZONE TOUCHDOWNS	50–82, 61%	28–58, 48%
PAT–ATTEMPTS	39–40, 98%	20–20, 100%
ATTENDANCE	1469660	725150
Games/Avg Per Game	14/104976	10/72515
Neutral Site Games / Avg Att	2/72047	

2008 Review

SCORE BY QUARTERS

	1st	2nd	3rd	4th	Total
Ohio State	97	90	47	125	359
Opponents	24	60	51	46	181

INDIVIDUAL STATISTICS
RUSHING

	GP	Att	Gain	Loss	Tot	Net Avg	TD	Long	Avg/G
Wells, Chris	10	207	1242	45	1197	5.8	8	59	119.7
Pryor, Terrelle	13	139	853	222	631	4.5	6	38	48.5
Herron, Dan	11	89	452	13	439	4.9	6	49	39.9
Wells, Maurice	12	39	139	10	129	3.3	0	18	10.8
Saine, Brandon	12	26	73	8	65	2.5	1	14	5.4
Hartline, Brian	13	3	24	7	17	5.7	0	18	1.3
Bauserman, Joe	5	3	16	0	16	5.3	0	8	3.2
Williams, Marcus	13	2	11	0	11	5.5	0	8	0.8
Trapasso, A.J.	13	1	9	0	9	9.0	0	9	0.7
Boeckman, Todd	8	23	58	50	8	0.3	0	16	1.0
Gantz, Joe	1	1	3	0	3	3.0	0	3	3.0
Small, Ray	11	1	0	1	-1	-1.0	0	0	-0.1
TEAM	9	6	0	22	-22	-3.7	0	0	-2.4
Total	13	540	2880	378	2502	4.6	21	59	192.5
Opponents	13	406	1781	348	1433	3.5	7	32	110.2

PASSING

	GP	Effic	Cmp–Att–Int	Pct	Yds	TD	Lng	Avg/G
Pryor, Terrelle								
	13	146.50	100–165–4	60.6	1311	12	56	100.8
Boeckman, Todd								
	8	130.73	57–93–2	61.3	620	5	48	77.5
Bauserman, Joe								
	5	80.80	3–6–0	50.0	22	0	11	4.4
TEAM								
	9	0.00	0–3–0	0.0	0	0	0	0.0
Total								
	13	137.88	160–267–6	59.9	1953	17	56	150.2
Opponents								
	13	105.23	253–440–15	57.5	2386	12	49	183.5

RECEIVING

	GP	No.	Yds	Avg	TD	Long	Avg/G
Robiskie, Brian							
	13	42	535	12.7	8	48	41.2
Hartline, Brian							
	13	21	479	22.8	4	56	36.8
Sanzenbacher, Dane							
	12	21	272	13.0	1	53	22.7
Small, Ray							
	11	18	149	8.3	0	23	13.5
Posey, DeVier							
	12	11	117	10.6	1	25	9.8
Smith, Brandon							
	13	8	79	9.9	0	21	6.1
Wells, Chris							
	10	8	47	5.9	0	21	4.7
Nicol, Rory							
	11	6	60	10.0	2	22	5.5
Wells, Maurice							
	12	6	42	7.0	0	18	3.5

2008 Review

Herron, Dan						
	11	6	29	4.8	0	12	2.6
Ballard, Jake						
	13	5	73	14.6	0	25	5.6
Thomas, Lamaar						
	10	4	29	7.2	0	16	2.9
Saine, Brandon						
	12	3	37	12.3	0	20	3.1
Pryor, Terrelle						
	13	1	5	5.0	1	5	0.4
Total	13	160	1953	12.2	17	56	150.2
Opponents						
	13	253	2386	9.4	12	49	183.5

PUNT RETURNS

	No.	Yds	Avg	TD	Long
Small, Ray	24	364	15.2	1	80
Robiskie, Brian	4	17	4.2	0	9
Hartline, Brian	4	22	5.5	0	8
Jenkins, Malcolm	2	28	14.0	0	0
Posey, DeVier	1	4	4.0	0	4
Sabino, Etienne	0	20	0.0	1	20
Total	35	455	13.0	2	80
Opponents	16	66	4.1	0	13

INTERCEPTIONS

	No.	Yds	Avg	TD	Long
Coleman, Kurt	4	18	4.5	0	18
Jenkins, Malcolm	3	7	2.3	0	7
Russell, Anderson	2	15	7.5	0	15
Laurinaitis, James	2	0	0.0	0	0
Chekwa, Chimdi	1	0	0.0	0	0
Rolle, Brian	1	7	7.0	0	7
Washington, Donald	1	34	34.0	0	34
Wilson, Lawrence	1	24	24.0	0	24

KICK RETURNS	No.	Yds	Avg	TD	Long
Thomas, Lamaar	16	345	21.6	0	37
Saine, Brandon	8	141	17.6	0	28
Herron, Dan	4	73	18.2	0	24
Wells, Maurice	3	53	17.7	0	35
Robiskie, Brian	1	11	11.0	0	11
Nicol, Rory	1	10	10.0	0	10
Total	33	633	19.2	0	37
Opponents	58	1015	17.5	0	32

FUMBLE RETURNS	No.	Yds	Avg	TD	Long
Hines, Jermale	1	48	48.0	1	48
Washington, Donald	1	44	44.0	0	44
Gibson, Thaddeus	1	69	69.0	1	69
Total	3	161	53.7	2	69
Opponents	0	0	0.0	1	0

SCORING

	TD	FGs	Kick	Rush	Rcv	Pass	DXP	Saf	Points
Pretorius, Ryan									
	0	15–19	38–39	0–0	0	0–0	0	0	83
Robiskie, Brian									
	8	0–0	0–0	0–0	0	0–0	0	0	48
Wells, Chris									
	8	0–0	0–0	0–0	0	0–0	0	0	48
Pryor, Terrelle									
	7	0–0	0–0	0–0	0	0–2	0	0	42
Herron, Dan									
	6	0–0	0–0	0–0	0	0–0	0	0	36
Hartline, Brian									
	4	0–0	0–0	0–0	0	0–0	0	0	24
Pettrey, Aaron									
	0	7–8	1–1	0–0	0	0–0	0	0	22
Nicol, Rory									
	2	0–0	0–0	0–0	0	0–0	0	0	12

Gibson, Thaddeus								
1	0–0	0–0	0–0	0	0–0	0	0	6
Sanzenbacher, Dane								
1	0–0	0–0	0–0	0	0–0	0	0	6
Posey, DeVier								
1	0–0	0–0	0–0	0	0–0	0	0	6
Small, Ray								
1	0–0	0–0	0–0	0	0–0	0	0	6
Saine, Brandon								
1	0–0	0–0	0–0	0	0–0	0	0	6
Sabino, Etienne								
1	0–0	0–0	0–0	0	0–0	0	0	6
Hines, Jermale								
1	0–0	0–0	0–0	0	0–0	0	0	6
TEAM								
0	0–0	0–0	0–0	0	0–0	0	1	2
Total								
42	22–27	39–40	0–0	0	0–2	0	1	359
Opponents								
21	11–14	20–20	0–0	1	1–1	0	0	181

TOTAL OFFENSE

	G	Plays	Rush	Pass	Total	Avg/G
Pryor, Terrelle						
	13	304	631	1311	1942	149.4
Wells, Chris						
	10	207	1197	0	1197	119.7
Boeckman, Todd						
	8	116	8	620	628	78.5
Herron, Dan						
	11	89	439	0	439	39.9
Wells, Maurice						
	12	39	129	0	129	10.8

Saine, Brandon						
	12	26	65	0	65	5.4
Bauserman, Joe						
	5	9	16	22	38	7.6
Hartline, Brian						
	13	3	17	0	17	1.3
Williams, Marcus						
	13	2	11	0	11	0.8
Trapasso, A.J.						
	13	1	9	0	9	0.7
Gantz, Joe						
	1	1	3	0	3	3.0
Small, Ray						
	11	1	−1	0	−1	−0.1
TEAM						
	9	9	−22	0	−22	−2.4
Total						
	13	807	2502	1953	4455	342.7
Opponents						
	13	846	1433	2386	3819	293.8

FIELD GOALS

	FGM-FGA	Pct	01-19	20-29	30-39	40-49	50-99	Lg	Blk
Pretorius, Ryan									
	15-19	78.9	0-0	8-8	5-6	1-3	1-2	50	0
Pettrey, Aaron									
	7-8	87.5	0-0	0-0	1-1	4-4	2-3	54	0

2008 Review

PUNTING

	No.	Yds	Avg	Long	TB	FC	I20	Blkd
Trapasso, A.J.								
	58	2390	41.2	67	5	14	21	0
Thoma, Jon								
	2	55	27.5	32	0	0	2	0

KICKOFFS

	No.	Yds	Avg	TB	OB	Retn	Net	YdLn
Pettrey, Aaron								
	74	4657	62.9	13	0			
Pretorius, Ryan								
	1	70	70.0	1	0			
Trapasso, A.J.								
	1	70	70.0	1	0			
Total								
	76	4797	63.1	15	0	1015	45.8	24
Opponents								
	42	2659	63.3	7	2	633	44.9	25

DEFENSIVE LEADERS—TACKLES

	GP	Solo	Ast	Total
33 Laurinaitis, James	13	52	78	130
1 Freeman, Marcus	13	39	45	84
4 Coleman, Kurt	12	43	35	78
21 Russell, Anderson	13	38	29	67
51 Homan, Ross	13	35	32	67
2 Jenkins, Malcolm	13	34	23	57
97 Heyward, Cameron	13	13	23	36
84 Worthington, Doug	13	11	23	34
93 Abdallah, Nader	13	12	21	33
7 Hines, Jermale	11	23	8	31
5 Chekwa, Chimdi	13	28	2	30
29 Lane, Shaun	13	19	8	27

Player				
90 Gibson, Thaddeus	13	14	12	26
20 Washington, Donald	11	18	4	22
36 Rolle, Brian	12	8	13	21
43 Williams, Nathan	9	9	9	18
87 Wilson, Lawrence	7	8	10	18
26 Moeller, Tyler	11	8	10	18
72 Larimore, Dexter	13	3	12	15
38 Spitler, Austin	10	5	6	11
10 Torrence, Devon	13	7	3	10
01 Rose, Rob	13	4	6	10
1D Oliver, Nate	13	3	5	8
92 Denlinger, Todd	12	2	5	7
8 Gant, Aaron	13	1	6	7
99 Terry, Curtis	9	4	2	6
11 Sabino, Etienne	13	4	2	6
42 Sweat, Andrew	9	2	3	5
3 O'Neal, Jamario	11	2	1	3
98 Thomas, Solomon	5	2	1	3
49 Lukens, Ryan	13	2	1	3
24 Williams, Marcus	13	3	0	3
44 Johnson, Mark	1	0	2	2
0C Saine, Brandon	12	1	0	1
0E Washington, Taurian	10	1	0	1
23 Patterson, Nick	8	0	1	1
9 Hartline, Brian	13	0	1	1
0B Pryor, Terrelle	13	1	0	1
TEAM	9	1	0	1
Total	13	460	442	902
Opponents	13	479	440	919

STARTING LINEUPS
OFFENSE/OPENER

OFFENSE/OPENER	LAST GAME
LT 75 Alex Boone	LT 75 Alex Boone
LG 71 Steve Rehring	LG 63 Ben Person
C 64 Jim Cordle	C 50 Mike Brewster
RG 63 Ben Person	RG 71 Steve Rehring
RT 70 Bryant Browning	RT 70 Bryant Browning
TE 88 Rory Nicol	TE 88 Rory Nicol
WR 80 Brian Robiskie	WR 80 Brian Robiskie
QB 17 Todd Boeckman	QB 17 Todd Boeckman
TB 28 Chris Wells	WR 2 Terrelle Pryor
FB 87 Brandon Smith	FB 87 Brandon Smith
WR 9 Brian Hartline	WR 9 Brian Hartline

DEFENSE

DEFENSE	
DE 87 Lawrence Wilson	DE 97 Cameron Heyward
DT 97 Cameron Heyward	DT 8 Doug Worthington
DT 92 Todd Denlinger	DT 93 Nader Abdallah
DE 72 Dexter Larimore	DE 90 Thaddeus Gibson
LB 33 James Laurinaitis	LB 33 James Laurinaitis
LB 1 Marcus Freeman	LB 1 Marcus Freeman
LB 51 Ross Homan	DB 20 Donald Washington
CB 2 Malcolm Jenkins	CB 2 Malcolm Jenkins
S 5 Chimdi Chekwa	S 5 Chimdi Chekwa
S 21 Anderson Russell	S 21 Anderson Russell
CB 7 Jermale Hines	CB 4 Kurt Coleman

2

Times Terrelle Pryor has been recognized by the Big Ten. After his sensational freshman campaign he was named Big Ten Freshman of the Year and was Honorable Mention All-Big Ten.

BIG TEN STANDINGS

	Conference			Overall		
	W-L	PF	PA	W-L	PF	PA
Penn State	7–1	271	109	11–1	482	149
Ohio State	7–1	238	98	10–2	338	157
Michigan State	6–2	201	208	9–3	314	263
Northwestern	5–3	191	187	9–3	294	232
Iowa	5–3	238	130	8–4	363	159
Minnesota	3–5	136	210	7–5	281	280
Wisconsin	3–5	206	227	7–6	357	345
Illinois	3–5	218	206	5–7	344	319
Purdue	2–6	175	196	4–8	296	301
Michigan	2–6	177	268	3–9	243	347
Indiana	1–7	116	328	3–9	246	423

2008 Review

9

Games lost by Michigan in the 2008 season. The Wolverines had never lost more games in their 129 years of playing football.

0

THROUGH THE YEARS

1890
1-3

May 3	at Ohio Wesleyan	Delaware	W	20-14
Nov. 1	Wooster	Columbus	L	64-0
Nov. 14	at Denison	Granville	L	14-0
Nov. 27	Kenyon	Columbus	L	18-10
Coach:	Alexander S. Lilley			30-110
Captains: Jesse L. Jones, Paul M. Lincoln				

Football became a varsity sport, with Alexander Lilley named the program's first head coach. Ohio State won its first game, 20–14, at Ohio Wesleyan in front of approximately 700 fans. ... The Kenyon game was Ohio State's first Thanksgiving game.

1891
2-2

Nov. 11	Western Reserve	Columbus	L	50-6
Nov. 14	at Kenyon	Gambier	L	26-0
Nov. 28	Denison	Columbus	W	8-4
Dec. 5	at Akron	Akron	W	6-0
Coach: Alexander S. Lilley				20-80
Captain: Richard T. Ellis				

The Denison victory was the program's first at home, and the shutout at Akron was also an Ohio State first.

OSU undergrad George Cole was the key figure in organizing OSU's football program and convincing Alexander Lilley to become the team's first head coach.

John Heisman got his coaching start at Oberlin College in 1892, debuting with a 40–4 loss to Ohio State. The trophy that now bears his name was modeled after the University of Chicago's Jay Berwanger, seen posing in 1934.

1892
5–3

Oct. 15	at Oberlin	Oberlin	L	40–4
Oct. 22	at Akron	Akron	W	62–0
Oct. 29	Marietta	Columbus	W	80–0
Nov. 5	at Denison	Granville	W	32–0
Nov. 7	Oberlin	Columbus	L	50–0
Nov. 12	Dayton YMCA	Columbus	W	42–4
Nov. 19	at Western Reserve Cleveland		L	40–18
Nov. 24	Kenyon	Columbus	W	26–10
Coach: Jack Ryder				260–144
Captain: Richard T. Ellis				

Jack Ryder's first game as Ohio State's head coach was against John Heisman at Oberlin. It was Heisman's first game as a coach. He was 23. ... Despite the loss, OSU recorded its first winning season. ... A small set of stands were set up on the south side of the football field for spectators. ... One of Ohio State's volunteer coaches was Samuel P. Bush, great-grandfather of President George W. Bush.

John Heisman is credited with several innovations in the way football is played. He was the first to have offensive linemen pull, was an early advocate of the forward pass, and was the driving force behind dividing the game into quarters instead of halves.

Through the Years

1893
4–5

Sept. 30	at Otterbein	Westerville	L	22–16
Oct. 14	Wittenberg	Columbus	W	36–10
Oct. 21	Oberlin	Columbus	L	38–10
Oct. 28	at Kenyon	Gambier	L	42–6
Nov. 4	Western Reserve	Columbus	L	30–16
Nov. 11	Akron	Columbus	W	32–18
Nov. 18	Cincinnati	Columbus	W	38–0
Nov. 25	Marietta	Columbus	W	40–8
Nov. 30	Kenyon	Columbus	L	10–8
Coach: Jack Ryder				202–178
Captain: A.P. Gillen				

According to Ohio State lore, a student who was enrolled tried out for the football team and stuck around just long enough to learn the plays. Weeks later, he was spotted on the Kenyon team. "Kenyon just seemed to have all of our signals down pat," quarterback Charles Wood later recalled. ... Fans stormed the field during the home game against Kenyon and tore down part of the fence surrounding the field. Play was halted until police were able to clear the field.

1894
6–5

Sept. 15	at Akron	Ohio State Fair	L	12–6
Sept. 17	at Wittenberg	Ohio State Fair	L	6–0
Oct. 6	Antioch	Columbus	W	32–0
Oct. 13	at Wittenberg	Ohio State Fair	L	18–6
Oct. 20	at Columbus Barracks	Columbus	W	30–0
Oct. 27	Western Reserve	Columbus	L	24–4
Nov. 3	Marietta	Columbus	W	10–4
Nov. 10	at Case	Cleveland	L	38–0
Nov. 17	at Cincinnati	Cincinnati	W	6–4
Nov. 24	17th Regiment	Columbus	W	46–4
Nov. 29	Kenyon	Columbus	W	20–4
Coach: Jack Ryder				160–114
Captain: W.G. Nagel				

The Ohio State Board of Agriculture arranged for three games to be played at the State Fair to introduce football to new fans. ... Ohio State held its first closed practices, except for reporters and school officials.

1895
4-4-2

Oct. 5	Akron	Columbus	W	14-6
Oct. 12	at Otterbein	Westerville	L	14-6
Oct. 19	Oberlin	Columbus	L	12-0
Oct. 26	at Denison	Granville	T	4-4
Nov. 2	Ohio Wesleyan	Columbus	T	8-8
Nov. 9	at Cincinnati	Cincinnati	W	4-0
Nov. 15	at Kentucky	Lexington	W	8-6
Nov. 16	at Central Kentucky	Danville	L	18-0
Nov. 23	at Marietta	Marietta	L	24-0
Nov. 28	Kenyon	Columbus	W	12-10
Coach: Jack Ryder				62-102
Captain: Renick W. Dunlap				

Coach Jack Ryder was 22–22–2 as a head coach. ... The Kentucky game marked the first time Ohio State crossed the state border. The next day it played Central Kentucky for the program's only back-to-back scheduled games.

$45

The weekly salary paid to Jack Ryder during his coaching tenure at Ohio State. He was the first paid head coach in school history, and his seasonal earnings totaled $150.

1896
5-5-1

Oct. 3	Ohio Medical	Columbus	W	24-0
Oct. 10	at Cincinnati	Cincinnati	L	8-6
Oct. 17	at Otterbein	Canton	W	12-0
Oct. 23	at Oberlin	Oberlin	L	16-0
Oct. 30	Case	Columbus	W	30-10
Nov. 5	Ohio Wesleyan	Columbus	L	10-4
Nov. 7	Columbus Barracks	Columbus	W	10-2
Nov. 11	Ohio Medical	Columbus	T	0-0
Nov. 14	Wittenberg	Columbus	L	24-6
Nov. 21	Ohio Medical	Columbus	W	12-0
Nov. 26	Kenyon	Columbus	L	34-18
Coach: Charles Hickey				122-104
Captains: Edward H. French, William A. Reed				

The October 17 game against Otterbein was moved from Columbus to Canton to aid the campaign of presidential candidate William McKinley, a Canton native. ... Ohio State played four games in 10 days and went 1-1-2.

1897
1-7-1

Oct. 6	Ohio Medical	Columbus	W	6-0
Oct. 9	Case	Columbus	L	14-0
Oct. 16	at Michigan	Ann Arbor	L	34-0
Oct. 23	Otterbein	Columbus	T	12-12
Oct. 26	Columbus Barracks	Columbus	L	6-0
Oct. 30	Oberlin	Columbus	L	44-0
Nov. 6	at West Virginia	Morgantown	L	28-0
Nov. 13	at Cincinnati	Cincinnati	L	24-0
Nov. 25	Ohio Wesleyan	Columbus	L	6-0
Coach: David F. Edwards				18-168
Captain: Harry C. Hawkins				

Ohio State played Michigan for the first time. ... The 1897 season marked the only season Ohio State has lost seven or more games.

1898
3–5

Oct. 1	Heidelberg	Columbus	W	17–0
Oct. 8	Ohio Medical	Columbus	L	10–0
Oct. 15	Denison	Columbus	W	34–0
Oct. 22	Marietta	Columbus	L	10–0
Nov. 5	at Western Reserve	Cleveland	L	49–0
Nov. 12	Case	Columbus	L	23–5
Nov. 19	Kenyon	Columbus	L	29–0
Nov. 24	Ohio Wesleyan	Columbus	W	24–0
Coach: David F. Edwards				80–121
Captain: John Segrist				

A portion of the proceeds from the Ohio Medical game were donated to build a monument honoring the 4th Ohio Volunteer Infantry, which served in the Spanish-American War. … Due to injuries, Marietta had to borrow a player—believed to be halfback Bob Hager—to finish the game. Hager scored a 67-yard touchdown on his first carry.

1899
9–0–1

Sept. 30	Otterbein	Columbus	W	30–0
Oct. 7	Wittenberg	Columbus	W	28–0
Oct. 14	at Case	Cleveland	T	5–5
Oct. 21	Ohio University	Columbus	W	41–0
Oct. 28	at Oberlin	Oberlin	W	6–0
Nov. 4	Western Reserve	Columbus	W	6–0
Nov. 11	Marietta	Columbus	W	17–0
Nov. 18	Ohio Medical	Columbus	W	12–0
Nov. 25	at Muskingum	New Concord	W	34–0
Nov. 30	Kenyon	Columbus	W	5–0
Coach: John Eckstrom				184–5
Captain: D.B. Sayers				

John Eckstrom was hired as head coach. The previous year his Kenyon team defeated OSU 29–0. … Ohio State registered its first unbeaten season and won its first championship of the Ohio colleges. … The five points allowed were the fewest in program history.

The Indiana Hoosiers won their first contest with Ohio
State, but the series has been one-sided ever since. More
than a century later, Maurice Clarett ran over, around,
and through the Hoosiers for three first half touchdowns.

1900
8–1–1

Sept. 29	Otterbein	Columbus	W	20–0
Oct. 6	Ohio University	Columbus	W	20–0
Oct. 13	at Cincinnati	Cincinnati	W	29–0
Oct. 20	Ohio Wesleyan	Columbus	W	47–0
Oct. 27	Oberlin	Columbus	W	17–0
Nov. 3	West Virginia	Columbus	W	27–0
Nov. 10	Case	Columbus	W	24–10
Nov. 17	Ohio Medical	Columbus	L	11–6
Nov. 24	at Michigan	Ann Arbor	T	0–0
Nov. 29	Kenyon	Columbus	W	23–5
Coach: John Eckstrom				213–26
Captain: J.H. Tilton				

The tie against Michigan snapped a 14-game winning streak, which included 13 shutouts.

1901
5–3–1

Sept. 28	Otterbein	Columbus	T	0–0
Oct. 5	Wittenberg	Columbus	W	30–0
Oct. 12	Ohio University	Columbus	W	17–0
Oct. 19	Marietta	Columbus	W	24–0
Oct. 26	Western Reserve	Columbus	W	6–5
Nov. 9	Michigan	Columbus	L	21–0
Nov. 16	at Oberlin	Oberlin	L	6–0
Nov. 23	Indiana	Columbus	L	18–6
Nov. 28	Kenyon	Columbus	W	11–6
Coach: John Eckstrom				94–56
Captain: J.M. Kittle				

On the heels of two successful seasons—during which Ohio State went 17–1–2—the program's success was reflected in numerous ways, including the university athletic association turning a profit for the first time. ... Ohio State hosted Michigan for the first time, which was also the 100th game in program history. ... OSU played Indiana for the first time.

1902
6-2-2

Sept. 27	Otterbein	Columbus	W	5-0
Oct. 4	Ohio University	Columbus	W	17-0
Oct. 11	West Virginia	Columbus	W	30-0
Oct. 18	Marietta	Columbus	W	34-0
Oct. 25	at Michigan	Ann Arbor	L	86-0
Nov. 1	Kenyon	Columbus	W	51-5
Nov. 8	Case	Columbus	L	23-12
Nov. 15	Illinois	Columbus	T	0-0
Nov. 22	at Ohio Wesleyan	Delaware	W	17-16
Nov. 27	Indiana	Columbus	T	6-6
Coach: Perry Hale				172-136
Captain: W.F. Coover				

John Eckstrom, who helped guide the program to its first success, surprised university officials by announcing his resignation so he could coach Ohio Medical College. He went 22–4–3 during his three seasons, with a winning percentage of .810. ... Former Yale standout Perry Hale took over and enjoyed shutouts in each of his first four games. ... Ohio State played Illinois for the first time. ... The 86–0 loss to Michigan was the most lopsided defeat in Ohio State history.

1903
8-3

Sept. 26	Otterbein	Columbus	W	18-0
Oct. 3	Wittenberg	Columbus	W	28-0
Oct. 10	Denison	Columbus	W	24-5
Oct. 14	Muskingum	Columbus	W	30-0
Oct. 17	Kenyon	Columbus	W	59-0
Oct. 24	at Case	Cleveland	L	12-0
Oct. 31	West Virginia	Columbus	W	34-6
Nov. 7	at Michigan	Ann Arbor	L	36-0
Nov. 14	Oberlin	Columbus	W	27-5
Nov. 21	Ohio Wesleyan	Columbus	W	29-6
Nov. 26	Indiana	Columbus	L	17-16
Coach: Perry Hale				265-87
Captain: James R. Marker				

1904
6-5

Sept. 24	Otterbein	Columbus	W	34-0
Oct. 1	Miami	Columbus	W	80-0
Oct. 5	Muskingum	Columbus	W	46-0
Oct. 8	Denison	Columbus	W	24-0
Oct. 15	Michigan	Columbus	L	31-6
Oct. 22	Case	Columbus	W	16-6
Oct. 29	at Indiana	Bloomington	L	8-0
Nov. 5	Illinois	Columbus	L	46-0
Nov. 12	at Oberlin	Oberlin	L	4-2
Nov. 19	Kenyon	Columbus	W	11-5
Nov. 24	Carlisle Indians	Columbus	L	23-0
Coach: E.R. Sweetland				219-123
Captain: John D. Thrower				

E.R. Sweetland became Ohio State's first year-round football coach, but also coached track and field. ... An additional 1,500 bleacher seats were installed on the east side of University Field. ... Ticket prices ranged from 25 cents to a dollar for "deluxe" games with Michigan and the Carlisle Indians.

The Carlisle Indian School was a power in the early 1900s, and though head coach Glenn "Pop" Warner had left the school for a few years to coach at Cornell, the Indians were a tough opponent in 1904, going 9-2.

1905
8-2-2

Sept. 23	Otterbein	Columbus	T	6-6
Sept. 30	Heidelberg	Columbus	W	28-0
Oct. 4	Muskingum	Columbus	W	40-0
Oct. 7	Wittenberg	Columbus	W	17-0
Oct. 14	Denison	Columbus	W	2-0
Oct. 21	DePauw	Columbus	W	32-6
Oct. 28	Case	Columbus	T	0-0
Nov. 4	Kenyon	Columbus	W	23-0
Nov. 11	at Michigan	Ann Arbor	L	40-0
Nov. 18	Oberlin	Columbus	W	36-0
Nov. 25	Wooster	Columbus	W	15-0
Nov. 30	Indiana	Columbus	L	11-0
Coach: E.R. Sweetland				199-63
Captain: Ralph W. Hoyer				

Ohio State played its first 12-game schedule. ...
The first organized "rooters club" was formed, with
Harry E. Ewing as head cheerleader.

1906
8-1

Sept. 29	Otterbein	Columbus	W	41-0
Oct. 6	Wittenberg	Columbus	W	52-0
Oct. 10	Muskingum	Columbus	W	16-0
Oct. 20	Michigan	Columbus	L	6-0
Nov. 3	at Oberlin	Oberlin	W	6-0
Nov. 10	Kenyon	Columbus	W	6-0
Nov. 17	at Case	Cleveland	W	9-0
Nov. 24	Wooster	Columbus	W	12-0
Nov. 29	Ohio Medical	Columbus	W	11-8
Coach: A.E. Herrnstein				153-14
Captain: James F. Lincoln				

Chillicothe native and former Michigan player Al
Herrnstein was hired as head coach. The former
Purdue coach was one of the first non-East Coast
coaches to have success in college football. He was
the first Ohio State coach to employ the forward pass
when it scored on a 10-yard touchdown completion

against Wooster. ... The 11–8 Thanksgiving victory against Ohio Medical came against former OSU coach John Eckstrom. ... Ohio State didn't give up a touchdown, and allowed just 14 points all season.

1907
7-2-1

Sept. 28	Otterbein	Columbus	W	28-0
Oct. 5	Muskingum	Columbus	W	16-0
Oct. 12	Denison	Columbus	W	28-0
Oct. 19	Wooster	Columbus	T	6-6
Oct. 26	at Michigan	Ann Arbor	L	22-0
Nov. 2	Kenyon	Columbus	W	12-0
Nov. 9	Oberlin	Columbus	W	22-10
Nov. 16	Case	Columbus	L	11-9
Nov. 23	Heidelberg	Columbus	W	23-0
Nov. 28	Ohio Wesleyan	Columbus	W	16-0
Coach: A.E. Herrnstein				160-49
Captain: H.J. Schory				

Ohio State played Michigan for the first time at Ferry Field.

Though Ferry Field was replaced by Michigan Stadium in 1927, it still remains in use as a multi-purpose facility. Ohio State's Jesse Owens had perhaps the greatest single day in sports history at the site in 1935, setting three world records and tying a fourth in a span of 45 minutes at the Big Ten meet.

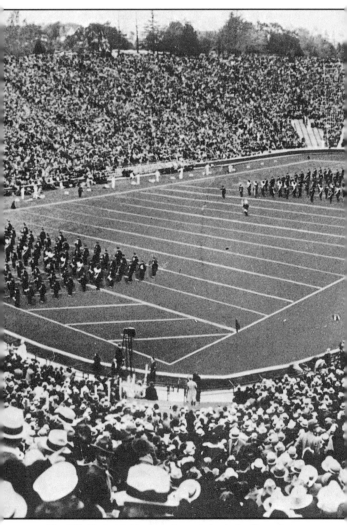

The Ohio State-Michigan rivalry was dominated in early years by the enemy from Ann Arbor. Ohio State would have to content itself with regular wins over the likes of Denison, Kenyon, Wittenberg, Wooster, and Otterbein.

1908
6–4

Sept. 26	Otterbein	Columbus	W	18–0
Oct. 3	Wooster	Columbus	L	8–0
Oct. 10	Denison	Columbus	W	16–2
Oct. 17	Western Reserve	Columbus	L	18–0
Oct. 24	Michigan	Columbus	L	10–6
Oct. 31	Ohio Wesleyan	Columbus	W	20–9
Nov. 7	at Case	Cleveland	L	18–8
Nov. 14	at Vanderbilt	Nashville	W	17–6
Nov. 21	Oberlin	Columbus	W	14–12
Nov. 26	Kenyon	Columbus	W	19–9
Coach: A.E. Herrnstein				118–92
Captain: W.D. Barrington				

The victory at Vanderbilt was No. 100 for the program. ... University Field was officially dedicated as Ohio Field on November 21. The wife of the school president used a flask of water from a campus spring to christen the field.

1909
7–3

Sept. 25	Otterbein	Columbus	W	14–0
Oct. 2	Wittenberg	Columbus	W	39–0
Oct. 9	Wooster	Columbus	W	74–0
Oct. 16	at Michigan	Ann Arbor	L	33–6
Oct. 23	Denison	Columbus	W	29–0
Oct. 30	Ohio Wesleyan	Columbus	W	21–6
Nov. 6	Case	Columbus	L	11–3
Nov. 13	Vanderbilt	Columbus	W	5–0
Nov. 20	at Oberlin	Oberlin	L	26–6
Nov. 25	Kenyon	Columbus	W	22–0
Coach: A.E. Herrnstein				219–76
Captain: Thomas H. Jones				

Center Chelsea Boone scored Ohio State's only points against Michigan by picking up a loose punt near the goal line and running into the end zone. At the time, a punt was considered a live ball. ... After two decades, Ohio State's record was 109–65–11.

1910
6-1-3

Sept. 24	Otterbein	Columbus	W	14-5
Oct. 1	Wittenberg	Columbus	W	62-0
Oct. 8	Cincinnati	Columbus	W	23-0
Oct. 15	Western Reserve	Columbus	W	6-0
Oct. 22	Michigan	Columbus	T	3-3
Oct. 29	Denison	Columbus	T	5-5
Nov. 5	at Case	Cleveland	L	14-10
Nov. 12	Ohio Wesleyan	Columbus	W	6-0
Nov. 19	Oberlin	Columbus	T	0-0
Nov. 24	Kenyon	Columbus	W	53-0
Coach: Howard Jones				182-27
Captain: Leslie R. Wells				

Additional bleachers bumped Ohio Field's capacity to 10,000. ... Season tickets were sold for $2.50. ... Howard Jones, an All-American from Yale, was named head coach, but stayed only one season. In 29 years as head coach, he compiled a 194-64-21 record. In 16 seasons at Southern California, he won seven Pacific Coast Conference titles, four national championships, and five Rose Bowls. ... The 3-3 tie vs. Michigan ended a nine-game losing streak in the series.

1911
5-3-2

Sept. 30	Otterbein	Columbus	W	6-0
Oct. 7	Miami	Columbus	W	3-0
Oct. 14	Western Reserve	Columbus	T	0-0
Oct. 21	at Michigan	Ann Arbor	L	19-0
Oct. 28	Ohio Wesleyan	Columbus	W	3-0
Nov. 4	Case	Columbus	L	9-0
Nov. 11	Kenyon	Columbus	W	24-0
Nov. 18	at Oberlin	Oberlin	T	0-0
Nov. 25	Syracuse	Columbus	L	6-0
Nov. 30	at Cincinnati	Cincinnati	W	11-6
Coach: Harry Vaughn				47-40
Captain: Frank P. Markley				

On the recommendation of Howard Jones, the athletic board hired Harry Vaughn as head football coach. Vaughn, who like Jones was also from Yale, stayed only one season and resigned after finishing 5–3–2. He returned to Yale to study law.

1912
6–3

Oct. 5	at Otterbein	Westerville	W	55–0
Oct. 12	Denison	Columbus	W	34–0
Oct. 19	Michigan	Columbus	L	14–0
Oct. 26	Cincinnati	Columbus	W	47–7
Nov. 2	at Case	Cleveland	W	31–6
Nov. 9	Oberlin	Columbus	W	23–17
Nov. 16	Penn State	Columbus	L	37–0
Nov. 23	at Ohio Wesleyan	Delaware	W	36–6
Nov. 28	Michigan State	Columbus	L	35–20
Coach: John R. Richards			246–122	
Captain: Don B. Barricklow				

Ohio State joined the Western Conference, which later became the Big Ten, but did not compete in the conference in football until 1913. ... After three different coaches during the previous three seasons, the athletic board looked for a long-term hire who would also serve as director of athletics. Former Wisconsin coach John Richards was hired, but resigned after one season. ... With five minutes remaining in the Penn State game, Richards pulled his players from the field because of alleged rough play. Penn State was awarded the victory. ... OSU scored 199 more points than the previous season. ... Homecoming was held for the first time, but was called "Ohio State Day."

Through the Years

Ohio State players hit the sled under Coach Woody Hayes. The tradition of "Senior Tackle," usually done on a tackling, rather than blocking, sled was born in 1913, the same year as Hayes.

1913
4–2–1

Oct. 4	Ohio Wesleyan	Columbus	W	58–0
Oct. 11	Western Reserve	Columbus	W	14–8
Oct. 18	Oberlin	Columbus	T	0–0
Nov. 1	Indiana	Columbus	L	7–6
Nov. 8	at Wisconsin	Madison	L	12–0
Nov. 15	Case	Columbus	W	18–0
Nov. 22	Northwestern	Columbus	W	58–0
Coach: John W. Wilce				154–27
Captain: W. Irving Geissman				

After Carl Rothgeb of Colorado College turned
down the head coaching job, Ohio State turned to
former Wisconsin standout John W. Wilce, who
held the position for 16 years and won three Big
Ten titles. ... The Buckeyes made their football
debut in the Western Conference, which would
eventually become the Big Ten. Their first league
victory was 58–0 against Northwestern. ... Ohio
Field's capacity was increased to 14,000. ... The
"Senior Tackle" tradition began. Senior players
hit the tackling sled once during the final practice
before Michigan. ... Woody Hayes was born on
February 14.

3

Western Conference titles won by
John Wilce's Buckeyes in his 16 seasons at the helm. Only Woody Hayes
has coached longer at the school.

1914
5-2

Oct. 3	Ohio Wesleyan	Columbus	W	16-2
Oct. 10	at Case	Cleveland	W	7-6
Oct. 17	at Illinois	Champaign	L	37-0
Oct. 24	Wisconsin	Columbus	L	7-6
Nov. 7	at Indiana	Bloomington	W	13-3
Nov. 14	Oberlin	Columbus	W	39-0
Nov. 21	Northwestern	Columbus	W	27-0
Coach: John W. Wilce			108-55	
Captain: Campbell J. Graf				
All-American: Boyd Cherry, E.				
All-Big Ten: Boyd Cherry, E.				

Ohio State had its first All-American, end Boyd Cherry.

1915
5-1-1

Oct. 2	Ohio Wesleyan	Columbus	W	19-6
Oct. 9	Case	Columbus	W	14-0
Oct. 16	Illinois	Columbus	T	3-3
Oct. 23	at Wisconsin	Madison	L	21-0
Nov. 6	Indiana	Columbus	W	10-9
Nov. 13	Oberlin	Columbus	W	25-0
Nov. 20	at Northwestern	Evanston	W	34-0
Coach: John W. Wilce			105-39	
Captain: Ivan B. Boughton				

Varsity manager William A. Dougherty wrote the fight song "Across the Field," which was first performed at the Illinois game. He dedicated it to Coach John W. Wilce.

1916
7–0, Big Ten champions

Oct. 7	Ohio Wesleyan	Columbus	W	12–0
Oct. 14	Oberlin	Columbus	W	128–0
Oct. 21	at Illinois	Champaign	W	7–6
Nov. 4	Wisconsin	Columbus	W	14–13
Nov. 11	Indiana	Columbus	W	46–7
Nov. 18	at Case	Cleveland	W	28–0
Nov. 25	Northwestern	Columbus	W	23–3
Coach: John W. Wilce				258–29
Captain: Frank Sorensen				
All-American: Charles "Chic" Harley, HB; Robert Karch, T.				
All-Big Ten: Charles "Chic" Harley, HB.				

Ohio State went a perfect 7–0 and captured its first Western Conference title, although the conference did not officially recognize football championships at that point. The deciding game was the 23–3 win against Northwestern. ... The 128–0 victory against Oberlin set a school record. The offense tallied 1,140 yards. ... Ohio State enjoyed its first victory against Wisconsin, at that point arguably the program's biggest win. ... Chic Harley was named an All-American for the first time. He was OSU's first three-time All-American, and sixth in program history.

Through the Years

128

The point total Ohio State put up against Oberlin in 1916. No other Ohio State team has matched that total in a single game. The game accounted for almost exactly half of Ohio State's points for the year.

1917
8–0–1, Big Ten champions

Sept. 29	Case	Columbus	W	49–0
Oct. 6	Ohio Wesleyan	Columbus	W	53–0
Oct. 13	Northwestern	Columbus	W	40–0
Oct. 27	Denison	Columbus	W	67–0
Nov. 3	at Indiana	Bloomington	W	26–3
Nov. 10	at Wisconsin	Madison	W	16–3
Nov. 17	Illinois	Columbus	W	13–0
Nov. 24	at Auburn	Montgomery	T	0–0
Nov. 29	Camp Sherman	Columbus	W	28–0
Coach: John W. Wilce				292–6

Captains: Harold J. Courtney, Howard Courtney

All-American: Charles "Shifty" Bolen, E; Harold "Hap" Courtney, E; Charles "Chic" Harley, HB; Kelley VanDyne, C.

All-Big Ten: Charles "Shifty" Bolen, E; Harold "Hap" Courtney, T; Charles "Chic" Harley, HB; Kelley VanDyne, C.

Ohio State successfully defended its Western Conference championship, although the conference was beginning to be called the Big Ten. ... OSU played in two postseason contests. The first was a 0–0 tie against Auburn in Montgomery, a benefit game for the Ohio National Guard training in the region. A few days later, Ohio State played Camp Sherman, a team from Chillicothe. ... Chic Harley scored four touchdowns at Indiana. ... Ohio State didn't yield a touchdown and recorded seven shutouts.

8.4

Chic Harley's average points scored per game in his Ohio State career, a school record. His 201 career points were a school record until the total was surpassed by "Hopalong" Cassady in 1955.

The Buckeyes have long enjoyed a one-sided relationship with the Northwestern Wildcats, regularly trouncing the squad from Evanston, Illinois. The 1917 matchup was no different, as the Ohio State squad crushed the Wildcats 40–0.

1918
3–3

Oct. 5	Ohio Wesleyan	Columbus	W	41–0
Oct. 12	Denison	Columbus	W	34–0
Oct. 26	Michigan	Columbus	L	14–0
Nov. 9	Case	Columbus	W	56–0
Nov. 16	at Illinois	Champaign	L	13–0
Nov. 23	Wisconsin	Columbus	L	14–3
Coach: John W. Wilce				134–41
Captain: Clarence A. MacDonald				
All-American: Clarence A. MacDonald, E.				
All-Big Ten: Clarence A. MacDonald, E.				

Many of Ohio State's players served in the military during World War I, but end Clarence MacDonald and halfback Roy Rife were assigned by the Navy to continue their education on campus. Coach John Wilce was inducted into the Army, but remained on campus to continue his study of medicine and coach the team.

1919
6–1

Oct. 4	Ohio Wesleyan	Columbus	W	38–0
Oct. 11	Cincinnati	Columbus	W	46–0
Oct. 18	Kentucky	Columbus	W	49–0
Oct. 25	at Michigan	Ann Arbor	W	13–3
Nov. 8	Purdue	Columbus	W	20–0
Nov. 15	at Wisconsin	Madison	W	3–0
Nov. 22	Illinois	Columbus	L	9–7
Coach: John W. Wilce				176–12
Captain: Charles "Chic" Harley				
All-American: Charles "Chic" Harley, B; Pete Stinchcomb, B.				
All-Big Ten: Charles "Chic" Harley, B; Pete Stinchcomb, B.				

Led by Chic Harley's key 40-yard run, Ohio State recorded its first win over Michigan, 13–3. The Wolverines had outscored the Buckeyes in the first 15 games 369–21. ... In three seasons, Harley, who in 1918 was a pilot in the Army Air Corps, tallied 23 touchdowns, 39 extra points, and eight field goals for 201 points—a school record that lasted 36 years until broken by Hopalong Cassady. ... Ohio State played Purdue for the first time. ... Nearly 20,000 were in attendance for Harley's last game against Illinois.

1920
7-1, Big Ten champions

Oct. 2	Ohio Wesleyan	Columbus	W	55-0
Oct. 9	Oberlin	Columbus	W	37-0
Oct. 16	Purdue	Columbus	W	17-0
Oct. 23	Wisconsin	Columbus	W	13-7
Nov. 30	at Chicago	Chicago	W	7-6
Nov. 6	Michigan	Columbus	W	14-7
Nov. 20	at Illinois	Champaign	W	7-0
Jan. 1	California	Rose Bowl	L	28-0
Coach: John W. Wilce				150-48
Captain: Iolas M. Huffman				
All-American: Iolas M. Huffman, G; Pete Stinchcomb, B.				
All-Big Ten: Pete Stinchcomb, B.				

Ohio State won its third Western Conference title and received its first invitation to play in the Rose Bowl, although there was a heated debate between the athletic board and athletics director Lynn Wilbur St. John about whether to accept. All-American Pete Stinchcomb had 82 rushing yards, but Cal easily won before a sellout crowd of 42,000. ... An extensive campaign was launched to build a new football stadium. It began Oct. 18, with a goal of reaching $600,000. By Nov. 26, more than $923,000 had been pledged. ... "Truck" Myers' dramatic 37-yard touchdown reception as time expired clinched the conference title.

1921
5-2

Oct. 1	Ohio Wesleyan	Columbus	W	28-0
Oct. 8	Oberlin	Columbus	L	7-6
Oct. 15	Minnesota	Columbus	W	27-0
Oct. 22	at Michigan	Ann Arbor	W	14-0
Nov. 5	at Chicago	Chicago	W	7-0
Nov. 12	Purdue	Columbus	W	28-0
Nov. 19	Illinois	Columbus	L	7-0
Coach: John W. Wilce				110-14
Captain: Cyril "Truck" Myers				
All-American: Iolas Huffman, T; Cyril "Truck" Myers, E.				
All-Big Ten: Cyril "Truck" Myers, E; Dean Trott, G.				

Ohio State enjoyed its third straight victory against Michigan. ... On Aug. 3, Gov. Harry Davis joined a crowd of more than 2,500 to officially break ground on the new stadium, just a few blocks from Ohio Field. The project was scheduled to take only 14 months and originally budgeted at a cost of $1,341,017. Upon completion, the final cost exceeded $1.5 million, of which roughly $1 million was raised by fans. Critics took issue with the "needless" seating capacity of 60,000. ... Coach John Wilce was so upset after the Oberlin loss that he ordered the team back onto the field for a night practice. Ohio State shut out its next four opponents. ... The term "Fighting Illini" came from the Ohio State game, used by Harvey Woodruff of the *Chicago Tribune*.

1922
3-4

Oct. 7	Ohio Wesleyan	Columbus	W	5-0
Oct. 14	Oberlin	Columbus	W	14-0
Oct. 21	Michigan	Columbus	L	19-0
Oct. 28	at Minnesota	Minneapolis	L	9-0
Nov. 11	Chicago	Columbus	L	14-9
Nov. 18	Iowa	Columbus	L	12-9
Nov. 25	at Illinois	Champaign	W	6-3
Coach: John W. Wilce				43-57
Captain: Lloyd A. Pixley				

The new stadium was dedicated before the Michigan game on October 21. Temporary stands were erected in the south end of the stadium, resulting in an estimated crowd of 72,500. It was actually the third game played in Ohio Stadium, following wins against Ohio Wesleyan and Oberlin. The opener attracted 25,000 fans. ... Ohio State had its first losing season since 1898.

1923
3–4–1

Oct. 6	Ohio Wesleyan	Columbus	W	24–7
Oct. 13	Colgate	Columbus	T	23–23
Oct. 20	at Michigan	Ann Arbor	L	23–0
Oct. 27	Iowa	Columbus	L	20–0
Nov. 3	Denison	Columbus	W	42–0
Nov. 10	at Purdue	West Lafayette	W	32–0
Nov. 17	at Chicago	Chicago	L	17–3
Nov. 24	Illinois	Columbus	L	9–0
Coach: John W. Wilce				124–99
Captain: Boni Petcoff				
All-American: Harry "Hoge" Workman, QB.				
All-Big Ten: Harry "Hoge" Workman, QB.				

The Big Ten allowed teams to expand the schedule to eight games. ... Quarterback Ollie Klee sustained a shoulder injury in the opener against Ohio Wesleyan.

"Hoge" Workman was an All-American quarterback at Ohio State and an outstanding baseball player as well. He played for the Boston Red Sox in 1924 and later became a player-coach in the NFL.

Ohio Stadium eventually became "Home Sweet Home," as the Buckeyes enjoy one of the best home-field advantages in all of sports, but things were not always that way. The Buckeyes were well below average in the stadium's first three years, the only three consecutive losing seasons in school history.

1924
2-3-3

Oct. 4	Purdue	Columbus	W	7-0
Oct. 11	at Iowa	Iowa City	T	0-0
Oct. 18	Ohio Wesleyan	Columbus	W	10-0
Oct. 25	Chicago	Columbus	T	3-3
Nov. 1	Wooster	Columbus	T	7-7
Nov. 8	Indiana	Columbus	L	12-7
Nov. 15	Michigan	Columbus	L	16-6
Nov. 22	at Illinois	Champaign	L	7-0
Coach: John W. Wilce				40-45
Captain: Francis D. Young				
All-American: Harold Cunningham, E.				

The 7-7 tie against Wooster was the 300th game in program history. ... Ohio Stadium's first three seasons were the only time in program history Ohio State had three consecutive losing seasons. The victory against Purdue was the stadium's first Big Ten win. ... The tradition of the "Illibuck" was created, making it an annual trophy game.

3

Years the living turtle that represented the Illibuck rivalry lasted before passing away. The turtle had been chosen for its long life expectancy, but had to be replaced by the wooden Illy Illibuck.

1925
4-3-1

Oct. 3	Ohio Wesleyan	Columbus	W	10-3
Oct. 10	Chicago	Columbus	T	3-3
Oct. 17	Columbia	Columbus	W	9-0
Oct. 24	Iowa	Columbus	L	15-0
Oct. 31	Wooster	Columbus	W	17-0
Nov. 7	Indiana	Columbus	W	7-0
Nov. 14	at Michigan	Ann Arbor	L	10-0
Nov. 21	Illinois	Columbus	L	14-9
Coach: John W. Wilce				55-45
Captain: Harold B. Cunningham				
All-American: Edwin Hess, G.				
All-Big Ten: Edwin Hess, G.				

Through the Years

Ohio State recorded a big victory against East Coast power Columbia, which at the time was the largest university in the nation with an enrollment of 15,000. It was considered the first major victory at Ohio Stadium. ... Ohio State finished a four-year run of 12-14-5. ... The Illinois game featured the final collegiate game of Harold "Red" Grange. The paid attendance was 84,295.

1926
7-1

Oct. 2	Wittenberg	Columbus	W	40-0
Oct. 9	Ohio Wesleyan	Columbus	W	47-0
Oct. 16	at Columbia	New York City	W	32-7
Oct. 23	Iowa	Columbus	W	23-6
Oct. 30	at Chicago	Chicago	W	18-0
Nov. 6	Wilmington	Columbus	W	13-7
Nov. 13	Michigan	Columbus	L	17-16
Nov. 20	at Illinois	Champaign	W	7-6
Coach: John W. Wilce				196-43
Captain: Marty G. Karow				
All-American: Edwin Hess, G; Martin Karow, HB; Leo Raskowski, T.				
All-Big Ten: Edwin Hess, G; Marty Karow, HB; Leo Raskowski, T.				

The only loss came against Michigan, in front of

90,411 fans at Ohio Stadium. ... A group of students led a movement to elect Maudine Ormsby as homecoming queen, who turned out to be a cow.

1927
4-4

Oct. 1	Wittenberg	Columbus	W	31-0
Oct. 8	at Iowa	Iowa City	W	13-6
Oct. 15	Northwestern	Columbus	L	19-13
Oct. 22	at Michigan	Ann Arbor	L	21-0
Oct. 29	Chicago	Columbus	W	13-7
Nov. 5	at Princeton	Princeton	L	20-0
Nov. 12	Denison	Columbus	W	61-6
Nov. 19	Illinois	Columbus	L	13-0
Coach: John W. Wilce				131-92
Captain: Theodore R. Meyer				
All-American: Leo Raskowski, T.				
All-Big Ten: Leo Raskowski, T.				

A wooden replica of Illibuck was introduced for the trophy game against Illinois. Initially, Illibuck was a live turtle.

1927 was a big year for Ohio State's big rival, Illinois. The Illini won the national championship, beating OSU in the regular season finale. The Buckeyes also lost to Michigan for the sixth straight year.

In addition to being named an All-American by Grantland Rice in 1928, Wes Fesler was also a standout basketball player. He was twice named All-Western Conference on the hardwood, running the Ohio State offense as a guard.

1928
5–2–1

Oct. 6	Wittenberg	Columbus	W	41–0
Oct. 13	at Northwestern	Evanston	W	10–0
Oct. 20	Michigan	Columbus	W	19–7
Oct. 27	at Indiana	Bloomington	W	13–0
Nov. 3	Princeton	Columbus	T	6–6
Nov. 10	Iowa	Columbus	L	14–7
Nov. 17	Muskingum	Columbus	W	39–0
Nov. 24	Illinois	Columbus	L	8–0
Coach: John W. Wilce				135–35
Captain: Leo Raskowski				
All-American: Wesley Fesler, E.				
All-Big Ten: Wesley Fesler, E.				

Coach John W. Wilce (78–33–9) announced his resignation. "Football was becoming too much of a business," he said. "The game was being taken away from the boys. I was a faculty-type coach who believed educational aspects were more important than winning games." Wilce went on to do post-graduate research at Harvard and Columbia before becoming the director of the Ohio State University Student Health Services in 1934. ... Athletics director Lynn Wilbur St. John announced that all stadium debt had been paid, just eight years after it opened.

6

Different colleges Wes Fesler coached after his playing days were done. He coached football at Wesleyan, Pitt, OSU, and Minnesota; he also coached basketball at Harvard and Princeton.

1929
4-3-1

Oct. 5	Wittenberg	Columbus	W	19-0
Oct. 12	Iowa	Columbus	W	7-6
Oct. 19	at Michigan	Ann Arbor	W	7-0
Oct. 26	Indiana	Columbus	T	0-0
Nov. 2	at Pittsburgh	Pittsburgh	L	18-2
Nov. 9	Northwestern	Columbus	L	18-6
Nov. 16	Kenyon	Columbus	W	54-0
Nov. 23	Illinois	Columbus	L	27-0
Coach: Sam S. Willaman				95-69
Captain: Alan M. Holman				
All-American: Wesley Fesler, E.				
All-Big Ten: Wesley Fesler, E.				

Sam Willaman, an assistant on John W. Wilce's staff and a 1913 Ohio State graduate (he scored four touchdowns in his last game), was named head coach after four years at Iowa State. ... Against Northwestern, Wesley Fesler grabbed a fumble and returned it 86 yards for Ohio State's only points in the game.

1930
5-2-1

Sept. 27	Mt. Union	Columbus	W	59-0
Oct. 4	Indiana	Columbus	W	23-0
Oct. 11	at Northwestern	Evanston	L	19-2
Oct. 18	Michigan	Columbus	L	13-0
Nov. 1	Wisconsin	Columbus	T	0-0
Nov. 8	at Navy	Baltimore	W	27-0
Nov. 15	Pittsburgh	Columbus	W	16-7
Nov. 22	at Illinois	Champaign	W	12-9
Coach: Sam S. Willaman				139-48
Captain: Wesley Fesler				
All-American: Wesley Fesler, E; Lew Hinchman, HB.				
All-Big Ten: Wesley Fesler, E; Lew Hinchman, HB.				

Wes Fesler became the second three-time All-American in Ohio State history, and was also the first recorded winner of the team's Most Valuable Player award. Fesler earned nine total varsity

Through the Years

letters, three each in football, basketball, and baseball. Pittsburgh's Jock Sutherland called him "a one man team. It is unbelievable how that boy can do so many things."

1931
6–3

Oct. 3	Cincinnati	Columbus	W	67–6
Oct. 10	Vanderbilt	Columbus	L	26–21
Oct. 17	at Michigan	Ann Arbor	W	20–7
Oct. 24	Northwestern	Columbus	L	10–0
Oct. 31	at Indiana	Bloomington	W	13–0
Nov. 7	Navy	Columbus	W	20–0
Nov. 14	at Wisconsin	Madison	W	6–0
Nov. 21	Illinois	Columbus	W	40–0
Nov. 28	at Minnesota	Minneapolis	L	19–7
Coach: Sam S. Willaman				194–68
Captain: Stuart K. Holcomb				
All-American: Carl Cramer, QB; Lew Hinchman, HB.				
All-Big Ten: Lew Hinchman, HB; Carl Cramer, QB.				

After being located in the Athletic House for years, the athletic department headquarters moved to a new physical education building. ... Earle Bruce was born on March 8.

1931

Captain Stu Holcomb was well-traveled after his playing days. He coached football at Findlay, Muskigum, Washington & Jefferson, Miami, and Purdue; coached basketball at West Point; was the athletics director at Northwestern; and later became the general manager of the Chicago White Sox.

1932
4-1-3

Oct. 1	Ohio Wesleyan	Columbus	W	34-7
Oct. 8	Indiana	Columbus	T	7-7
Oct. 15	Michigan	Columbus	L	14-0
Oct. 22	at Pittsburgh	Pittsburgh	T	0-0
Oct. 29	Wisconsin	Columbus	T	7-7
Nov. 5	at Northwestern	Evanston	W	20-6
Nov. 12	Pennsylvania	Columbus	W	19-0
Nov. 19	at Illinois	Champaign	W	3-0
Coach: Sam S. Willaman				90-41
Captain: Lewi Hinchman				
All-American: Joseph Gailus, G; Sid Gillman, E; Lew Hinchman, HB; Ted Rosequist, T.				
All-Big Ten: Joseph Gailus, G; Sid Gillman, E; Lew Hinchman, HB; Ted Rosequist T.				

The origins of the pregame "Skull Session" date back to 1932, when band director Eugene Weigel began having the marching band memorize the music they would be playing that week. Before game time, the band would go through its routine as a final rehearsal. ... Lew Hinchman became Ohio State's third three-time All-American.

1933
7-1

Oct. 7	Virginia	Columbus	W	75-0
Oct. 14	Vanderbilt	Columbus	W	20-0
Oct. 21	at Michigan	Ann Arbor	L	13-0
Oct. 28	Northwestern	Columbus	W	12-0
Nov. 4	Indiana	Columbus	W	21-0
Nov. 11	at Pennsylvania	Philadelphia	W	20-7
Nov. 18	at Wisconsin	Madison	W	6-0
Nov. 25	Illinois	Columbus	W	7-6
Coach: Sam S. Willaman				161-26
Captains: Joseph Gailus, Sid Gillman				
All-American: Joseph Gailus, G.				
All-Big Ten: Joseph Gailus, G.				

After going just 2–3 against Michigan, Sam Willaman (21–10–5) resigned to become the head coach at Western Reserve, but soon after died unexpectedly following an emergency operation. ... The Buckeyes had their best season since 1920, with the defense allowing just 26 points, but didn't win the Big Ten title. Nevertheless, the Dunkel College Football Index named the Buckeyes its national champion.

1934
7–1

Oct. 6	Indiana	Columbus	W	33–0
Oct. 13	at Illinois	Champaign	L	14–13
Oct. 20	Colgate	Columbus	W	10–7
Oct. 27	at Northwestern	Evanston	W	28–6
Nov. 3	at Western Reserve	Cleveland	W	76–0
Nov. 10	Chicago	Columbus	W	33–0
Nov. 17	Michigan	Columbus	W	34–0
Nov. 24	Iowa	Columbus	W	40–7
Coach: Francis Schmidt				267–34
Captain: Regis Monahan				
All-American: Regis Monahan, G; Merle Wendt, E.				
All-Big Ten: Regis Monahan, G; Merle Wendt, E.				

Francis Schmidt was named head coach, and brought a "razzle-dazzle" offense from TCU to Ohio State. It included double and triple reverses, laterals, and passes, en route to 267 points scored, the second-most in school history. ... Schmidt, the first coach signed to a multiyear contract, made immediate news after being hired when he was asked how he'll deal with rival Michigan: "They put their pants on one leg at a time same as everybody else." It led to the formation of the "Gold Pants Club," which awarded miniature gold football pants to all players who participated in a victory over the Wolverines. ... Ohio State began the tradition of planting a tree for each All-American in Buckeye Grove.

Francis A. Schmidt won a pair of Western Conference
titles at Ohio State, his greatest success in coaching.
Known for his use of colorful trick plays, Schmidt was
dubbed Francis "Close the Gates of Mercy" Schmidt.

1935

7–1, Big Ten champions (tied)

Oct. 5	Kentucky	Columbus	W	19–6
Oct. 12	Drake	Columbus	W	85–7
Oct. 19	Northwestern	Columbus	W	28–7
Oct. 26	at Indiana	Bloomington	W	28–6
Nov. 2	Notre Dame	Columbus	L	18–13
Nov. 9	at Chicago	Chicago	W	20–13
Nov. 16	Illinois	Columbus	W	6–0
Nov. 23	at Michigan	Ann Arbor	W	38–0
Coach: Francis Schmidt				237–57
Captain: Gomer Jones				
All-American: Gomer Jones, C; Merle Wendt, E.				
All-Big Ten: Gomer Jones, C; Merle Wendt, E.				

Ohio State claimed a share of the Big Ten title for the first time in 14 years. ... The Michigan game was moved to the season finale, with Ohio State winning 38–0. ... OSU held a 13–0 lead entering the fourth quarter against Notre Dame, but the Fighting Irish scored three times, including twice in the last two minutes, for an 18–13 win. ... Ohio State came back from a 13–0 fourth-quarter deficit to win at Chicago. ... Center/linebacker Gomer Thomas Jones was the team's most valuable player. He was 5-foot-8, 210 pounds.

72

Points scored by Francis Schmidt's Buckeyes against Michigan in his first two seasons at the helm. By contrast, the Wolverines failed to score a single point in those two matchups.

1936
5–3

Oct. 3	New York University	Columbus	W	60–0
Oct. 10	Pittsburgh	Columbus	L	6–0
Oct. 17	at Northwestern	Evanston	L	14–13
Oct. 24	Indiana	Columbus	W	7–0
Oct. 31	at Notre Dame	South Bend	L	7–2
Nov. 7	Chicago	Columbus	W	44–0
Nov. 14	at Illinois	Champaign	W	13–0
Nov. 21	Michigan	Columbus	W	21–0
Coach: Francis Schmidt				160–27
Captain: Merle E. Wendt				
All-American: Charles Hamrick, T; Inwood Smith, G; Merle Wendt, E.				
All-Big Ten: Charles Hamrick, T; Inwood Smith, T; Merle Wendt, E.				

Ohio State was ranked 18th after winning at Illinois, but still fell out of the Associated Press Poll (top 20) after defeating Michigan. It was also the 400th game in OSU history. … The Ohio State Marching Band performed "Script Ohio" for the first time at Pittsburgh. After losing its Big Ten opener to Northwestern, OSU shut out its other four conference opponents.

1937
6–2

Sept. 25	Texas Christian	Columbus	W	14–0
Oct. 2	Purdue	Columbus	W	13–0
Oct. 9	at Southern California	Los Angeles	L	13–12
Oct. 23	Northwestern	Columbus	W	7–0
Oct. 30	at Chicago	Chicago	W	39–0
Nov. 6	Indiana	Columbus	L	10–0
Nov. 13	Illinois	Columbus	W	19–0
Nov. 20	at Michigan	Ann Arbor	W	21–0
Coach: Francis Schmidt				125–23
Captains: Ralph Wolf, Jim McDonald				
Ranking (AP): Preseason No. 12; Postseason No. 13.				
All-American: Carl Kaplanoff, T; Jim McDonald, QB; Ralph Wolf, C; Gust Zarnas, G.				
All-Big Ten: Carl Kaplanoff, T; Jim McDonald, QB; Esco Sarkkinen, E; Ralph Wolf, C; Gust Zarnas, G.				

Through the Years

Coach Francis Schmidt was known for trick plays, and against Indiana Gust Zarnas pulled out of his guard position, took a handoff from one of the backs, and threw a 57-yard completion to Fred Crow. Zarnas was born in Greece, came to America with his parents, and became a Hall of Fame player. ... Ohio State enjoyed its fourth consecutive shutout against Michigan, by a combined score of 114–0.

1938
4–3–1

Oct. 1	Indiana	Columbus	W	6–0
Oct. 8	Southern California	Columbus	L	14–7
Oct. 15	at Northwestern	Evanston	T	0–0
Oct. 22	Chicago	Columbus	W	42–7
Oct. 29	at N.Y. University	New York City	W	32–0
Nov. 5	Purdue	Columbus	L	12–0
Nov. 12	at Illinois	Champaign	W	32–14
Nov. 19	Michigan	Columbus	L	18–0
Coach: Francis Schmidt				119–65
Captains: Michael Kabealo, Carl G. Kaplanoff				

For the seventh consecutive year, the Michigan game was a shutout. Ohio State was 4–3 in those games. .... Hall of Fame coach Sid Gillman joined Francis Schmidt's staff. ... Cheerleader Clancy Isaac began the "Block O" tradition, although instead of the student section being in the south stands it was in the closed (north) end of Ohio Stadium. An actual "Block O" was painted on the stadium seats in this area. ... With 67,397 fans in the stands, Ohio State pulled out a tough 6–0 victory against Indiana in the season opener. Said the *Cleveland Plain Dealer*: "No Ohio team ever came through as hard a game, battered, tattered but victorious."

Through the Years

1939
6–2, Big Ten champions

Oct. 7	Missouri	Columbus	W	19–0
Oct. 14	Northwestern	Columbus	W	13–0
Oct. 21	at Minnesota	Minneapolis	W	23–20
Oct. 28	Cornell	Columbus	L	23–14
Nov. 4	Indiana	Columbus	W	24–0
Nov. 11	at Chicago	Chicago	W	61–0
Nov. 18	Illinois	Columbus	W	21–0
Nov. 25	at Michigan	Ann Arbor	L	21–14
Coach: Francis Schmidt				189–64
Captain: Steven F. Andrako				
Ranking (AP): Preseason No. 10; Postseason No. 15.				
All-American: Vic Marino, G; Esco Sarkkinen, E; Don Scott, HB.				
All-Big Ten: Vic Marino, G; Esco Sarkkinen, E; Don Scott, HB.				

Ohio State climbed to No. 4, its highest ranking ever at the time, prior to hosting No. 7 Cornell for its first top 10 matchup. ... Versitile back Don Scott was named an All-American the first of two times. He died October 1, 1943, when his bomber crashed while he was training as a pilot in England during World War II. "I can't remember a back as dangerous in so many departments of play," Coach Francis Schmidt later said.

1940
4–4

Sept. 28	Pittsburgh	Columbus	W	30–7
Oct. 5	Purdue	Columbus	W	17–14
Oct. 12	at Northwestern	Evanston	L	6–3
Oct. 19	Minnesota	Columbus	L	13–7
Oct. 26	at Cornell	Ithaca	L	21–7
Nov. 2	Indiana	Columbus	W	21–6
Nov. 16	at Illinois	Champaign	W	14–6
Nov. 23	Michigan	Columbus	L	40–0
Coach: Francis Schmidt				99–113
Captain: E. James Langhurst				
Ranking (AP): Preseason No. 15; Postseason NR.				
All-American: Donald Scott, QB.				
All-Big Ten: Donald Scott, QB.				

For the first time in its history, Ohio State faced a team ranked No. 1, Cornell. ... Hall of Fame Coach Sid Gillman resigned from Francis Schmidt's staff at the end of the season and coached Idaho in 1941–42 before the school banned football during World War II. ... According to the *Mansfield News Journal*, Frank Chapman said his friend James Langhurst used to tell him: "I have an obsession when it comes to that. If any publication writes up a boy or girl, and he or she is a captain of their team, it should be so announced. It's the greatest honor a guy or girl can have."

1941
6-1-1

Sept. 27	Missouri	Columbus	W	12-7
Oct. 4	at Southern California	Los Angeles	W	33-0
Oct. 18	Purdue	Columbus	W	16-14
Oct. 25	Northwestern	Columbus	L	14-7
Nov. 1	at Pittsburgh	Pittsburgh	W	21-14
Nov. 8	Wisconsin	Columbus	W	46-34
Nov. 15	Illinois	Columbus	W	12-7
Nov. 22	at Michigan	Ann Arbor	T	20-20
Coach: Paul Brown				167-110
Captain: Jack W. Stephenson				
Ranking (AP): Preseason No. 10; Postseason No. 13.				

After a stellar coaching career at Massillon-Washington High School (80–8–2), Paul Brown was named Ohio State's head coach. His team went 6-1-1, and Ohio State recorded its first West Coast victory, 33–0 at Southern California in Brown's second game. ... "Big Jim" Daniell's blocked punt through the end zone for a safety proved to be the difference against Purdue. During World War II, Daniell served as naval lieutenant on a destroyer in the Pacific, where he earned the Silver Star, the Bronze Star, and a Presidential Citation.

Before moving on to the professional ranks, Paul Brown
(right) sharpened his teeth in the college game. He led
the Buckeyes to the 1942 national championship, and
remained head coach in abstensia through World War II,
even though he coached the Great Lakes Naval Station's
team against the Buckeyes in 1945.

1942

9–1, Big Ten champions, national champions

Sept. 26	Fort Knox	Columbus	W	59–0
Oct. 3	Indiana	Columbus	W	32–21
Oct. 10	Southern California	Columbus	W	28–12
Oct. 17	Purdue	Columbus	W	26–0
Oct. 24	at Northwestern	Evanston	W	20–6
Oct. 31	at Wisconsin	Madison	L	17–7
Nov. 7	Pittsburgh	Columbus	W	59–19
Nov. 14	Illinois	Cleveland	W	44–20
Nov. 21	Michigan	Columbus	W	21–7
Nov. 28	Iowa Seahawks	Columbus	W	41–12
Coach: Paul Brown				337–114
Captain: George M. Lynn				

Ranking (AP): Preseason No. 1; Postseason No. 1.

All-American: Robert Shaw, E; Charles Csuri, T; Lindell Houston, G; Paul Sarringhaus, HB; Gene Fekete, FB

All-Big Ten: Lindell Houston, G; Paul Saringhaus, HB; Robert Shaw, E.

Led by a star-studded backfield that included Les Horvath, Paul Sarringhaus, and Gene Fekete, Ohio State claimed its first national title. ... The only loss, 17–7 at Wisconsin, came after several key players and coaches caught a virus from a drinking fountain on the train from Chicago to Madison. ... The 337 points set a team record that stood until 1969. ... The offense averaged 218.2 yards per game and 5.2 per carry. ... Fekete led the Big Ten in scoring with 92 points, while Sarringhaus was second at 72.

1943
3–6

Sept. 25	Iowa Seahawks	Columbus	L	28–13
Oct. 2	Missouri	Columbus	W	27–6
Oct. 9	at Great Lakes	Crestwood, Ill.	L	13–6
Oct. 16	Purdue	Cleveland	L	30–7
Oct. 23	Northwestern	Columbus	L	13–0
Oct. 30	Indiana	Columbus	L	20–14
Nov. 6	at Pittsburgh	Pittsburgh	W	46–6
Nov. 13	Illinois	Columbus	W	29–26
Nov. 20	at Michigan	Ann Arbor	L	45–7
Coach: Paul Brown				149–187
Captains: John R. Dugger, Charles A. Csuri				
Ranking (AP): Preseason No. 18; Postseason NR.				
All-American: Bill Willis, T.				
All-Big Ten: Bill Willis, T.				

With the game apparently ending in a 26-all tie, Ohio State and Illinois left the field, only to be called back 20 minutes later when it was discovered that the Illini were called for a penalty on the Buckeyes' final play. John Stungis kicked a 27-yard field goal, the first of his career, for the victory. ... Coach Paul Brown, a lieutenant junior-grade, left Ohio State for the Great Lakes Naval Training Station in April 1944. ... Les Horvath was in dental school and not eligible for football. When the rules were changed he returned in 1944 and won the Heisman Trophy. ... Bill Willis was Ohio State's first black All-Ameican, an honor he earned again in 1944.

1944
9–0, Big Ten champions

Sept. 30	Missouri	Columbus	W	54–0
Oct. 7	Iowa	Columbus	W	34–0
Oct. 14	at Wisconsin	Madison	W	20–7
Oct. 21	Great Lakes	Columbus	W	26–6
Oct. 28	Minnesota	Columbus	W	34–14
Nov. 4	Indiana	Columbus	W	21–7
Nov. 11	Pittsburgh	Columbus	W	54–19

| Nov. 18 | Illinois | Cleveland | W | 26-12 |
| Nov. 25 | Michigan | Columbus | W | 18-14 |

Coach: Carroll C. Widdoes   287-79

Captain: Gordon Appleby

Ranking (AP): Preseason No. 8; Postseason No. 2.

Major Awards: Les Horvath, Heisman Trophy

All-American: Jack Dugger, E; Bill Willis, T; Bill Hackett, G; Les Horvath, QB/HB.

All-Big Ten: Jack Dugger, E; Bill Hackett, G; Les Horvath, QB/HB; Bill Willis, T.

Leaders: Rushing—Les Horvath (924 yards, 163 carries); Passing—Les Horvath (14 of 32, 344 yards).

Carroll Widdoes, an assistant coach for Paul Brown at both Massillon High School and Ohio State, was named acting head coach. The Buckeyes claimed the Big Ten championship, but finished No. 2 in the Associated Press poll behind Army. ... Les Horvath became the school's first Heisman Trophy winner. He had 905 rushing yards and 345 passing to rank second in the nation in rushing and third in total offense. ... Ohio State received an invitation to the Rose Bowl, but faculty representatives from around the Big Ten disallowed the trip. ... Brown returned as coach of the Great Lakes Naval Center.

Fully half of the final poll in 1944 consisted of service teams, squads comprised of military men being trained for war service. The Buckeyes were the highest ranked traditional school in '44, finishing second in the final AP poll to the Army Cadets. The next five teams in the poll were service teams.

1945
7-2

Sept. 29	Missouri	Columbus	W	47-6
Oct. 6	Iowa	Columbus	W	42-0
Oct. 13	Wisconsin	Columbus	W	12-0
Oct. 20	Purdue	Columbus	L	35-13
Oct. 27	at Minnesota	Minneapolis	W	20-7
Nov. 3	Northwestern	Columbus	W	16-14
Nov. 10	at Pittsburgh	Pittsburgh	W	14-0
Nov. 17	Illinois	Columbus	W	27-2
Nov. 24	at Michigan	Ann Arbor	L	7-3
Coach: Carroll C. Widdoes				194-71
Captain: William C. Hackett				
Ranking (AP): Preseason No. 4; Postseason No. 12.				
All-American: Warren Amling, G; Ollie Cline, FB; Russell Thomas, T.				
All-Big Ten: Warren Amling, G/T; Ollie Cline, FB; Russell Thomas, T.				
Leaders: Rushing—Ollie Cline (936 yards, 181 carries);				
Passing—Dick Fisher (9 of 28, 245 yards).				

Warren Amling earned All-America honors at guard, a year before being named an All-American tackle. ... Coach Carroll Widdoes went 16-2 over two seasons, giving him the highest winning percentage (.889) in Ohio State history.

1946
4-3-2

Sept. 28	Missouri	Columbus	T	13-13
Oct. 5	at Southern California	Los Angeles	W	21-0
Oct. 12	at Wisconsin	Madison	L	20-7
Oct. 19	Purdue	Columbus	T	14-14
Oct. 26	Minnesota	Columbus	W	39-9
Nov. 2	at Northwestern	Evanston	W	39-27
Nov. 9	Pittsburgh	Columbus	W	20-13
Nov. 16	at Illinois	Champaign	L	16-7
Nov. 23	Michigan	Columbus	L	58-6
Coach: Paul Bixler				166-170
Captain: Warren Amling				
Ranking (AP): Preseason No. 14; Postseason NR.				
All-American: Warren Amling, T; Cecil Souders, E.				

All-Big Ten: Warren Amling G/T; Cecil Souders, E.

Leaders: Rushing—Joseph Whisler (544 yards, 129 carries);
Passing—George Spencer (25 of 51, 398 yards); Receiving—
Cecil Soudere (9 catches, 157 yards).

Offensive coordinator Paul Bixler and head coach
Carroll Widdoes switched roles prior to the season. However, Bixler turned in his resignation at
the end of the season to take the same position
at Colgate. ... Paul Brown signed his former Ohio
State player Bill Willis to the Cleveland Browns for
a starting salary of $4,000 to permanently break
professional football's race barrier. The NFL broke
its color barrier a few months earlier by signing
Kenny Washington and Woody Strode, who were
both near the end of their careers. Willis was an
immediate starter and had a Hall of Fame career.
"I think he knew what he was doing and how important it was because he used other avenues," Willis
said. "And when he told me to suit up, he told me
he'd let it be known in his own time."

Through the Years

After his one and only season as head coach at
Ohio State, Paul Bixler moved on to coach at
Colgate. He later became director of player per-
sonnel for the Cleveland Browns.

Wes Fesler had a coaching career unlike many that have graced the sidelines. A basketball and football coach at the collegiate level, Fesler had starred at Ohio State in the 1930s before returning to coach in 1947 after a year at Pittsburgh.

1947
2-6-1

Sept. 27	Missouri	Columbus	W	13-7
Oct. 4	at Purdue	West Lafayette	L	24-20
Oct. 11	Southern California	Columbus	L	32-0
Oct. 18	Iowa	Columbus	T	13-13
Oct. 25	at Pittsburgh	Pittsburgh	L	12-0
Nov. 1	Indiana	Columbus	L	7-0
Nov. 8	Northwestern	Columbus	W	7-6
Nov. 15	Illinois	Columbus	L	28-7
Nov. 22	at Michigan	Ann Arbor	L	21-0
Coach: Wesley E. Fesler				60-150
Captain: Robert O. Jabbusch				

Leaders: Rushing—Ollie Cline (332 yards, 80 carries); Passing—Dick Slager (19 of 69, 236 yards); Receiving—Fred Morrison (7 catches, 113 yards).

Wes Fesler, a three-time All-American end/fullback at Ohio State (1928–30), was named the fifth head coach in eight years. The previous season, he coached Pitt against Ohio State. ... In an unusual game, Ohio State was awarded three plays after time expired against Northwestern because of penalties (12 men, and two offsides calls) and came away with a 7–6 victory in Ohio Stadium.

3 Teams, including Michigan, that finished unbeaten and untied in 1947. Despite their perfect seasons, the Wolverines and Penn State played bridesmaid to Notre Dame, which repeated as champions.

1948
6–3

Sept. 25	Missouri	Columbus	W	21–7
Oct. 2	Southern California	Columbus	W	20–0
Oct. 9	Iowa	Columbus	L	14–7
Oct. 16	at Indiana	Bloomington	W	17–0
Oct. 23	Wisconsin	Columbus	W	34–32
Oct. 30	at Northwestern	Evanston	L	21–7
Nov. 6	Pittsburgh	Columbus	W	41–0
Nov. 13	at Illinois	Champaign	W	34–7
Nov. 20	Michigan	Columbus	L	13–3

Coach: Wesley E. Fesler   184–94

Captain: David I. Templeton

Ranking (AP): Preseason No. 11; Postseason NR.

Leaders: Rushing—Joseph Whisler (579 yards, 132 carries);
Passing—Pandel Savic (36 of 69, 486 yards); Receiving—Alex
Verdova (12 catches, 117 yards).

**The two-point victory against Wisconsin was Ohio
State's 500th all-time game.**

1949
7–1–2, Big Ten champions (tied)

Sept. 24	Missouri	Columbus	W	35–34
Oct. 1	Indiana	Columbus	W	46–7
Oct. 8	at Southern California	Los Angeles	T	13–13
Oct. 15	Minnesota	Columbus	L	27–0
Oct. 22	at Wisconsin	Madison	W	21–0
Oct. 29	Northwestern	Columbus	W	24–7
Nov. 5	at Pittsburgh	Pittsburgh	W	14–10
Nov. 12	Illinois	Columbus	W	30–17
Nov. 19	at Michigan	Ann Arbor	T	7–7
Jan. 2	California	Rose Bowl	W	17–14

Coach: Wesley E. Fesler   207–136

Captain: A. Jack Wilson

Ranking (AP): Preseason No. 11; Postseason No. 6.

All-Big Ten: Jack Lininger, C; Gerry Krall, HB.

Through the Years

Leaders: Rushing—Gerry Krall (606 yards, 128 carries);
Passing—Pandel Savic (35 of 84, 581 yards); Receiving—Ray
Hamilton (15 catches, 347 yards).

Ohio State enjoyed its first victory at the Rose
Bowl, defeating previously unbeaten Cal and Coach
Pappy Waldorf. The Buckeyes scored the winning
points with slightly more than two minutes remaining on a 17-yard field goal by James Hague. Fred
"Curly" Morrison had 113 rushing yards on 25 carries, and Jerry Krall had 80 yards in 28 attempts.
Defensive back Victor Janowicz had two interceptions. ... The victory against Missouri was the first
televised game from Ohio Stadium.

Through the Years

**Career wins for Wes Fesler against
Michigan. The tie in 1949 was the best
performance his Buckeyes had against
the Wolverines.**

1950
6–3

Sept. 30	Southern Methodist	Columbus	L	32–27
Oct. 7	Pittsburgh	Columbus	W	41–7
Oct. 14	at Indiana	Bloomington	W	26–14
Oct. 21	at Minnesota	Minneapolis	W	48–0
Oct. 28	Iowa	Columbus	W	83–21
Nov. 4	at Northwestern	Evanston	W	32–0
Nov. 11	Wisconsin	Columbus	W	19–14
Nov. 18	at Illinois	Champaign	L	14–7
Nov. 25	Michigan	Columbus	L	9–3
Coach: Wesley E. Fesler				286–111

Captain: Henry "Bill" Trautwein

Ranking (AP): Preseason 11; Postseason No. 14.

Major Awards: Victor Janowicz, Heisman Trophy

All-American: Robert Momsen, T; Robert McCullough, C; Victor Janowicz, HB.

All-Big Ten: Bill Trautwein, T; John Biltz, G; Vic Janowicz, HB.

Leaders: Rushing—Walt Klevay (520 yards, 66 carries); Passing—Vic Janowicz (32 of 77, 561 yards); Receiving—Thomas Watson (23 catches, 461 yards).

Ohio State was ranked No. 1 after defeating No. 15 Wisconsin, and voters opted to bump Army down to No. 3 despite being undefeated. ... Against Iowa, Heisman Trophy winner Vic Janowicz recovered two fumbles on defense, scored on an 11-yard touchdown run, returned a punt 61 yards for a touchdown, threw a 12-yard touchdown pass, kicked three extra points, and sent two kickoffs out of the end zone for touchbacks, all in the first five minutes of the game. He scored 46 points. ... The versatile Janowicz made a 27-yard field goal in the "Snow Bowl" game against Michigan. ... Coach Wesley Fesler stepped down December 9. Six weeks later he accepted the job at Minnesota. ... The school made "Buckeyes" the official team nickname.

1951
4–3–2

Sept. 29	Southern Methodist	Columbus	W	7–0
Oct. 6	Michigan State	Columbus	L	24–20
Oct. 13	at Wisconsin	Madison	T	6–6
Oct. 20	Indiana	Columbus	L	32–10
Oct. 27	Iowa	Columbus	W	47–21
Nov. 3	Northwestern	Columbus	W	3–0
Nov. 10	at Pittsburgh	Pittsburgh	W	16–14
Nov. 17	Illinois	Columbus	T	0–0
Nov. 24	at Michigan	Ann Arbor	L	7–0

Coach: Wayne Woodrow "Woody" Hayes — 109–104

Captain: Robert C. Heid

Ranking (AP): Preseason No. 3; Postseason NR.

All-Big Ten: Vic Janowicz, HB.

Leaders: Rushing—Vic Janowicz (376 yards, 106 carries); Passing—Tony Curcillo (58 of 133, 912 yards); Receiving—Bob Joslin (18 catches, 281 yards).

Wayne Woodrow "Woody" Hayes, a lieutenant commander in the navy, began his 28-year tenure as head coach. His first season, though, the Buckeyes struggled to adjust to his T formation offense, and Vic Janowicz failed to repeat as an All-American.

If the college football ranking system collected a vote after the bowl games in 1951, it is likely that Michigan State would have become national champions instead of Tennessee. Tennessee had lost their bowl game to Maryland, and Michigan State did not play in a bowl, finishing unbeaten.

Assistant Ernie Godfrey planted a kiss on the game ball that Ohio State used in its upset win over Wisconsin in 1952. The victory was the school's first over a team ranked first in the country, and the team later capped off its season with a then-rare win over Michigan.

1952
6–3

Sept. 27	Indiana	Columbus	W	33–13
Oct. 4	Purdue	Columbus	L	21–14
Oct. 11	Wisconsin	Columbus	W	23–14
Oct. 18	Washington State	Columbus	W	35–7
Oct. 25	at Iowa	Iowa City	L	8–0
Nov. 1	at Northwestern	Evanston	W	24–21
Nov. 8	Pittsburgh	Columbus	L	21–14
Nov. 15	at Illinois	Champaign	W	27–7
Nov. 22	Michigan	Columbus	W	27–7

Coach: Wayne Woodrow "Woody" Hayes   197–119

Captain: Bernie G. Skvarka

Ranking (AP): Preseason No. 20; Postseason No. 17.

All-American: Mike Takacs, G.

All-Big Ten: George Jacoby, T; James Reichenbach, G; Tony Curcillo, FB; Fred Bruney, HB.

Leaders: Rushing—John Hlay (535 yards, 133 carries); Passing—John Borton (115 of 196, 1,555 yards); Receiving—Bob Grimes (39 catches, 534 yards).

Ohio State enjoyed its first victory against a team ranked No. 1, Wisconsin. At the time, the Buckeyes were unranked. ... After winning just 12 of 48 games against Michigan, Coach Woody Hayes began a remarkable 16–7–1 run to turn the tables, with 13 of those games deciding the Big Ten title. The 1952 win over Michigan resulted in Wisconsin representing the conference in the Rose Bowl. ... John Borton's 1,555 passing yards set a school record that stood until 1979.

Through the Years

1953
6–3

Sept. 26	Indiana	Columbus	W	36–12
Oct. 3	at California	Berkeley	W	33–19
Oct. 10	Illinois	Columbus	L	41–20
Oct. 17	at Pennsylvania	Philadelphia	W	12–6
Oct. 24	at Wisconsin	Madison	W	20–19
Oct. 31	Northwestern	Columbus	W	27–13
Nov. 7	Michigan State	Columbus	L	28–13
Nov. 14	Purdue	Columbus	W	21–6
Nov. 21	at Michigan	Ann Arbor	L	20–0
Coach: Wayne Woodrow "Woody" Hayes				182–164
Captains: Robert V. Joslin, George Jacoby				
Ranking (AP): Preseason No. 7; Postseason NR.				
All-Big Ten: George Jacoby, T.				
Leaders: Rushing—Bob Watkins (875 yards, 153 carries); Passing—John Borton (45 of 86, 522 yards); Receiving—Thomas Hague (19 catches, 275 yards).				

Ohio State was ranked 20th in the final coaches' poll, but not by the Associated Press. ... The NCAA eliminated two-platoon football, so players had to play both offense and defense. ... Howard "Hopalong" Cassady's first collegiate pass was a 25-yard touchdown to end Tommy Hague against Northwestern. ... Chic Harley was honored at half-time of the Michigan State game for his induction into the College Football Hall of Fame.

1954
10–0, Big Ten champions, national champions

Sept. 25	Indiana	Columbus	W	28–0
Oct. 2	California	Columbus	W	21–13
Oct. 9	at Illinois	Champaign	W	40–7
Oct. 16	Iowa	Columbus	W	20–14
Oct. 23	Wisconsin	Columbus	W	31–14
Oct. 30	at Northwestern	Evanston	W	14–7
Nov. 6	Pittsburgh	Columbus	W	26–0
Nov. 13	at Purdue	West Lafayette	W	28–6
Nov. 20	Michigan	Columbus	W	21–7

Jan. 1	Southern California Rose Bowl	W	20–7

Coach: Wayne Woodrow "Woody" Hayes   249–75

Captains: C. Richard Brubaker, John R. Borton

Ranking (AP): Preseason No. 20; Postseason No. 1.

All-American: Dean Dugger, E; Howard Cassady, HB; Jim Reichenbach, G.

All-Big Ten: Dean Dugger, E; Dick Hilinski, T; Francis Machinsky, T; Howard Cassady, HB.

Leaders: Rushing—Howard Cassady (609 yards, 102 carries); Passing—Bill Leggett (46 of 95, 578 yards); Receiving—Howard Cassady (12 catches, 137 yards).

Ohio State claimed its second national championship after defeating Southern California in a rainy, mud-soaked Rose Bowl, 20–7. Hopalong Cassady, Bob Watkins, and Dick Harkrader all scored touchdowns against the Trojans, who had seven fumbles and just six first downs. ... A rift between West Coast writers and Woody Hayes was created when the coach criticized the Tournament of Roses Association for not covering the field before the game and allowing the bands to perform at halftime. ... After the Cal victory, Ohio State began the tradition of ringing the 2,420-pound Victory Bell in the stadium's southeast tower after wins. ... The defense gave up an average of 7.5 points and 110 rushing yards, recovered 17 fumbles, and made 18 interceptions.

6

First downs by the USC offense in the 1955 Rose Bowl. The Trojans' only score came on an 86-yard punt return.

1955

7–2, Big Ten champions

Sept. 24	Nebraska	Columbus	W	28–20
Oct. 1	at Stanford	Stanford	L	6–0
Oct. 8	Illinois	Columbus	W	27–12
Oct. 15	Duke	Columbus	L	20–14
Oct. 22	at Wisconsin	Madison	W	26–16
Oct. 29	Northwestern	Columbus	W	49–0
Nov. 5	Indiana	Columbus	W	20–13
Nov. 12	Iowa	Columbus	W	20–10
Nov. 19	at Michigan	Ann Arbor	W	17–0

Coach: Wayne Woodrow "Woody" Hayes   201–97

Captains: Frank C. Machinsky, Kenneth W. Vargo

Ranking (AP): Preseason No. 4; Postseason No. 5.

Major Awards: Howard Cassady, Heisman Trophy, Maxwell Award (offensive player)

All-American: Jim Parker, G; Howard Cassady, HB.

All-Big Ten: Howard Cassady, HB; Jim Parker, G; Ken Vargo, C.

Leaders: Rushing—Howard Cassady (958 yards, 161 carries); Passing—Frank Ellwood (9 of 23, 60 yards); Receiving—Paul Michael (4 catches, 50 yards).

Howard "Hopalong" Cassady became Ohio State's third Heisman Trophy winner. He finished his career with 2,374 yards and 37 touchdowns. Coach Woody Hayes said Cassady "was the most inspirational player I have ever seen." ... The 17–0 shutout of Michigan resulted in the second-consecutive Big Ten championship. ... During the season, the controversial Hayes voiced his displeasure over several other conferences awarding scholarships to student-athletes, while the Big Ten did not. After a series of meetings and discussions, the conference adopted a complicated grant-in-aid program based on financial need.

Howard "Hopalong" Cassady finished his memorable Ohio State career by winning the school's third Heisman Trophy in 1955. He capped his final season by helping the Buckeyes to a Big Ten championship, including a shutout win over Michigan.

1956
6–3

Sept. 29	Nebraska	Columbus	W	34–7
Oct. 6	Stanford	Columbus	W	32–20
Oct. 13	at Illinois	Champaign	W	26–6
Oct. 20	Penn State	Columbus	L	7–6
Oct. 27	Wisconsin	Columbus	W	21–0
Nov. 3	at Northwestern	Evanston	W	6–2
Nov. 10	Indiana	Columbus	W	35–14
Nov. 17	at Iowa	Iowa City	L	6–0
Nov. 24	Michigan	Columbus	L	19–0

Coach: Wayne Woodrow "Woody" Hayes   160–81

Captains: Franklin D. R. Ellwood, P. William Michael

Major Awards: Jim Parker, Outland Trophy (outstanding lineman)

Ranking (AP): Preseason No. 5; Postseason No. 15.

All-American: Jim Parker, G.

All-Big Ten: Jim Parker, G.

Leaders: Rushing—Don Clark (797 yards, 139 carries); Passing—Don Clark (3 of 7, 88 yards); Receiving—Leo Brown (8 catches, 151 yards).

Ohio State set a Big Ten record with 17-consecutive victories, breaking Michigan's previous mark of 15. ... Offensive guard Jim Parker became the first Ohio State player to win the Outland Trophy.

1957
9–1, Big Ten champions, national champions

Sept. 28	Texas Christian	Columbus	L	18–14
Oct. 5	at Washington	Seattle	W	35–7
Oct. 12	Illinois	Columbus	W	21–7
Oct. 19	Indiana	Columbus	W	56–0
Oct. 26	at Wisconsin	Madison	W	16–13
Nov. 2	Northwestern	Columbus	W	47–6
Nov. 9	Purdue	Columbus	W	20–7
Nov. 16	Iowa	Columbus	W	17–13
Nov. 23	at Michigan	Ann Arbor	W	31–14
Jan. 1	Oregon	Rose Bowl	W	10–7

Coach: Wayne Woodrow "Woody" Hayes	267-92
Captains: Galen B. Cisco, Leo M. Brown	
Ranking (AP): Preseason No. 17; Postseason No. 2.	
All-American: Aurealius Thomas, G.	
All-Big Ten: Leo Brown, E; Aurealius Thomas, G; Don Clark, B.	

Leaders: Rushing—Don Clark (737 yards, 132 carries); Passing—Frank Kremblas (20 of 47, 337 yards); Receiving—Dick LeBeau (7 catches, 91 yards); Leo Brown (7 catches, 83 yards).

After losing the season opener to TCU, Ohio State won nine straight to stake a claim for the national title, although Auburn was the consensus champion. OSU was No. 1 in the final coaches' poll, but second to Auburn according to the Associated Press. ... The Buckeyes were outgained by Oregon in the Rose Bowl, but a 34-yard field goal by Don Sutherin and a late fumble recovery resulted in a 10–7 victory. ... The offense ranked 11th nationally, while the defense allowed only 9.2 points per game and just six points in the fourth quarter all season. ... Ohio State was placed on one-year probation by the NCAA for extra benefits and illicit recruiting.

66

Yards of 68 that fullback Bob White carried for on the deciding drive of the game against unbeaten Iowa.

1958
6-1-2

Sept. 27	Southern Methodist	Columbus	W	23-20
Oct. 4	Washington	Columbus	W	12-7
Oct. 11	at Illinois	Champaign	W	19-13
Oct. 18	Indiana	Columbus	W	49-8
Oct. 25	Wisconsin	Columbus	T	7-7
Nov. 1	at Northwestern	Evanston	L	21-0
Nov. 8	Purdue	Columbus	T	14-14
Nov. 15	at Iowa	Iowa City	W	38-28
Nov. 22	Michigan	Columbus	W	20-14

Coach: Wayne Woodrow "Woody" Hayes 182-132

Captains: Francis T. Kremblas, Richard P. Schafrath

Ranking (AP): Preseason No. 1; Postseason No. 8.

All-American: James Houston, E; Jim Marshall, T; Bob White, FB.

All-Big Ten: Don Clark, B; Jim Houston, E; Jim Marshall, T; Bob White, FB.

Leaders: Rushing—Bob White (859 yards, 218 carries); Passing—Frank Kremblas (16 of 42, 281 yards); Receiving—Dick LeBeau (8 catches, 110 yards); Donald Clark (8 catches, 110 yards).

Ohio State led the nation in attendance for the first of 14 straight years, through 1971. ... The two-point conversion was introduced and in the season opener Coach Woody Hayes surprised a lot of fans by calling for a two-point attempt after Don Clark's first of two touchdowns. Quarterback Frank Kremblas passed 3 yards to halfback Dick LeBeau. ... Despite leading the nation in total offense, Iowa lost to Ohio State, but went on to rout Cal in the Rose Bowl.

1959
3-5-1

Sept. 26	Duke	Columbus	W	14-13
Oct. 2	at Southern California	Los Angeles	L	17-0
Oct. 10	Illinois	Columbus	L	9-0
Oct. 17	Purdue	Columbus	W	15-0
Oct. 24	at Wisconsin	Madison	L	12-3
Oct. 31	Michigan State	Columbus	W	30-24
Nov. 7	Indiana	Columbus	T	0-0
Nov. 14	Iowa	Columbus	L	16-7
Nov. 21	at Michigan	Ann Arbor	L	23-14

Coach: Wayne Woodrow "Woody" Hayes   83-114

Captain: James E. Houston

Ranking (AP): Preseason No. 7; Postseason NR.

All-American: Jim Houston, E.

All-Big Ten: Jim Houston, E.

Leaders: Rushing—Bob Ferguson (371 yards, 61 carries); Passing—Tom Matte (28 of 51, 439 yards); Receiving—Charles Bryant (11 catches, 153 yards); Jim Houston (11 catches, 214 yards).

Jim Houston concluded his illustrious career after playing both offensive and defensive end. He was a two-time team MVP and an All-American, and in 1959 actually led the team in receiving. The Cleveland Browns selected Houston with the eighth-overall selection in the 1960 NFL Draft. He played 13 years and was selected to four Pro Bowls.

214
Yards receiving for Jim Houston in 1959. Despite being an end, he led the team in that category and caught four touchdown passes.

1960
7-2

Sept. 24	Southern Methodist	Columbus	W	24-0
Oct. 1	Southern California	Columbus	W	20-0
Oct. 8	at Illinois	Champaign	W	34-7
Oct. 15	at Purdue	West Lafayette	L	24-21
Oct. 22	Wisconsin	Columbus	W	34-7
Oct. 29	at Michigan State	East Lansing	W	21-10
Nov. 5	Indiana	Columbus	W	36-7
Nov. 12	at Iowa	Iowa City	L	35-12
Nov. 19	Michigan	Columbus	W	7-0
Coach: Wayne Woodrow "Woody" Hayes				209-90
Captains: James Tyrer, James Herbstreit				
Ranking (AP): Preseason No. 16; Postseason No. 8.				
All-American: Bob Ferguson, FB.				
All-Big Ten: Jim Tyrer, T; Tom Matte, QB; Bob Ferguson, FB.				
Leaders: Rushing—Bob Ferguson (853 yards, 160 carries); Passing—Tom Matte (50 of 95, 737 yards); Receiving—Charles Bryant (17 catches, 336 yards).				

Fullback Bob Ferguson, who averaged five yards every time he carried the ball, scored 13 touchdowns, one year before he scored 11 and won the Maxwell Award as offensive player of the year.

1961
8-0-1, Big Ten champions, national champions

Sept. 30	Texas Christian	Columbus	T	7-7
Oct. 7	UCLA	Columbus	W	13-3
Oct. 14	Illinois	Columbus	W	44-0
Oct. 21	at Northwestern	Evanston	W	10-0
Oct. 28	at Wisconsin	Madison	W	30-21
Nov. 4	Iowa	Columbus	W	29-13
Nov. 11	at Indiana	Bloomington	W	16-7
Nov. 18	Oregon	Columbus	W	22-12
Nov. 25	at Michigan	Ann Arbor	W	50-20
Coach: Wayne Woodrow "Woody" Hayes				221-83
Captains: Thomas Perdue, Michael Ingram				
Ranking (AP): Preseason No. 2; Postseason No. 2.				
Major Awards: Bob Ferguson, Maxwell Award (offensive player)				

All-American: Bob Ferguson, FB

All-Big Ten: Bob Ferguson, FB; Mike Ingram, G.

Leaders: Rushing—Bob Ferguson (938 yards, 202 carries); Passing—Joe Sparma (16 of 38, 341 yards); Receiving—Charles Bryant (15 catches, 270 yards).

After defeating Michigan, 50–20, Ohio State finished 8–0–1, won the Big Ten title, and was named national champion by the Football Writers Association. However, Alabama, which went 10–0 and defeated No. 9 Arkansas in the Sugar Bowl, was the consensus No. 1. ... By a narrow margin (28–25), the school's faculty council voted not to accept an invitation to the Rose Bowl, claiming there was too much emphasis on football at Ohio State. Hayes claimed for years the decision hampered his recruiting efforts, but had the team captains tell protesters on campus to accept it.

1962
6–3

Sept. 29	North Carolina	Columbus	W	41–7
Oct. 6	at UCLA	Los Angeles	L	9–7
Oct. 13	at Illinois	Champaign	W	51–15
Oct. 20	Northwestern	Columbus	L	18–14
Oct. 27	Wisconsin	Columbus	W	14–7
Nov. 3	at Iowa	Iowa City	L	28–14
Nov. 10	Indiana	Columbus	W	10–7
Nov. 17	Oregon	Columbus	W	26–7
Nov. 24	Michigan	Columbus	W	28–0
Coach: Wayne Woodrow "Woody" Hayes			205–98	
Captains: Gary Moeller, Robert Vogel				
Ranking (AP): Preseason No. 1; Postseason NR.				
All-Big Ten: Bill Armstrong, C; Paul Warfield, HB.				

Leaders: Rushing—David Francis (624 yards, 119 carries); Passing—Joe Sparma (30 of 71, 288 yards); Receiving—Paul Warfield (8 catches, 139 yards).

Paul Warfield was a halfback for the Buckeyes in 1961 and 1962, but moved to tight end in 1963 and played that position in the NFL.

1963
5-3-1

Sept. 28	Texas A&M	Columbus	W	17-0
Oct. 5	at Indiana	Bloomington	W	21-0
Oct. 12	Illinois	Columbus	T	20-20
Oct. 19	at Southern California	Los Angeles	L	32-3
Oct. 26	at Wisconsin	Madison	W	13-10
Nov. 2	Iowa	Columbus	W	7-3
Nov. 9	Penn State	Columbus	L	10-7
Nov. 16	Northwestern	Columbus	L	17-8
Nov. 23	at Michigan	Ann Arbor	W	14-10

Coach: Wayne Woodrow "Woody" Hayes   110-102

Captains: Ormonde Ricketts, Matthew Snell

Ranking (AP): Preseason No. 10 (tied); Postseason NR.

All-Big Ten: Paul Warfield, HB.

Leaders: Rushing—Matt Snell (491 yards, 134 carries);
Passing—Don Unverferth (48 of 117 , 586 yards); Receiving—
Paul Warfield (22 catches, 266 yards).

**Ohio State won its fourth straight against Michigan
after the game was delayed a week following the
assassination of President John F. Kennedy. The
36,424 in attendance was the smallest crowd at
Michigan Stadium in 20 years.**

1964
7-2

Sept. 26	Southern Methodist	Columbus	W	27-8
Oct. 3	Indiana	Columbus	W	17-9
Oct. 10	at Illinois	Champaign	W	26-0
Oct. 17	Southern California	Columbus	W	17-0
Oct. 24	Wisconsin	Columbus	W	28-3
Oct. 31	at Iowa	Iowa City	W	21-19
Nov. 7	Penn State	Columbus	L	27-0
Nov. 14	Northwestern	Columbus	W	10-0
Nov. 21	Michigan	Columbus	L	10-0

Coach: Wayne Woodrow "Woody" Hayes   146-76

Captains: James Davidson, William Spahr, Thomas Kiehfuss

Ranking (AP): Preseason No. 5; Postseason No. 9.

All-American: Jim Davidson, T; Ike Kelley, LB; Arnie Chonko, DB.

Coach Hayes is on the phone with assistants during the 1963 game against Southern California. One tradition that Hayes started that every coach at OSU has tried to match is Hayes' dedication to winning by playing hard, tough football.

All-Big Ten: Jim Davidson, T; Dan Poretta, G; Bill Spahr, E; Ike Kelley, LB; Tom Bugel, T; Arnie Chonko, DB.

Leaders: Rushing—William Sander (626 yards, 147 carries); Passing—Don Unverferth (73 of 160, 871 yards); Receiving—Bo Rein (22 catches, 320 yards).

The loss to Michigan was particularly painful for Ohio State fans. The Wolverines won their first Big Ten title since 1950 after finishing no higher than fifth during the previous seven years, and went on to rout Oregon State in the Rose Bowl.

1965
7–2

Sept. 25	North Carolina	Columbus	L	14–3
Oct. 2	at Washington	Seattle	W	23–21
Oct. 9	Illinois	Columbus	W	28–14
Oct. 16	at Michigan State	East Lansing	L	32–7
Oct. 23	at Wisconsin	Madison	W	20–10
Oct. 30	Minnesota	Columbus	W	11–10
Nov. 6	Indiana	Columbus	W	17–10
Nov. 13	Iowa	Columbus	W	38–0
Nov. 20	at Michigan	Ann Arbor	W	9–7

Coach: Wayne Woodrow "Woody" Hayes — 156–118

Captains: Dwight Kelley, Gregory Lashutka

Ranking (AP): Preseason No. 10; Postseason NR.

All-American: Doug Van Horn, G; Ike Kelley, LB.

All-Big Ten: Ike Kelly, LB; Doug Van Horn, G; Ray Pryor, C; John Fill, HB.

Leaders: Rushing—Tom Barrington (554 yards, 139 carries); Passing—Don Unverferth (91 of 191, 1,061 yards); Receiving—Bo Rein (29 catches, 328 yards).

Brutus Buckeye, a student with a big head shaped like a buckeye nut, made his first appearance. ... The song "Hang on Sloopy" was played by the marching band for the first time during the Illinois game. It's regularly played before the start of the fourth quarter, with fans performing an O-H-I-O chant in the intervals between the refrains. It's also been heard late in games to encourage the defense.

So many Ohio State traditions started under the watch of Woody Hayes, it's impossible to recount all of them at once. His legacy is still stamped on every game played by the Buckeyes.

1966
4–5

Sept. 24	Texas Christian	Columbus	W	14–7
Oct. 1	Washington	Columbus	L	38–22
Oct. 8	at Illinois	Champaign	L	10–9
Oct. 15	Michigan State	Columbus	L	11–8
Oct. 22	Wisconsin	Columbus	W	24–13
Oct. 29	at Minnesota	Minneapolis	L	17–7
Nov. 5	Indiana	Columbus	W	7–0
Nov. 12	at Iowa	Iowa City	W	14–10
Nov. 19	Michigan	Columbus	L	17–3

Coach: Wayne Woodrow "Woody" Hayes   108–123

Captains: John Fill, Mike Current, Ray Pryor

All-American: Ray Pryor, C.

All-Big Ten: Ray Pryor, C; Dick Himes, T.

Leaders: Rushing—Bo Rein (456 yards, 139 carries); Passing—Bill Long (106 of 192, 1,180 yards); Receiving—Billy Anders (55 catches, 671 yards).

Walk-on Billy Ray Anders, who didn't play high school football, set a school record with 55 receptions. The record stood for nearly 20 years (Cris Carter, 1985). ... With Ohio State finishing with a losing record, speculation grew that Woody Hayes would be replaced.

1967
6–3

Sept. 30	Arizona	Columbus	L	14–7
Oct. 7	at Oregon	Eugene	W	30–0
Oct. 14	Purdue	Columbus	L	41–6
Oct. 21	at Northwestern	Evanston	W	6–2
Oct. 28	Illinois	Columbus	L	17–13
Nov. 4	at Michigan State	East Lansing	W	21–7
Nov. 11	Wisconsin	Columbus	W	17–15
Nov. 18	Iowa	Columbus	W	21–10
Nov. 25	at Michigan	Ann Arbor	W	24–14

Coach: Wayne Woodrow "Woody" Hayes   145–120

Captains: Billy Ray Anders, Samuel Elliott

All-Big Ten: Dick Himes, T; Billy Anders, E.

Leaders: Rushing—Jim Otis (530 yards, 141 carries); Passing—Bill Long (44 of 102, 563 yards); Receiving—Billy Anders (28 catches, 403 yards).

Coach Woody Hayes was quoted as saying after the 2–3 start, "That's the greatest freshman team I've had here in 17 years." At the time, NCAA rules made freshmen ineligible for the varsity. Apparently he had reason to smile, because the Buckeyes were about to start a 22-game winning streak.

Through the Years

Dick Himes was the only player from the young 1967 team to get drafted the next season into the NFL. He played tackle for 10 seasons with the Green Bay Packers.

1968

10–0, Big Ten champions, national champions

Sept. 28	Southern Methodist	Columbus	W	35–14
Oct. 5	Oregon	Columbus	W	21–6
Oct. 12	Purdue	Columbus	W	13–0
Oct. 19	Northwestern	Columbus	W	45–21
Oct. 26	at Illinois	Champaign	W	31–24
Nov. 2	Michigan State	Columbus	W	25–20
Nov. 9	at Wisconsin	Madison	W	43–8
Nov. 16	at Iowa	Iowa City	W	33–27
Nov. 23	Michigan	Columbus	W	50–14
Jan. 1	Southern California	Rose Bowl	W	27–16
Coach: Wayne Woodrow "Woody" Hayes				323–150

Captains: David Foley, Dirk Worden

Ranking (AP): Preseason No. 11; Postseason No. 1.

All-American: Dave Foley, OT; Rufus Mayes, T.

All-Big Ten: Dave Foley, OT; Rufus Mayes, T; Jack Tatum, CB; Ted Provost, HB.

Leaders: Rushing—Jim Otis (985 yards, 219 carries); Passing—Rex Kern (75 of 131, 972 yards); Receiving—Bruce Jankowski (31 catches, 328 yards).

Many fans believe the 1968 team was the finest in Ohio State history, despite starting five sophomores on offense and six on defense. The Buckeyes shut out No. 1 Purdue ("It was the greatest effort I've ever seen," Hayes said), crushed Michigan, 50–14, and came from behind to beat Southern California in the Rose Bowl, 27–16. Although O.J. Simpson had 171 rushing yards on 28 carries, he was involved in three of USC's five turnovers. .... Before the final polls were released, Coach Woody Hayes left for Vietnam on a volunteer trip to talk football with U.S. servicemen. ... Eleven players earned All-American honors during their careers, with six becoming first-round NFL draft picks. ... Hayes began the tradition of awarding buckeye leaves to players who made good plays in games.

1969
8–1, Big Ten champions

Sept. 27	Texas Christian	Columbus	W	62–0
Oct. 4	at Washington	Seattle	W	41–14
Oct. 11	Michigan State	Columbus	W	54–21
Oct. 18	at Minnesota	Minneapolis	W	34–7
Oct. 25	Illinois	Columbus	W	41–0
Nov. 1	at Northwestern	Evanston	W	35–6
Nov. 8	Wisconsin	Columbus	W	62–7
Nov. 15	Purdue	Columbus	W	42–14
Nov. 22	at Michigan	Ann Arbor	L	24–12

Coach: Wayne Woodrow "Woody" Hayes   383–93

Captains: David Whitfield, Alan Jack

Ranking (AP): Preseason No. 1; Postseason No. 4.

All-American: Jim Stillwagon, G; Rex Kern, QB; Jim Otis, FB; Ted Provost, CB; Jack Tatum, CB.

All-Big Ten: Jack Tatum, CB; Ted Provost, CB; Charles Hutchinson, T; Brian Donovan, C; Jim Otis, FB; Dave Whitfield, E; Mark Debevec, E; Paul Schmidlin, T; Jim Stillwagon, G; Doug Adams, LB; Mike Sensibaugh, S.

Leaders: Rushing—Jim Otis (1,027 yards, 225 carries); Passing—Rex Kern (68 of 135, 1,002 yards); Receiving—Bruce Jankowski (23 catches, 404 yards); Jan White (23 catches, 308 yards).

Coach Woody Hayes called the 1969 Buckeyes "the best team we ever put together, probably the best team that ever played college football." However, after a 9–0 start, Ohio State's 22-game unbeaten streak and effort to defend its national title ended with a heartbreaking 24–12 loss at Michigan. Although coming in Ohio State hadn't trailed all season and was averaging 46 points and 512 yards of offense, the Wolverines intercepted six passes and out-rushed OSU 266–22. It sparked "The Ten Year War."

Through the Years

1970

9–1, Big Ten champions, national champions

Sept. 26	Texas A&M	Columbus	W	56–13
Oct. 3	Duke	Columbus	W	34–10
Oct. 10	at Michigan State	East Lansing	W	29–0
Oct. 17	Minnesota	Columbus	W	28–8
Oct. 24	at Illinois	Champaign	W	48–29
Oct. 31	Northwestern	Columbus	W	24–10
Nov. 7	at Wisconsin	Madison	W	24–7
Nov. 14	at Purdue	West Lafayette	W	10–7
Nov. 21	Michigan	Columbus	W	20–9
Jan. 1	Stanford	Rose Bowl	L	27–17
Coach: Wayne Woodrow "Woody" Hayes				290–120

Captains: Rex Kern, Jan White, James Stillwagon, Douglas Adams

Ranking (AP): Preseason No. 1; Postseason No. 5.

Major Awards: Jim Stillwagon, Outland Trophy (interior lineman), Vince Lombardi Trophy (lineman)

All-American: Jan White, TE; Jim Stillwagon, MG; John Brockington, FB; Jack Tatum, CB; Mike Sensibaugh, S; Tim Anderson, CB.

All-Big Ten: Jack Tatum, CB; Mark Debevec, E; Jim Stillwagon, MG; Mike Sensibaugh, S; Dave Cheney, T; Phil Strickland, LB; Tom DeLeone, C; John Brockington, FB.

Leaders: Rushing—John Brockington (1,142 yards, 261 carries); Passing—Rex Kern (45 of 98, 470 yards); Receiving—Jan White (17 catches, 171 yards).

After an undefeated regular season, including an emotional 20–9 victory against Michigan, the Rose Bowl was a quarterback duel of contrasting styles. Jim Plunkett completed 20 of 23 passes to lead Stanford, while Rex Kern ran for 129 yards on 20 carries. With Randy Vataha catching a touchdown pass and Bob Moore setting up Jackie Brown's touchdown run, Stanford rallied from a 17–13 deficit in the fourth quarter. ... Ohio State still was awarded a national championship by the National Football Foundation, but Nebraska was the consensus choice. ... Jim Stillwagon won both the Outland Trophy and the first Lombardi Award. ... The senior class had a three-year 27–2 record.

Stanford's Jim Plunkett gave the OSU defense fits during the 1971 Rose Bowl. The star pivot led his team to a pair of fourth-quarter touchdowns in a 27-17 upset, preventing Ohio State from capturing the consensus national championship.

1971
6–4

Sept. 11	Iowa	Columbus	W	52–21
Sept. 25	Colorado	Columbus	L	20–14
Oct. 2	California	Columbus	W	35–3
Oct. 9	at Illinois	Champaign	W	24–10
Oct. 16	at Indiana	Bloomington	W	27–7
Oct. 23	Wisconsin	Columbus	W	31–6
Oct. 30	at Minnesota	Minneapolis	W	14–12
Nov. 6	Michigan State	Columbus	L	17–10
Nov. 13	Northwestern	Columbus	L	14–10
Nov. 20	at Michigan	Ann Arbor	L	10–7

Coach: Wayne Woodrow "Woody" Hayes   224–120

Captains: Harry Howard, Tom DeLeone

Ranking (AP): Preseason No. 11; Postseason NR.

All-American: Tom DeLeone, C.

All-Big Ten: Tom DeLeone, C; Rick Simon, T; Stan White, LB; George Hasenohrl, DT; Randy Gradishar, LB.

Leaders: Rushing—Rick Galbos (540 yards, 141 carries); Passing—Don Lamka (54 of 107, 718 yards); Receiving—Dick Wakefield (31 catches, 432 yards).

The three-game losing streak was the first since 1966, and second in a single season since 1943. ... Standout tackle John Hicks missed the season due to a preseason knee injury. He came back to be an All-American in 1972, and as a senior won the Outland Trophy as best interior lineman, the Lombardi Award as best lineman, and placed second in Heisman Trophy voting.

The three close losses to end the 1971 season cost the Buckeyes a Big Ten championship. Their only other loss came to the Colorado Buffaloes.

1972

9–2, Big Ten champions (tied)

Sept. 16	Iowa	Columbus	W	21–0
Sept. 30	North Carolina	Columbus	W	29–14
Oct. 7	at California	Berkeley	W	35–18
Oct. 14	Illinois	Columbus	W	26–7
Oct. 21	Indiana	Columbus	W	44–7
Oct. 28	at Wisconsin	Madison	W	28–20
Nov. 4	Minnesota	Columbus	W	27–19
Nov. 11	at Michigan State	East Lansing	L	19–12
Nov. 18	at Northwestern	Evanston	W	27–14
Nov. 25	Michigan	Columbus	W	14–11
Jan. 1	Southern California	Rose Bowl	L	42–17

Coach: Wayne Woodrow "Woody" Hayes 280–171

Captains: Richard Galbos, George Hasenohrl

Ranking (AP): Preseason No. 3; Postseason No. 9.

All-American: John Hicks, OT; Randy Gradishar, LB.

All-Big Ten: George Hasenohrl, DT; Randy Gradishar, LB; Charles Bonica, G; John Hicks, OT.

Leaders: Rushing—Archie Griffin (867 yards, 159 carries); Passing—Greg Hare (55 of 111, 815 yards); Receiving—Rick Galbos (11 catches, 235 yards).

Freshmen were cleared to play for the first time, and at the urging of backfield coach Rudy Hubbard, Archie Griffin came off the bench against North Carolina and rushed for 239 yards, an Ohio State record. ... Two goal-line stands keyed the 14–11 victory against Michigan. ... Griffin made the first of four Rose Bowl starts, but Sam Cunningham scored four touchdowns to lead Southern California, which featured 23 players who would play pro football.

Through the Years

The Ohio State defense was quick to collapse on USC's Anthony Davis on this play. The Buckeyes were able to avenge their embarrassing defeat from a year prior, doubling up the Trojans by a final of 42–21.

1973

10–0–1, Big Ten champions (tied)

Sept. 15	Minnesota	Columbus	W	56–7
Sept. 29	Texas Christian	Columbus	W	37–3
Oct. 6	Washington State	Columbus	W	27–3
Oct. 13	at Wisconsin	Madison	W	24–0
Oct. 20	at Indiana	Bloomington	W	37–7
Oct. 27	Northwestern	Columbus	W	60–0
Nov. 3	at Illinois	Champaign	W	30–0
Nov. 10	Michigan State	Columbus	W	35–0
Nov. 17	Iowa	Columbus	W	55–13
Nov. 24	at Michigan	Ann Arbor	T	10–10
Jan. 1	Southern California	Rose Bowl	W	42–21

Coach: Wayne Woodrow "Woody" Hayes — 413–64

Captains: Greg Hare, Richard Middleton

Ranking (AP): Preseason No. 2; Postseason No. 2.

Major Awards: John Hicks, Outland Trophy (interior lineman), Vince Lombardi Trophy (lineman)

All-American: Van Ness DeCree, DE; John Hicks, T; Randy Gradishar, LB; Archie Griffin, TB.

All-Big Ten: Randy Gradishar, LB; John Hicks, T; Jim Kregel, G; Vic Koegel, LB; Rick Middleton, LB; Kurt Schumacher, T; Van Ness DeCree, DE; Pete Cusick, DT; Neal Colzie, CB; Archie Griffin, TB.

Leaders: Rushing—Archie Griffin (1,577 yards, 247 carries); Passing—Cornelius Greene (20 of 46, 343 yards); Receiving—Fred Pagac (9 catches, 159 yards).

Pete Johnson scored three touchdowns and Archie Griffin had 149 yards, including a 47-yard touchdown as Ohio State got revenge on Southern California in the Rose Bowl. ... Tackle John Hicks finished second to Penn State running back John Cappelletti in Heisman Trophy balloting. Griffin placed fifth and linebacker Randy Gradishar sixth. ... Of Gradishar, athletics director Ed Weaver said, "No more outstanding young man has participated in our athletic program." ... Griffin had 246 rushing yards against Iowa.

1974

10–2, Big Ten champions (tied)

Sept. 14	at Minnesota	Minneapolis	W	34–19
Sept. 21	Oregon State	Columbus	W	51–10
Sept. 28	Southern Methodist	Columbus	W	28–9
Oct. 5	at Washington State	Seattle	W	42–7
Oct. 12	Wisconsin	Columbus	W	52–7
Oct. 19	Indiana	Columbus	W	49–9
Oct. 26	at Northwestern	Evanston	W	55–7
Nov. 2	Illinois	Columbus	W	49–7
Nov. 9	at Michigan State	East Lansing	L	16–13
Nov. 16	at Iowa	Iowa City	W	35–10
Nov. 23	Michigan	Columbus	W	12–10
Jan. 1	Southern California	Rose Bowl	L	18–17

Coach: Wayne Woodrow "Woody" Hayes — 437–129

Captains: Steve Myers, Archie Griffin, Arnold Jones, Neal Colzie, Pete Cusick

Ranking (AP): Preseason No. 2; Postseason No. 4.

Major Awards: Archie Griffin, Heisman Trophy; Walter Camp Award (outstanding player)

All-American: Van Ness DeCree, DE; Kurt Schumacher, T; Pete Cusick, DT; Steve Myers, C; Archie Griffin, TB; Neal Colzie, CB; Tom Skladany, P.

All-Big Ten: Kurt Schumacher, CT; Van Ness De Cree, DE; Pete Cusick, DT; Neal Colzie, CB; Archie Griffin, TB; Steve Myers, C; Steve Luke, CB; Doug France, TE; Dick Mack, G; Cornelius Greene, QB.

Leaders: Rushing—Archie Griffin (1,695 yards, 256 carries); Passing—Cornelius Greene (58 of 97, 939 yards); Receiving—Brian Baschnagel (19 catches, 244 yards).

Coach Woody Hayes had a heart attack on June 5, but returned to lead Ohio State to its third-consecutive Big Ten championship. ... Touchdowns by Champ Henson and Cornelius Greene, along with a Tom Klaban field goal, give Ohio State a 17–10 lead in the Rose Bowl, but Pat Haden's 36-yard touchdown pass and a two-point conversion pass to a diving Shelton Diggs gave Southern California a last-minute victory. ... Archie Griffin won the Heisman Trophy, becoming the fifth non-senior to win the award. ... Ohio State fans still believe Brian Baschnagel scored from 1-yard out on the final play of the controversial Michigan State loss.

1975

11–1, Big Ten champions

Sept. 13	at Michigan State	East Lansing	W	21–0
Sept. 20	Penn State	Columbus	W	17–9
Sept. 27	North Carolina	Columbus	W	32–7
Oct. 4	at UCLA	Los Angeles	W	41–20
Oct. 11	Iowa	Columbus	W	49–0
Oct. 18	Wisconsin	Columbus	W	56–0
Oct. 25	at Purdue	West Lafayette	W	35–6
Nov. 1	Indiana	Columbus	W	24–14
Nov. 8	at Illinois	Champaign	W	40–3
Nov. 15	Minnesota	Columbus	W	38–6
Nov. 22	Michigan	Columbus	W	21–14
Jan. 1	UCLA	Rose Bowl	L	23–10

Coach: Wayne Woodrow "Woody" Hayes   384–102

Captains: Archie Griffin, Brian Baschnagel, Tim Fox, Ken Kuhn

Ranking (AP): Preseason No. 4; Postseason No. 4.

Major Awards: Archie Griffin, Heisman Trophy, Walter Camp Award (outstanding player), Maxwell Award (offensive player)

All-American: Ted Smith, G; Archie Griffin, TB; Tim Fox, S; Tom Skladany, P.

All-Big Ten: Archie Griffin, TB; Cornelius Greene, QB; Scott Dannelley, T; Ted Smith, G; Tim Fox, S; Bob Brudzinski, DE; Ed Thompson, LB; Pete Johnson, FB; Nick Buonamici, DT; Chris Ward, T; Tom Skladany, P.

Leaders: Rushing—Archie Griffin (1,450 yards, 262 carries); Passing—Cornelius Greene (68 of 121, 1,066 yards); Receiving—Brian Baschnagel (24 catches, 362 yards).

Despite being 5-foot-9, 180 pounds, Archie Griffin (nicknamed Duckfoot) extended his record of consecutive 100-yard games to 31, his overall yardage to 5,589, and became the only player ever to win the Heisman Trophy twice. Despite this, he cast the deciding vote to name quarterback Cornelius Greene team MVP. ... Said Woody Hayes about Griffin, "He's a better young man than he is a football player, and he's the best football player I've ever seen." ... Ohio State completely dominated the first half of the Rose Bowl, but only took a 3–0 lead. UCLA came back to win 23–10. ... Griffin's four Rose Bowl appearances amounted to 412 yards on 79 carries.

1976

9–2–1, Big Ten champions (tied)

Sept. 11	Michigan State	Columbus	W	49–21
Sept. 18	at Penn State	University Park	W	12–7
Sept. 25	Missouri	Columbus	L	22–21
Oct. 2	UCLA	Columbus	T	10–10
Oct. 9	at Iowa	Iowa City	W	34–14
Oct. 16	at Wisconsin	Madison	W	30–20
Oct. 23	Purdue	Columbus	W	24–3
Oct. 30	at Indiana	Bloomington	W	47–7
Nov. 6	Illinois	Columbus	W	42–10
Nov. 13	at Minnesota	Minneapolis	W	9–3
Nov. 20	Michigan	Columbus	L	22–0
Jan. 1	Colorado	Orange Bowl	W	27–10

Coach: Wayne Woodrow "Woody" Hayes   305–149

Captains: Bill Lukens, Ed Thompson, Tom Skladany

Ranking (AP): Preseason No. 4; Postseason No. 6.

All-American: Bob Brudzinski, DE; Chris Ward, OT; Tom Skladany, P.

All-Big Ten: Bob Brudzinski, DE; Nick Buonamici, DT; Chris Ward, OT; Tom Skladany, P; Bill Lukens, G; Aaron Brown, MG; Tom Cousineau, LB.

Leaders: Rushing—Jeff Logan (1,248 yards, 218 carries); Passing—Jim Pacenta (28 of 54, 404 yards); Receiving—James Harrell (14 catches, 288 yards).

One year after the Big Ten changed its rule to allow more than just the conference champion to attend a bowl game, the Buckeyes beat Colorado in the Orange Bowl, 27–10. Rod Gerald, who had been sidelined by a bone chip in his lower back, came off the bench to tally 81 rushing yards on 14 carries, and sparked Ohio State's comeback from a 10–0 deficit. ... Fullback Pete Johnson ended his career with 2,308 rushing yards and a school-record 58 touchdowns. ... Punter Tom Skladany, the first kicking specialist to receive a football scholarship at Ohio State, finished his career with a 42.7 yard average.

This pass was bobbled, but James Harrell held on for a catch that set up a Buckeye score during the Orange Bowl. Ohio State had tied for the Big Ten championship, setting up a meeting with the Colorado Buffaloes on New Year's Day.

1977

9–3, Big Ten champions (tied)

Sept. 10	Miami (Fla.)	Columbus	W	10-0
Sept. 17	Minnesota	Columbus	W	38-7
Sept. 24	Oklahoma	Columbus	L	29-28
Oct. 1	at Southern Methodist	Dallas	W	35-7
Oct. 8	Purdue	Columbus	W	46-0
Oct. 15	at Iowa	Iowa City	W	27-6
Oct. 22	Northwestern	Columbus	W	35-15
Oct. 29	Wisconsin	Columbus	W	42-0
Nov. 5	at Illinois	Champaign	W	35-0
Nov. 12	Indiana	Columbus	W	35-7
Nov. 19	at Michigan	Ann Arbor	L	14-6
Jan. 2	Alabama	Sugar Bowl	L	35-6

Coach: Wayne Woodrow "Woody" Hayes   343–120

Captains: Chris Ward, Jeff Logan, Aaron Brown, Ray Griffin

Ranking (AP): Preseason No. 5; Postseason No. 11.

All-American: Chris Ward, T; Aaron Brown, NG; Tom Cousineau, LB; Ray Griffin, S.

All-Big Ten: Chris Ward, T; Aaron Brown, NG; Tom Cousineau, LB; Jimmy Moore, TE; Rod Gerald, QB; Ron Springs, TB; Jeff Logan, FB; Kelton Dansler, DE; Ray Griffin, S; Mike Guess, CB.

Leaders: Rushing—Ron Springs (1,166 yards, 200 carries); Passing—Ron Gerald (67 of 114, 1,016 yards); Receiving—Ron Springs (16 catches, 90 yards).

The Sugar Bowl, Ohio State's first, was the first meeting between Woody Hayes and Paul W. "Bear" Bryant. At that point they had combined for 501 victories. OSU caused 10 fumbles, but recovered only two. ... In the final moments of the Michigan loss, Hayes hit an ABC cameraman.

1978

7-4-1

Sept. 16	Penn State	Columbus	L	19-0
Sept. 23	at Minnesota	Minneapolis	W	27-10
Sept. 30	Baylor	Columbus	W	34-28
Oct. 7	Southern Methodist	Columbus	T	35-35
Oct. 14	at Purdue	West Lafayette	L	27-16

Oct. 21	Iowa	Columbus	W	31–7
Oct. 28	Northwestern	Columbus	W	63–20
Nov. 4	at Wisconsin	Madison	W	49–14
Nov. 11	Illinois	Columbus	W	45–7
Nov. 18	at Indiana	Bloomington	W	21–18
Nov. 25	Michigan	Columbus	L	14–3
Dec. 29	Clemson	Gator Bowl	L	17–15

Coach: Wayne Woodrow "Woody" Hayes   339–216

Captains: Ron Springs, Tim Vogler, Tom Cousineau, Byron Cato

Ranking (AP): Preseason No. 7; Postseason NR.

All-American: Tom Cousineau, LB.

All-Big Ten: Tom Cousineau, LB; Kelton Dansler, DE; Mike Guess, S; Ken Fritz, G; Joe Robinson, T; Tom Orosz, P; Vince Skillings, DB.

Leaders: Rushing—Paul Campbell (591 yards, 142 carries); Passing—Art Schlichter (87 of 175, 1,250 yards); Receiving—Doug Donley (24 catches, 510 yards).

Hayes was fired by Ohio State president Harold Enarson for punching Clemson nose guard Charlie Bauman after his interception sealed Clemson's victory in the Gator Bowl. His OSU teams went 205–61–10, won 13 Big Ten titles, three national championships, three Heisman Trophies, and included 51 first-team All-Americans. ... "All good commanders want to die in the field," Hayes once said.

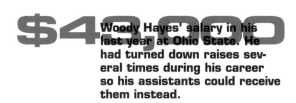

$49,000 Woody Hayes' salary in his last year at Ohio State. He had turned down raises several times during his career so his assistants could receive them instead.

1979

11–1, Big Ten champions

Sept. 8	Syracuse	Columbus	W	31–8
Sept. 15	at Minnesota	Minneapolis	W	21–17
Sept. 22	Washington State	Columbus	W	45–29
Sept. 29	at UCLA	Los Angeles	W	17–13
Oct. 6	Northwestern	Columbus	W	16–7
Oct. 13	Indiana	Columbus	W	47–6
Oct. 20	Wisconsin	Columbus	W	59–0
Oct. 27	Michigan State	Columbus	W	42–0
Nov. 3	at Illinois	Champaign	W	44–7
Nov. 10	Iowa	Columbus	W	34–7
Nov. 17	at Michigan	Ann Arbor	W	18–15
Jan. 1	Southern California	Rose Bowl	L	17–16
Coach: Earle Bruce				390–126

Captains: Jim Laughlin, Mike Guess, Ken Fritz, Tom Waugh

Ranking (AP): Preseason NR; Postseason No. 4.

All-American: Ken Fritz, G; Art Schlichter, QB.

All-Big Ten: Mike Guess, CB; Ken Fritz, G; Vince Skillings, S; Vlade Janakievski, K; Jim Laughlin, LB; Luther "Champ" Henson, DT; Todd Bell, LB; Tom Waugh, C; Art Schlichter, QB; Doug Donley, FL.

Leaders: Rushing—Calvin Murray (872 yards, 173 carries); Passing—Art Schlichter (105 of 200, 1,816 yards); Receiving—Doug Donley (37 catches, 800 yards).

Former Ohio State player and assistant coach Earle Bruce was named head coach. ... The Buckeyes came within a point—and two yards—of a national championship, falling 17–16 to Southern California in the Rose Bowl. Art Schlichter's long pass to Gary Williams gave OSU the ball at the 2, but USC successfully made a goal-line stand. The Buckeyes scored on a 67-yard Williams touchdown reception and three Vlade Janakievski field goals. Charles White set a Rose Bowl rushing record with 242 yards. ... Bruce was named the Big Ten and national coach of the year.

1980
9-3

Sept. 13	Syracuse	Columbus	W	31-21
Sept. 20	Minnesota	Columbus	W	47-0
Sept. 27	Arizona State	Columbus	W	38-21
Oct. 4	UCLA	Columbus	L	17-0
Oct. 11	at Northwestern	Evanston	W	63-0
Oct. 18	Indiana	Columbus	W	27-17
Oct. 25	at Wisconsin	Madison	W	21-0
Nov. 1	at Michigan State	East Lansing	W	48-16
Nov. 8	Illinois	Columbus	W	49-42
Nov. 15	at Iowa	Iowa City	W	41-7
Nov. 22	Michigan	Columbus	L	9-3
Dec. 26	Penn State	Fiesta Bowl	L	31-19
Coach: Earle Bruce				387-181

Captains: Doug Donley, Calvin Murray, Ray Ellis, Keith Ferguson

Ranking (AP): Preseason No. 1; Postseason No. 15.

All-Big Ten: Vlade Janakievski, K; Todd Bell, DB; Doug Donley, FL; Calvin Murray, TB; Joe Lukens, G; Ray Ellis, CB; Marcus Marek, LB; Vince Skillings, CB; Jerome Foster, DT.

Leaders: Rushing—Calvin Murray (1,267 yards, 195 carries); Passing—Art Schlichter (122 of 226, 1,930 yards); Receiving—Doug Donley (43 catches, 887 yards).

Ohio State and Illinois combined for 1,057 yards and 91 points in a 49–42 win for the Buckeyes. ... Penn State's Curt Warner ran 64 yards for a touchdown on the first play of the Fiesta Bowl. The Nittany Lions gave up just 73 yards in the second half to come back from a 19–10 deficit.

Ohio State missed out on a second Big Ten title in as many years in 1980 on the last day of their regular season. The defensive battle with Michigan sent the Wolverines to the Rose Bowl and dropped OSU into a second-place tie in the conference with Purdue.

1981

9–3, Big Ten champions (tied)

Sept. 12	Duke	Columbus	W	34–13
Sept. 19	Michigan State	Columbus	W	27–13
Sept. 26	at Stanford	Stanford	W	24–19
Oct. 3	Florida State	Columbus	L	36–27
Oct. 10	at Wisconsin	Madison	L	24–21
Oct. 17	Illinois	Columbus	W	34–27
Oct. 24	Indiana	Columbus	W	29–10
Oct. 31	at Purdue	West Lafayette	W	45–33
Nov. 7	at Minnesota	Minneapolis	L	35–31
Nov. 14	Northwestern	Columbus	W	70–6
Nov. 21	at Michigan	Ann Arbor	W	14–9
Dec. 30	Navy	Liberty Bowl	W	31–28
Coach: Earle Bruce				387–253

Captains: Art Schlichter, Glen Cobb

Ranking (AP): Preseason No. 11; Postseason No. 15.

All-Big Ten: Art Schlichter, QB; Joe Lukens, G; Marcus Marek, LB; Tim Spencer, TB.

Leaders: Rushing—Tim Spencer (1,217 yards, 226 carries); Passing—Art Schlichter (183 of 350, 2,551 yards); Receiving—Gary Williams (50 catches, 941 yards).

Ohio State earned a share of its second Big Ten championship in three years under Earle Bruce. ... Art Schlichter completed 31 of 52 passes for 458 yards—all OSU records—against Florida State. He had career touchdown passes No. 49 and 50 at the Liberty Bowl.

5

Field goals made by Bob Atha against Illinois. Atha, who was also the Buckeyes' backup quarterback, led the team in scoring in 1981. His Ohio Stadium record for field goals in a game has been tied twice but never beaten.

Art Schlichter battles through a facemask during the 1980 Rose Bowl. Schlichter had a third straight unsuccessful run at the Heisman Trophy in 1981, leading the Buckeyes to their second Big Ten title in three years.

1982
9–3

Sept. 11	Baylor	Columbus	W	21–14
Sept. 18	at Michigan State	East Lansing	W	31–10
Sept. 25	Stanford	Columbus	L	23–20
Oct. 2	Florida State	Columbus	L	34–17
Oct. 9	Wisconsin	Columbus	L	6–0
Oct. 16	at Illinois	Champaign	W	26–21
Oct. 23	at Indiana	Bloomington	W	49–25
Oct. 30	Purdue	Columbus	W	38–6
Nov. 6	Minnesota	Columbus	W	35–10
Nov. 13	at Northwestern	Evanston	W	40–28
Nov. 20	Michigan	Columbus	W	24–14
Dec. 17	Brigham Young	Holiday Bowl	W	47–17
Coach: Earle Bruce				348–208

Captains: Glen Cobb, Marcus Marek, Joe Luken, Jerome Foster, Gary Williams, Tim Spencer

Ranking (AP): Preseason No. 14; Postseason No. 12.

All-American: Marcus Marek, LB.

All-Big Ten: Joe Lukens, G; Marcus Marek, LB; Jerome Foster, DT; Tim Spencer, TB; John Frank, TE.

Leaders: Rushing—Tim Spencer (1,538 yards, 273 carries); Passing—Mike Tomczak (96 of 187, 1,602 yards); Receiving—Gary Williams (40 catches, 690 yards).

BYU led only once, 10–7, in the second quarter of the Holiday Bowl. Tim Spencer and Jimmy Gayle both scored two touchdowns, and linebacker Marcus Marek had eight tackles to pass Tom Cousineau as OSU's all-time leading tackler. ... Fans stormed the field after Ohio State ruined Michigan's undefeated season.

1983
9–3

Sept. 10	Oregon	Columbus	W	31–6
Sept. 17	at Oklahoma	Norman	W	24–14
Sept. 24	at Iowa	Iowa City	L	20–14
Oct. 1	Minnesota	Columbus	W	69–18
Oct. 8	Purdue	Columbus	W	33–22
Oct. 15	at Illinois	Champaign	L	17–13
Oct. 22	Michigan State	Columbus	W	21–11
Oct. 29	Wisconsin	Columbus	W	45–27
Nov. 5	at Indiana	Bloomington	W	56–17
Nov. 12	Northwestern	Columbus	W	55–7
Nov. 19	at Michigan	Ann Arbor	L	24–21
Jan. 2	Pittsburgh	Fiesta Bowl	W	28–23
Coach: Earle Bruce				410–206

Captains: Bill Roberts, John Frank, Rowland Tatum, Garcia Lane

Ranking (AP): Preseason No. 9; Postseason No. 9.

All-Big Ten: John Frank, TE; Garcia Lane, CB; Rowland Tatum, LB; Keith Byars, TB.

Leaders: Rushing—Keith Byars (1,199 yards, 222 carries); Passing—Mike Tomczak (131 of 237, 1,942 yards); Receiving—John Frank (45 catches, 641 yards).

Tight end John Frank finished his career with 121 catches for 1,481 yards and nine touchdowns. ... Ohio State and Pitt combined for 897 yards and 30 points during the fourth quarter. After a 37-yard field goal by the Panthers for their first lead with 2:37 remaining, the Buckeyes drove 89 yards for the winning score. Thad Jemison scored the winning touchdown, a 39-yard pass from Mike Tomczak. Jemison had eight receptions and Keith Byars scored two touchdowns, including a 99-yard kick return.

Keith Byars was an inspired player in 1984, running off several memorable performances and finishing second in Heisman Trophy balloting. Byars famously broke his toe the next year, and was unable to recapture the magic of 1984, though the season is still remembered fondly by OSU fans.

1984

9–3, Big Ten champions

Sept. 8	Oregon State	Columbus	W	22–14
Sept. 15	Washington State	Columbus	W	44–0
Sept. 22	Iowa	Columbus	W	45–26
Sept. 29	at Minnesota	Minneapolis	W	35–22
Oct. 6	at Purdue	West Lafayette	L	28–23
Oct. 13	Illinois	Columbus	W	45–38
Oct. 20	at Michigan State	East Lansing	W	23–20
Oct. 27	at Wisconsin	Madison	L	16–14
Nov. 3	Indiana	Columbus	W	50–7
Nov. 10	at Northwestern	Evanston	W	52–3
Nov. 17	Michigan	Columbus	W	21–6
Jan. 1	Southern California	Rose Bowl	L	20–17
Coach: Earle Bruce				391–200

Captains: Kirk Lowdermilk, Mike Tomczak, Mark Krerowicz, Thomas Johnson

Ranking (AP): Preseason No. 7; Postseason No. 13.

All-American: James Lachey, G; Keith Byars, TB.

All-Big Ten: Keith Byars, TB; Mark Krerowicz, T; Kirk Lowdermilk, C; Jim Lachey, G; Thomas "Pepper" Johnson, LB; Tom Tupa, P.

Leaders: Rushing—Keith Byars (1,764 yards, 336 carries); Passing—Mike Tomczak (145 of 244, 1,952 yards); Receiving—Keith Byars (42 catches, 479 yards).

In his debut, Chris Spielman came off the bench to make 10 tackles in the second half against Oregon State. ...Keith Byars rushed for a then school-record 274 yards and scored five touchdowns against Illinois. Byars also had a 67-yard touchdown run despite losing a shoe 35 yards from the goal line. ... Freshman Cris Carter set a Rose Bowl record with nine receptions for 172 yards.

1985
9-3

Sept. 14	Pittsburgh	Columbus	W	10-7
Sept. 21	at Colorado	Boulder	W	36-13
Sept. 28	Washington State	Columbus	W	48-32
Oct. 5	at Illinois	Champaign	L	31-28
Oct. 12	Indiana	Columbus	W	48-7
Oct. 19	Purdue	Columbus	W	41-27
Oct. 26	at Minnesota	Minneapolis	W	23-19
Nov. 2	Iowa	Columbus	W	22-13
Nov. 9	at Northwestern	Evanston	W	35-17
Nov. 16	Wisconsin	Columbus	L	12-7
Nov. 23	at Michigan	Ann Arbor	L	27-17
Dec. 28	Brigham Young	Citrus Bowl	W	10-7
Coach: Earle Bruce				325-212

Captains: Keith Byars, Mike Lanese, Thomas Johnson

Ranking (AP): Preseason No. 8; Postseason No. 14.

All-American: Thomas Johnson, LB.

All-Big Ten: Thomas Johnson, LB; Tom Tupa, P; Cris Carter, SE; Rory Graves, T; Bob Maggs, C; Chris Spielman, LB.

Leaders: Rushing—John Wooldridge (820 yards, 174 carries); Passing—Jim Karsatos (177 of 289, 2,311 yards); Receiving—Cris Carter (58 catches, 950 yards).

Ohio State defeated Pittsburgh 10-7 in the first night game in Ohio Stadium history. ... Flanker Mike Lanese became the first OSU football player to win a Rhodes scholarship. ... John Wooldridge emerged as the team's top ball carrier after Keith Byars sustained a preseason foot injury. ... Linebacker Pepper Johnson finished his career with 379 tackles. ... The Buckeyes made four interceptions in the Citrus Bowl—all in the second half—two by defensive lineman Larry Kolic, who returned one 41 yards for a touchdown.

1986

10–3, Big Ten champions (tied)

Aug. 27	Alabama	East Rutherford	L	16–10
Sept. 13	at Washington	Seattle	L	40–7
Sept. 20	Colorado	Columbus	W	13–10
Sept. 27	Utah	Columbus	W	64–6
Oct. 4	Illinois	Columbus	W	14–0
Oct. 11	at Indiana	Bloomington	W	24–22
Oct. 18	at Purdue	West Lafayette	W	39–11
Oct. 25	Minnesota	Columbus	W	33–0
Nov. 1	at Iowa	Iowa City	W	31–10
Nov. 8	Northwestern	Columbus	W	30–9
Nov. 15	at Wisconsin	Madison	W	30–17
Nov. 22	Michigan	Columbus	L	26–24
Jan. 1	Texas A&M	Cotton Bowl	W	28–12
Coach: Earle Bruce				347–179

Captains: Jim Karsatos, Sonny Gordon

Ranking (AP): Preseason No. 9; Postseason No. 7.

All-American: Cris Carter, SE; Chris Spielman, LB.

All-Big Ten: Cris Carter, SE; Bob Maggs, C; Chris Spielman, LB; Ed Taggart, TE; Jeff Uhlenhake, G; Eric Kumerow, LB; Sonny Gordon, DB.

Leaders: Rushing—Vince Workman (1,030 yards, 210 carries); Passing—Jim Karsatos (145 of 272, 2,122 yards); Receiving—Cris Carter (69 catches, 1,127 yards).

Ohio State was the first Big Ten team to play in the Cotton Bowl. The Buckeyes picked off five passes and returned two for touchdowns. The first was by Chris Spielman, who finished with 11 tackles and two interceptions. ... The Alabama game was the Kickoff Classic. ... Earle Bruce received a three-year contract, the first for the modern program. After the season he was offered the head coaching job at Arizona, but was persuaded to stay at his alma mater by athletics director Rick Bay. ... Ohio State opened with two losses for the first time in more than 90 years.

1987
6–4–1

Sept. 12	West Virginia	Columbus	W	24–3
Sept. 19	Oregon	Columbus	W	24–14
Sept. 26	at LSU	Baton Rogue	T	13–13
Oct. 3	at Illinois	Champaign	W	10–6
Oct. 10	Indiana	Columbus	L	31–10
Oct. 17	at Purdue	West Lafayette	W	20–17
Oct. 24	Minnesota	Columbus	W	42–9
Oct. 31	Michigan State	Columbus	L	13–7
Nov. 7	at Wisconsin	Madison	L	26–24
Nov. 14	Iowa	Columbus	L	29–27
Nov. 21	at Michigan	Ann Arbor	W	23–20
Coach: Earle Bruce				224–181

Captains: Chris Spielman, Eric Kumerow, William White, Tom Tupa

Ranking (AP): Preseason No. 4; Postseason NR.

Major Awards: Chris Spielman, Vince Lombardi Trophy (lineman)

All-American: Chris Spielman, LB; Tom Tupa, P.

All-Big Ten: Eric Kumerow, LB; Chris Spielman, LB; William White, DB; Tom Tupa, P.

Leaders: Rushing—Vince Workman (470 yards, 118 carries); Passing—Tom Tupa (134 of 242, 1,786 yards); Receiving—Everett Ross (29 catches, 585 yards).

Woody Hayes died on March 12 at age 74. President Richard Nixon, joined by a crowd of over 10,000, spoke at his memorial service. ... Linebacker Chris Spielman won the Lombardi Award. He had 546 career tackles and 283 solo stops. ... The Western Conference formally changed its name to the Big Ten. ... Earle Bruce (81–26–1) won or shared four Big Ten championships, took the Buckeyes to eight bowl games, and finished in the top 20 eight times.

Earle Bruce had already been fired before the Buckeyes took on Michigan in 1987, but his team delivered an inspired performance, winning one last game for their coach. Bruce was carried off the field by his players after his 81st win at OSU.

1988
4-6-1

Sept. 10	Syracuse	Columbus	W	26-9
Sept. 17	at Pittsburgh	Pittsburgh	L	42-10
Sept. 24	LSU	Columbus	W	36-33
Oct. 1	Illinois	Columbus	L	31-12
Oct. 8	at Indiana	Bloomington	L	41-7
Oct. 15	Purdue	Columbus	L	31-26
Oct. 22	at Minnesota	Minneapolis	W	13-6
Oct. 29	at Michigan State	East Lansing	L	20-10
Nov. 5	Wisconsin	Columbus	W	34-12
Nov. 12	at Iowa	Iowa City	T	24-24
Nov. 19	Michigan	Columbus	L	34-31
Coach: John Cooper				229-283

Captains: Jeff Uhlenhake, Vince Workman, Mike Sullivan, Michael McCray

All-American: Jeff Uhlenhake, C.

Leaders: Rushing—Carlos Snow (828 yards, 152 carries); Passing—Greg Frey (152 of 293, 2,028 yards); Receiving—Jeff Ellis (40 catches, 492 yards).

John Cooper was named the school's 21st head football coach. In his third game the Buckeyes upset No. 7 LSU. ... At the 20th reunion of the 1968 team the former players presented Ohio State with a $1.2 million endowment in memory of Coach Woody Hayes. ... The Buckeyes rallied from a 13-point deficit to upset No. 7 LSU.

1989
8-4

Sept. 16	Oklahoma State	Columbus	W	37-13
Sept. 23	at Southern California	Los Angeles	L	42-3
Sept. 30	Boston College	Columbus	W	34-29
Oct. 7	at Illinois	Champaign	L	34-14
Oct. 14	Indiana	Columbus	W	35-31
Oct. 21	Purdue	Columbus	W	21-3
Oct. 28	at Minnesota	Minneapolis	W	41-37
Nov. 4	at Northwestern	Evanston	W	52-27
Nov. 11	Iowa	Columbus	W	28-0

Nov. 18	Wisconsin	Columbus	W	42-22
Nov. 25	at Michigan	Ann Arbor	L	28-18
Jan. 1	Auburn	Hall of Fame	L	31-14
Coach: John Cooper				339-297

Captains: Joe Staysniak, Jeff Davidson, Zack Dumas, David Brown, Derek Isaman

Ranking (AP): Preseason NR; Postseason No. 24.

All-Big Ten: Joe Staysniak, T; Jeff Davidson, G.

Leaders: Rushing—Carlos Snow (990 yards, 190 carries); Passing—Greg Frey (144 of 246, 2,132 yards); Receiving—Jeff Graham (32 catches, 608 yards).

Ohio State celebrated its 100th season of collegiate football. ... The Buckeyes overcame a 31-0 deficit to win 41-37 at Minnesota, equaling the largest comeback in NCAA history. Quarterback Greg Frey finished off the Gophers with a 15-yard touchdown pass to Jeff Graham with 51 seconds remaining. ... Reggie Slack threw four touchdown passes for Auburn in the Hall of Fame Bowl. Graham had 103 yards on five receptions, but didn't play the second half due to a groin injury.

Through the Years

1987 was the final season for legendary Michigan coach and former Ohio State assistant Bo Schembechler. His Wolverines went 11-9-1 against Ohio State during his tenure.

1990
7-4-1

Sept. 8	Texas Tech	Columbus	W	17-10
Sept. 15	at Boston College	Chestnut Hill	W	31-10
Sept. 22	Southern California	Columbus	L	35-26
Oct. 6	Illinois	Columbus	L	31-20
Oct. 13	at Indiana	Bloomington	T	27-27
Oct. 20	at Purdue	West Lafayette	W	42-2
Oct. 27	Minnesota	Columbus	W	52-23
Nov. 3	Northwestern	Columbus	W	48-7
Nov. 10	at Iowa	Iowa City	W	27-26
Nov. 17	at Wisconsin	Madison	W	35-10
Nov. 24	Michigan	Columbus	L	16-13
Dec. 27	Air Force	Liberty Bowl	L	23-11
Coach: John Cooper				349-220

Captains: Jeff Graham, Dan Beatty, Mark Pelini, Vinnie Clark, Greg Frey

Ranking (AP): Preseason No. 17; Postseason NR.

All-Big Ten: Jeff Graham, WR; Steve Tovar, LB.

Leaders: Rushing—Robert Smith (1,126 yards, 177 carries); Passing—Greg Frey (139 of 276, 2,062 yards); Receiving—Bobby Olive (41 catches, 652 yards).

Natural grass was reinstalled at Ohio Stadium. ... Robert Smith gained 1,126 yards to break Archie Griffin's freshman rushing record at OSU. ... Ohio State jumped out to a 5–0 lead on Air Force in the Liberty Bowl due to a safety and field goal, but only reached the end zone once on Smith's 29-yard run. Air Force's wishbone offense tallied 254 rushing yards compared to the Buckeyes' 80.

Through the Years

John Cooper's Buckeyes struggled in the postseason early in his tenure, losing their first four bowls under the coach.

1991
8–4

Sept. 7	Arizona	Columbus	W	38–14
Sept. 14	Louisville	Columbus	W	23–15
Sept. 21	Washington State	Columbus	W	33–19
Oct. 5	Wisconsin	Columbus	W	31–16
Oct. 12	at Illinois	Champaign	L	10–7
Oct. 19	Northwestern	Cleveland	W	34–3
Oct. 26	Michigan State	Columbus	W	27–17
Nov. 2	Iowa	Columbus	L	16–9
Nov. 9	at Minnesota	Minneapolis	W	35–6
Nov. 16	Indiana	Columbus	W	20–16
Nov. 23	at Michigan	Ann Arbor	L	31–3
Jan. 1	Syracuse	Hall of Fame Bowl	L	24–17

Coach: John Cooper 277–187

Captains: Carlos Snow, Scottie Graham, John Kacherski

Ranking (AP): Preseason No. 23; Postseason NR.

All-American: Steve Tovar, LB.

All-Big Ten: Alan Kline, T; Jason Simmons, DE; Alonzo Spellman, DE; Steve Tovar, LB.

Leaders: Rushing—Carlos Snow (828 yards, 169 carries); Passing—Kent Graham (79 of 153, 1,018 yards); Receiving—Bernard Edwards (27 catches, 381 yards).

With the addition of 5,000 new bleacher seats, numerous attendance records were set including home total (654,500), average home (90,500), and single game (95,357 vs. Iowa). ... Steve Tovar's punt block recovered in the end zone by Tito Paul tied the Hall of Fame Bowl at 17, but less than a minute later Marvin Graves' 60-yard deep pass to Antonio Johnson burned Ohio State. ... Future coach Jim Tressel won his first I-AA national championship at Youngstown State.

1992
8–3–1

Sept. 5	Louisville	Columbus	W	20–19
Sept. 12	Bowling Green	Columbus	W	17–6
Sept. 19	at Syracuse	Syracuse	W	35–12

Oct. 3	at Wisconsin	Madison	L	20-16
Oct. 10	Illinois	Columbus	L	18-16
Oct. 17	Northwestern	Columbus	W	31-7
Oct. 24	at Michigan State	East Lansing	W	27-17
Oct. 31	at Iowa	Iowa City	W	38-15
Nov. 7	Minnesota	Columbus	W	17-0
Nov. 14	at Indiana	Bloomington	W	27-10
Nov. 21	Michigan	Columbus	T	13-13
Jan. 1	Georgia	Florida Citrus Bowl	L	21-14

Coach: John Cooper   271-158

Captains: Kirk Herbstreit, Steve Tovar

Ranking (AP): Preseason No. 19; Postseason No. 18.

All-American: Steve Tovar, LB.

All-Big Ten: Roger Harper, DB; Greg Smith, NG; Steve Tovar, LB; Dan Wilkinson, DT.

Leaders: Rushing—Robert Snow (819 yards, 147 carries); Passing—Kirk Herbstreit (155 of 264, 1,904 yards); Receiving—Brian Stablein (53 catches, 643 yards).

Linebacker Steve Tovar, the first John Cooper recruit at Ohio State to be named an All-American, led the Buckeyes in tackles for the third consecutive season. He finished his career with 414 total tackles and 239 solo stops. ... Ohio State played Georgia for the first time in the Florida Citrus Bowl. Garrison Hearst led the Bulldogs with 28 carries, 163 yards, and two touchdowns, and Eric Zeier passed for 241 yards.

271

Yards Kirk Herbstreit passed for against Michigan in 1992. His performance helped Ohio State to a tie in a game that is widely credited with saving John Cooper's job.

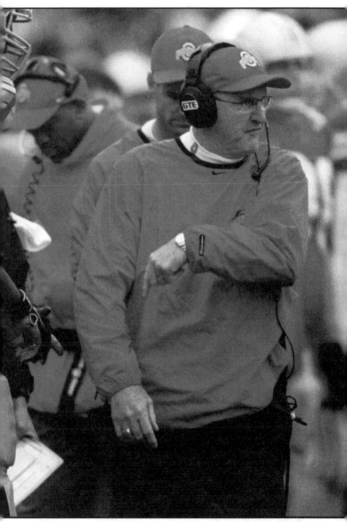

Head coach John Cooper famously, or perhaps infamously, guaranteed an Ohio State bowl win just two days after a loss to Michigan forced the Buckeyes to share the 1993 Big Ten championship. Cooper delivered on the promise, as OSU defeated BYU in the Holiday Bowl.

1993

10–1–1, Big Ten champions (tied)

Sept. 4	Rice	Columbus	W	34–7
Sept. 11	Washington	Columbus	W	21–12
Sept. 18	at Pittsburgh	Pittsburgh	W	63–28
Oct. 2	Northwestern	Columbus	W	51–3
Oct. 9	at Illinois	Champaign	W	20–12
Oct. 16	Michigan State	Columbus	W	28–21
Oct. 23	at Purdue	West Lafayette	W	45–24
Oct. 30	Penn State	Columbus	W	24–6
Nov. 6	at Wisconsin	Madison	T	14–14
Nov. 13	Indiana	Columbus	W	23–17
Nov. 20	at Michigan	Ann Arbor	L	28–0
Dec. 30	Brigham Young	Holiday Bowl	W	28–21
Coach: John Cooper				351–193

Captains: Alan Kline, Cedric Saunders, Jason Simmons, Chico Nelson

Ranking (AP): Preseason No. 17; Postseason No. 11.

All-American: Korey Stringer, T; Dan Wilkinson, DT.

All-Big Ten: Jason Winrow, G; Korey Stringer, T; Joey Galloway, SE; Tim Williams, K; Dan Wilkinson, DT; Lorenzo Styles, LB; Chico Nelson, SS.

Leaders: Rushing—Raymont Harris (1,344 yards, 273 carries); Passing—Bobby Hoying (109 of 202, 1,570 yards); Receiving—Joey Galloway (47 catches, 946 yards).

Ohio State (10–1–1) recorded its best record since 1979 and captured a share of the Big Ten title. .... Defensive tackle Dan "Big Daddy" Wilkinson made 44 tackles, 13 for a loss. In two seasons, he tallied 90 tackles, 23 for a loss, and 8.5 sacks. ... Raymont Harris had 39 carries for 235 yards and three touchdowns in the Holiday Bowl. Coach John Cooper guaranteed an Ohio State bowl victory during the team's awards banquet two days after losing to Michigan, and before the Buckeyes knew their postseason destination. The victory broke a four-game bowl losing streak under Cooper.

1994
9-4

Through the Years

Aug. 29	Fresno State	Anaheim	W	34–10
Sept. 10	at Washington	Seattle	L	25–16
Sept. 17	Pittsburgh	Columbus	W	27–3
Sept. 24	Houston	Columbus	W	52–0
Oct. 1	at Northwestern	Evanston	W	17–15
Oct. 8	Illinois	Columbus	L	24–10
Oct. 15	at Michigan State	East Lansing	W	23–7
Oct. 22	Purdue	Columbus	W	48–14
Oct. 29	at Penn State	University Park	L	63–14
Nov. 5	Wisconsin	Columbus	W	24–3
Nov. 12	at Indiana	Bloomington	W	32–17
Nov. 19	Michigan	Columbus	W	22–6
Jan. 2	Alabama	Florida Citrus Bowl	L	24–17

Coach: John Cooper   336–211

Captains: Joey Galloway, Marlon Kerner

Ranking (AP): Preseason No. 20; Postseason No. 14.

All-American: Korey Stringer, T.

All-Big Ten: Korey Stringer, T; Matt Finkes, DL; Mike Vrabel, T; Lorenzo Styles, LB.

Leaders: Rushing—Eddie George (1,442 yards, 276 carries); Passing—Bobby Hoying (170 of 301, 2,335 yards); Receiving—Joey Galloway (44 catches, 669 yards).

Ohio State defeated Michigan, 22–6, to end a six-game winless streak against the Wolverines. ... The Fresno State game was the Pigskin Classic. ... Despite Alabama having a yardage advantage of 521–276 in the Florida Citrus Bowl, Ohio State had three fumble recoveries, a blocked punt, a blocked field goal, and 12 tackles for a loss to keep the game close. Jay Barker's 50-yard touchdown pass to Sherman Williams with 42 seconds remaining snapped the 17-all tie. ... The "Tunnel of Pride" began with the Michigan game when all former players in attendance formed a tunnel through which the team ran to take the field. With Ohio State winning, the tradition stuck.

Bobby Hoying hands off to Eddie George during 1994's Pigskin Classic. George scored two early touchdowns to key the Buckeyes' 34–10 rout of Fresno State.

1995
11-2

Aug. 27	Boston College	East Rutherford	W	38-6
Sept. 16	Washington	Columbus	W	30-20
Sept. 23	at Pittsburgh	Pittsburgh	W	54-14
Sept. 30	Notre Dame	Columbus	W	45-26
Oct. 7	at Penn State	University Park	W	28-25
Oct. 14	at Wisconsin	Madison	W	27-16
Oct. 21	Purdue	Columbus	W	28-0
Oct. 28	Iowa	Columbus	W	56-35
Nov. 4	at Minnesota	Minneapolis	W	49-21
Nov. 11	Illinois	Columbus	W	41-3
Nov. 18	Indiana	Columbus	W	42-3
Nov. 25	at Michigan	Ann Arbor	L	31-23
Jan. 1	Tennessee	Florida Citrus Bowl	L	20-14
Coach: John Cooper				475-220

Captains: Matt Bonhaus, Eddie George, Bobby Hoying

Ranking (AP): Preseason No. 12; Postseason No. 6.

Major Awards: Eddie George, Heisman Trophy, Walter Camp Award (outstanding player), Doak Walker Award (running back); Orlando Pace, Vince Lombardi Trophy (lineman); Maxwell Award (offensive player); Terry Glenn, Fred Biletnikoff Award (receiver)

All-American: Eddie George, TB; Terry Glenn, FL; Orlando Pace, T; Mike Vrabel, DE.

All-Big Ten: Rickey Dudley, TE; Eddie George, TB; Terry Glenn, FL; Bobby Hoying, QB; Orlando Pace, T; Shawn Springs, CB; Mike Vrabel, DE.

Leaders: Rushing—Eddie George (1,927 yards, 328 carries); Passing—Bobby Hoying (211 of 341, 3,269 yards); Receiving—Terry Glenn (64 catches, 1,411 yards).

Ohio State dominated the postseason awards. Eddie George became the Buckeyes' sixth Heisman Trophy winner, tackle Orlando Pace was the first sophomore to win the Lombardi Award, and former walk-on Terry Glenn won the Biletnikoff Award. … George led the nation in scoring by averaging 12.1 points per game. He averaged 5.9 yards per carry, and set a school record for receptions by a running back with 47. … The 475 points scored set a school record. An Ohio Stadium record crowd of 95,537 watched Ohio State's win against Notre Dame.

Rickey Dudley gathers in a pass and is smacked in midair by Purdue's Willie Burroughs during the Buckeyes' 28-0 stomping on October 21, 1995, in Columbus.

1996

11–1, Big Ten champions (tied)

Sept. 7	Rice	Columbus	W	70–7
Sept. 21	Pittsburgh	Columbus	W	72–0
Sept. 28	at Notre Dame	South Bend	W	29–16
Oct. 5	Penn State	Columbus	W	38–7
Oct. 12	Wisconsin	Columbus	W	17–14
Oct. 19	at Purdue	West Lafayette	W	42–14
Oct. 26	at Iowa	Iowa City	W	38–26
Nov. 2	Minnesota	Columbus	W	45–0
Nov. 9	at Illinois	Champaign	W	48–0
Nov. 16	at Indiana	Bloomington	W	27–17
Nov. 23	Michigan	Columbus	L	13–9
Jan. 1	Arizona State	Rose Bowl	W	20–17
Coach: John Cooper				455–131

Captains: Juan Porter, Greg Bellisari

Ranking (AP): Preseason No. 9; Postseason No. 2.

Major Awards: Orlando Pace, Outland Trophy (interior lineman); Vince Lombardi Trophy (lineman)

All-American: Orlando Pace, T; Shawn Springs, CB; Mike Vrabel, DE.

All-Big Ten: Matt Finkes, DE; Andy Katzenmoyer, LB; Orlando Pace, T; Shawn Springs, CB; Mike Vrabel, DE.

Leaders: Rushing—Pepe Pearson (1,484 yards, 299 carries); Passing—Stanley Jackson (87 of 165, 1,298 yards); Receiving—Dimitrious Stanley (43 catches, 829 yards).

Joe Germaine of Mesa, Arizona, (who wasn't recruited as a quarterback by Arizona State because it already had Jake Plummer) tossed a 5-yard winning touchdown pass to freshman David Boston with 19 seconds remaining in the Rose Bowl. John Cooper, who used to coach Arizona State, became the first coach to win the Rose Bowl with both a Big Ten and Pac-10 team. ... Tackle Orlando Pace repeated as the Lombardi Award winner and won the Outland Trophy. He made "pancake block" a popular term, and was credited with 80 of them. ... More than 20,000 fans showed up at Ohio Stadium to watch the Senior Tackle tradition. ... With teams throwing away from him, cornerback Shawn Springs had no interceptions. ... Defensive end Mike Vrable had 13 sacks to finish his career with 36.

1997
10–3

Aug. 28	Wyoming	Columbus	W	24–10
Sept. 13	Bowling Green	Columbus	W	44–13
Sept. 20	Arizona	Columbus	W	28–20
Sept. 27	at Missouri	Columbia	W	31–10
Oct. 4	Iowa	Columbus	W	23–7
Oct. 11	at Penn State	University Park	L	31–27
Oct. 18	Indiana	Columbus	W	31–0
Oct. 25	Northwestern	Columbus	W	49–6
Nov. 1	at Michigan State	East Lansing	W	37–13
Nov. 8	at Minnesota	Minneapolis	W	31–3
Nov. 15	Illinois	Columbus	W	41–6
Nov. 22	at Michigan	Ann Arbor	L	20–14
Jan. 1	Florida State	Sugar Bowl	L	31–14
Coach: John Cooper				394–170

Captains: Stanley Jackson, Winfield Garnett

Ranking (AP): Preseason No. 9; Postseason No. 12.

Major Awards: Andy Katzenmoyer, Dick Butkus Award
(linebacker)

All-American: Andy Katzenmoyer, LB; Rob Murphy, G; Antoine
Winfield, CB.

All-Big Ten: Brent Bartholomew, P; David Boston, SE; Eric
Gohlstin, T; Andy Katzenmoyer, LB; Damon Moore, SS; Antoine
Winfield, CB.

Leaders: Rushing—Pepe Pearson (869 yards, 192 carries);
Passing—Joe Germaine (129 of 210, 1,847 yards); Receiving—
David Boston (73 catches, 970 yards).

**Andy Katzenmoyer won the Butkus Award as a
sophomore and went on to finish his three-year
career with 197 solo tackles, 256 total tackles
(50 for a loss), 18 sacks, and six interceptions. ...
Thad Busby passed for 334 yards for Florida State
in the Sugar Bowl. ... Michigan went on to finish
12–0, but Wolverines fans were outraged when the
coaches' poll flip-flopped and voted Nebraska No. 1
by a very narrow margin, resulting in a spilt title.**

1998

11–1, Big Ten champions (tied)

Sept. 5	at West Virginia	Morgantown	W	34–17
Sept. 12	Toledo	Columbus	W	49–0
Sept. 19	Missouri	Columbus	W	35–14
Oct. 3	Penn State	Columbus	W	28–9
Oct. 10	at Illinois	Champaign	W	41–0
Oct. 17	Minnesota	Columbus	W	45–15
Oct. 24	at Northwestern	Evanston	W	36–10
Oct. 31	at Indiana	Bloomington	W	38–7
Nov. 7	Michigan State	Columbus	L	28–24
Nov. 14	at Iowa	Iowa City	W	45–14
Nov. 21	Michigan	Columbus	W	31–16
Jan. 1	Texas A&M	Sugar Bowl	W	24–14
Coach: John Cooper				430–144

Captains: Joe Germaine, Jerry Rudzinski, Antoine Winfield

Ranking (AP): Preseason No. 1; Postseason No. 2.

Major Awards: Antoine Winfield, Jim Thorpe Award (defensive back)

All-American: David Boston, SE; Damon Moore, SS; Rob Murphy, G; Antoine Winfield, CB.

All-Big Ten: David Boston, SE; Na'il Diggs, LB; Joe Germaine, QB; Andy Katzenmoyer, LB; Rob Murphy G; Damon Moore, SS; Michael Wiley, TB; Antoine Winfield, CB.

Leaders: Rushing—Michael Wiley (1,235 yards, 198 carries); Passing—Joe Germaine (230 of 384, 3,330 yards); Receiving—David Boston (85 catches, 1,435 yards).

Ohio State was the preseason No. 1, a ranking it held for 10 weeks, and went 5–0 against top-25 teams, but an upset loss to Michigan State cost a shot at the national title. ... Quarterback Joe Germaine won the *Chicago Tribune's* Silver Football Award as the Big Ten's Most Valuable Player. ... Antoine Winfield won the Thorpe Award. He was also the first non-linebacker to make 200 solo tackles, and the first OSU defensive back to be named team MVP. ... David Boston set or tied 12 Ohio State receiving records. ... A punt block by Derek Ross off Texas A&M's Shane Leckler was recovered by Kevin Griffin for a 16-yard touchdown to pace the 21–14 victory in the Sugar Bowl.

1999
6–6

Aug. 29	Miami	East Rutherford	L	23–12
Sept. 11	UCLA	Columbus	W	42–20
Sept. 18	Ohio	Columbus	W	40–16
Sept. 25	Cincinnati	Columbus	W	34–20
Oct. 2	Wisconsin	Columbus	L	42–17
Oct. 9	Purdue	Columbus	W	25–22
Oct. 16	at Penn State	University Park	L	23–10
Oct. 23	at Minnesota	Minneapolis	W	20–17
Oct. 30	Iowa	Columbus	W	41–11
Nov. 6	at Michigan State	East Lansing	L	23–7
Nov. 13	Illinois	Columbus	L	46–20
Nov. 20	at Michigan	Ann Arbor	L	24–17
Coach: John Cooper				285–287

Captains: Matt Keller, Ahmed Plummer

Ranking (AP): Preseason No. 9; Postseason NR.

All-American: Na'il Diggs, LB.

All-Big Ten: Ahmed Plummer, CB.

Leaders: Rushing—Michael Wiley (952 yards, 183 carries); Passing—Steve Bellisari (101 of 224, 1,616 yards); Receiving—Reggie Germany (43 catches, 656 yards).

Archie Griffin's No. 45 was retired at the Iowa game. It was the first number retired in any sport in Ohio State history. ... The Miami game was the Kickoff Classic. On the Buckeyes' first possession Michael Wiley was run down from behind by linebacker Al Blades. The game may have signaled the beginning of the end for John Cooper's coaching reign.

2000
8–4

Sept. 2	Fresno State	Columbus	W	43–10
Sept. 9	at Arizona	Tucson	W	27–17
Sept. 16	Miami (Ohio)	Columbus	W	27–16
Sept. 23	Penn State	Columbus	W	45–6
Oct. 7	at Wisconsin	Madison	W	23–7
Oct. 14	Minnesota	Columbus	L	29–17
Oct. 21	at Iowa	Iowa City	W	38–10
Oct. 28	at Purdue	West Lafayette	L	31–27
Nov. 4	Michigan State	Columbus	W	27–13
Nov. 11	at Illinois	Champaign	W	24–21
Nov. 18	Michigan	Columbus	L	38–26
Jan. 1	South Carolina	Outback Bowl	L	24–7
Coach: John Cooper				331–222

Captains: Rodney Bailey, Steve Bellisari, Joe Cooper, Ken-Yon Rambo

Ranking (AP): Preseason No. 16; Postseason NR.

All-American: Mike Doss, SS.

All-Big Ten: Joe Cooper, LB; Mike Doss, SS; Dan Stultz, K.

Leaders: Rushing—Derek Combs (888 yards, 175 carries); Passing—Steve Bellisari (163 of 310, 2,319 yards); Receiving—Ken-Yon Rambo (53 catches, 794 yards).

The jersey numbers of former Heisman Trophy winners Vic Janowicz (31) and Howard "Hopalong" Cassady (40) were retired at home games against Penn State and Michigan, respectively. ... Ohio State lost to South Carolina in the Outback Bowl, the first meeting between the two teams. Ohio native Ryan Brewer led the Gamecocks with 214 all-purpose yards and three touchdowns. ... John Cooper was fired for a "deteriorating climate," despite compiling a 111–43–4 record (.715 winning percentage), in part because he was 2–10–1 against Michigan. He was replaced by former Ohio State assistant coach Jim Tressel.

2001
7–5

Sept. 8	Akron	Columbus	W	28–14
Sept. 22	at UCLA	Los Angeles	L	13–6
Sept. 29	at Indiana	Bloomington	W	27–14
Oct. 6	Northwestern	Columbus	W	38–20
Oct. 13	Wisconsin	Columbus	L	20–17
Oct. 20	San Diego State	Columbus	W	27–12
Oct. 27	at Penn State	University Park	L	29–27
Nov. 3	at Minnesota	Minneapolis	W	31–28
Nov. 10	Purdue	Columbus	W	35–9
Nov. 17	Illinois	Columbus	L	34–22
Nov. 24	at Michigan	Ann Arbor	W	26–20
Jan. 1	South Carolina	Outback Bowl	L	31–28
Coach: Jim Tressel				312–244

Captains: Jamar Martin, Steve Bellisari, Joe Cooper, Mike Collins

Ranking (AP): Preseason No. 23; Postseason NR.

Major Awards: LeCharles Bentley, Dave Rimington Award (center)

All-American: LeCharles Bentley, C; Mike Doss, SS.

All-Big Ten: LeCharles Bentley, C; Mike Doss, SS; Tyson Walter, T.

Leaders: Rushing—Jonathan Wells (1,294 yards, 251 carries); Passing—Steve Bellisari (119 of 220, 1,919 yards); Receiving—Michael Jenkins (49 catches, 988 yards).

The jerseys of Les Horvath (22) and Eddie George (27), Ohio State's first and at that time most recent Heisman Trophy winners, respectively, were retired. ... The Buckeyes defeated Michigan in Ann Arbor, their first win there since 1987. ... The three-year, $194 million renovation of "The Horseshoe" was completed, bumping capacity to 101,568. ... In a rematch from the previous year, South Carolina defeated Ohio State again in the Outback Bowl on Daniel Weaver's 42-yard field goal as time expired. OSU's Steve Bellisari was 21 of 35 for 320 yards and two touchdowns.

2002

14–0, Big Ten champions (tied), national champions

Aug. 24	Texas Tech	Columbus	W	45–21
Sept. 7	Kent State	Columbus	W	51–17
Sept. 14	Washington State	Columbus	W	25–7
Sept. 21	vs. Cincinnati	Paul Brown Stadium	W	23–19
Sept. 28	Indiana	Columbus	W	45–17
Oct. 5	at Northwestern	Evanston	W	27–16
Oct. 12	San Jose State	Columbus	W	50–7
Oct. 19	at Wisconsin	Madison	W	19–14
Oct. 26	Penn State	Columbus	W	13–7
Nov. 2	Minnesota	Columbus	W	34–3
Nov. 9	at Purdue	West Lafayette	W	10–6
Nov. 16	at Illinois	Champaign	W OT	23–16
Nov. 23	Michigan	Columbus	W	14–9
Jan. 3	Miami (Fla.)	Fiesta Bowl	W 2OT	31–24
Coach: Jim Tressel				410–183

Captains: Michael Doss, Donnie Nickey

Ranking (AP): Preseason No. 13; Postseason No. 1.

All-American: Mike Doss, SS; Andy Groom, P; Mike Nugent, K; Matt Wilhelm, LB.

All-Big Ten: Maurice Clarett, RB; Mike Doss, SS; Chris Gamble, CB; Andy Groom, P; Mike Nugent, K; Darrion Scott, DL; Matt Wilhelm, LB.

Leaders: Rushing—Maurice Clarett (1,237 yards, 222 carries); Passing—Craig Krenzel (148 of 249, 2,110 yards); Receiving—Michael Jenkins (61 catches, 1,076 yards).

Ohio State captured the school's seventh national championship after defeating Miami in the Fiesta Bowl, a controversial 31–24 double-overtime victory. Running back Maurice Clarett scored the decisive points on a 5-yard touchdown run. "We've always had the best damn band in the land, now we've got the best damn team in the land," Coach Jim Tressel said. ... Quarterback Craig Krenzel and flanker/cornerback Chris Gamble shared team MVP honors. Krenzel was offensive MVP of the Fiesta Bowl, with Mike Doss the defensive MVP. ... The 14 victories set an NCAA Division I-A record, although Ohio State won five games by six points or less.

Jim Tressel hoists the national championship trophy after one of the finest seasons in college football history. Ohio State's 14 wins in 2002 set a national record, and the nail-biting Fiesta Bowl became an instant classic.

2003
11–2

Aug. 30	Washington	Columbus	W	28–9
Sept. 6	San Diego State	Columbus	W	16–13
Sept. 13	North Carolina State	Columbus	W 3OT	44–38
Sept. 20	Bowling Green	Columbus	W	24–17
Sept. 27	Northwestern	Columbus	W	20–0
Oct. 11	at Wisconsin	Madison	L	17–10
Oct. 18	Iowa	Columbus	W	19–10
Oct. 25	at Indiana	Bloomington	W	35–6
Nov. 1	at Penn State	University Park	W	21–20
Nov. 8	Michigan State	Columbus	W	33–23
Nov. 15	Purdue	Columbus	W OT	16–13
Nov. 22	at Michigan	Ann Arbor	L	35–21
Jan. 1	Kansas State	Fiesta Bowl	W	35–28
Coach: Jim Tressel				322–229

Captains: Craig Krenzel, Michael Jenkins, Will Smith, Tim Anderson

Ranking (AP): Preseason No. 2; Postseason No. 4.

Major Awards: Jake Grove, Dave Rimington Award (center); B.J. Sander, Ray Guy Award (punter).

All-American: Will Allen, SS; Will Smith, DE; B.J. Sander, P.

All-Big Ten: Will Smith, DE; Will Allen, SS; Alex Stepanovich, G; Ben Hartsock, TE; Tim Anderson, DT; A.J. Hawk, LB; Chris Gamble, CB; B.J. Sander, P.

Leaders: Rushing—Lydell Ross (826 yards, 193 carries); Passing—Craig Krenzel (153 of 278, 2,040 yards); Receiving—Michael Jenkins (55 catches, 834 yards).

Ohio State's winning streak reached 19, the second longest in school history. ... The Buckeyes played their first overtime game in Ohio Stadium, a 44-38 triple-overtime victory over North Carolina State. It was the longest game in OSU history, lasting 4 hours and 17 minutes. ... Controversial running back Maurice Clarett was suspended for violating 14 NCAA rules—12 for receiving improper benefits and two for lying to investigators—and would never play another down for Ohio State. ... Craig Krenzel improved to 24-3 as a starter with the victory in the Fiesta Bowl.

2004
8–4

Sept. 4	Cincinnati	Columbus	W	27–6
Sept. 11	Marshall	Columbus	W	24–21
Sept. 18	at North Carolina State	Raleigh	W	22–14
Oct. 2	at Northwestern	Evanston	L OT	33–27
Oct. 9	Wisconsin	Columbus	L	24–13
Oct. 16	at Iowa	Iowa State	L	33–7
Oct. 23	Indiana	Columbus	W	30–7
Oct. 30	Penn State	Columbus	W	21–10
Nov. 6	at Michigan State	East Lansing	W	32–19
Nov. 13	at Purdue	West Lafayette	L	24–17
Nov. 20	Michigan	Columbus	W	37–21
Dec. 29	Oklahoma State	Alamo Bowl	W	33–7
Coach: Jim Tressel				267–219

Captains: Lydell Ross, Dustin Fox, Simon Fraser, Mike Nugent

Ranking (AP): Preseason No. 9; Postseason No. 20.

Major Awards: Mike Nugent, Lou Groza Award (kicker)

All-American: Mike Nugent, PK; A.J. Hawk, LB.

All-Big Ten: A.J. Hawk, LB; Mike Nugent, PK.

Leaders: Rushing—Lydell Ross (475 yards, 117 carries);
Passing—Justin Zwick (98 of 187, 1,209 yards); Receiving—
Santonio Holmes (55 catches, 769 yards).

After 14 players were selected in the NFL draft, and the team lost 28 seniors, the young Buckeyes won five of their last six games. ... The senior class was just the second class in Ohio State history to post winning records against Michigan (3–1) and in bowls (3–1). ... Mike Nugent became the school's first Lou Groza Award winner and became Ohio State's all-time leading scorer. ... Chic Harley, Ohio State's first three-time All-American, had his jersey retired. ... Former running back Maurice Clarett accused Jim Tressel and school officials of several improprieties. Quarterback Troy Smith was suspended from the Alamo Bowl for accepting cash from a booster.

Through the Years

2005

10–2, Big Ten champions (tied)

Sept. 3	Miami (Ohio)	Columbus	W	34–14
Sept. 10	Texas	Columbus	L	25–22
Sept. 17	San Diego State	Columbus	W	27–6
Sept. 24	Iowa	Columbus	W	31–6
Oct. 8	at Penn State	University Park	L	17–10
Oct. 15	Michigan State	Columbus	W	35–24
Oct. 22	at Indiana	Bloomington	W	41–10
Oct. 29	at Minnesota	Minneapolis	W	45–31
Nov. 5	Illinois	Columbus	W	40–2
Nov. 12	Northwestern	Columbus	W	48–7
Nov. 19	at Michigan	Ann Arbor	W	25–21
Jan. 2	Notre Dame	Fiesta Bowl	W	34–20

Coach: Jim Tressel   392–183

Captains: A.J. Hawk, Nick Mangold, Nate Salley, Rob Sims

Ranking (AP): Preseason No. 6; Postseason No. 4.

Major Awards: A.J. Hawk, Vince Lombardi Trophy (lineman)

All-American: A.J. Hawk, LB; Donte Whitner, SS; Nick Mangold, C.

All-Big Ten: A.J. Hawk, LB; Mike Kudla, DE; Nate Salley, FS;
Rob Sims, G; Josh Huston, PK; Santonio Holmes, WR; Donte
Whitner, SS; Ashton Youboty, CB.

Leaders: Rushing—Antonio Pittman (1,331 yards, 243 carries);
Passing—Troy Smith (149 of 237, 2,282 yards); Receiving—
Santonio Holmes (53 catches, 977 yards).

Ohio State won its last seven games and secured a
share of the Big Ten title. The Buckeyes also pulled off
back-to-back wins against Michigan and Notre Dame.
The latter came in the Fiesta Bowl, where quarterback
Troy Smith accounted for 408 yards of total offense
to be named game MVP. ... Linebacker A.J. Hawk won
the Lombardi Award. Center Nick Mangold and safety
Donte Whitner were also accorded first-team All-
American honors. ... "Burned out" Andy Geiger retired
as athletics director.

2006

12–1, Big Ten champions

Sept. 2	Northern Illinois	Columbus	W	35–12
Sept. 9	at Texas	Austin	W	24–7
Sept. 16	Cincinnati	Columbus	W	37–7
Sept. 23	Penn State	Columbus	W	28–6
Sept. 30	at Iowa	Iowa City	W	38–17
Oct. 7	Bowling Green	Columbus	W	35–7
Oct. 14	at Michigan State	East Lansing	W	38–7
Oct. 21	Indiana	Columbus	W	44–3
Oct. 28	Minnesota	Columbus	W	44–0
Nov. 4	at Illinois	Champaign	W	17–10
Nov. 11	at Northwestern	Evanston	W	54–10
Nov. 18	Michigan	Columbus	W	42–39
Jan. 8	Florida	BCS Championship	L	41–14
Coach: Jim Tressel				450–166

Captains: Troy Smith, Doug Datish, Quinn Pitcock, David Patterson

Ranking (AP): Preseason No. 1; Postseason No. 2.

Major Awards: Troy Smith, Heisman Trophy, Walter Camp Award (outstanding player), Davey O'Brien Award (quarterback); James Laurinaitis, Bronco Nagurski Award (defensive)

All-American: Troy Smith, QB; James Laurinaitis, LB; Quinn Pitcock, DL.

All-Big Ten: Troy Smith, QB; Antonio Pittman, RB; Anthony Gonzalez, WR; Doug Datish. C; T.J. Downing, G; Ted Ginn Jr., WR; Quinn Pitcock, DL; James Laurinaitis, LB; Malcolm Jenkins, DB; Antonio Smith, DB.

Leaders: Rushing—Antonio Pittman (1,233 yards, 242 carries); Passing—Troy Smith (203 of 311, 2,542 yards); Receiving—Ted Ginn Jr. (59 catches, 781 yards).

Ohio State was the preseason No. 1, a ranking it held until the national championship game. The Buckeyes defeated No. 2 Texas in Austin and No. 2 Michigan in Columbus, the first No. 1 vs. No. 2 matchup in the history of the rivalry. ... Senior quarterback Troy Smith threw a school-record 30 touchdowns and became Ohio State's seventh Heisman Trophy winner. ... Line-backer James Laurinaitis won the Nagurski Award as the best defensive player in the country and was one of three finalists for the Butkus Award. ... Ted Ginn Jr.'s 93-yard kick return for a touchdown was the highlight for Ohio State in the BCS Championship. It was outscored 41–7 the rest of the game.

2007

11–2, Big Ten champions

Sept. 1	Youngstown State	Columbus	W	38–6
Sept. 8	Akron	Columbus	W	20–2
Sept. 15	at Washington	Seattle	W	33–14
Sept. 22	Northwestern	Columbus	W	58–7
Sept. 29	at Minnesota	Minneapolis	W	30–7
Oct. 6	at Purdue	West Lafayette	W	23–7
Oct. 13	Kent State	Columbus	W	48–3
Oct. 20	Michigan State	Columbus	W	24–17
Oct. 27	at Penn State	University Park	W	37–17
Nov. 3	Wisconsin	Columbus	W	38–17
Nov. 10	Illinois	Columbus	L	28–21
Nov. 17	at Michigan	Ann Arbor	W	14–3
Jan. 7	LSU	BCS Championship	L	38–24
Coach: Jim Tressel				408–166

Captains: Kirk Barton, Dionte Johnson, James Laurinaitis

Ranking (AP): Preseason No. 11; Postseason No. 4.

Major Awards: James Laurinaitis, Butkus Award (linebacker)

All-American: James Laurinaitis, LB; Kirk Barton, T; Vernon Gholston, DE; Malcolm Jenkins, DB.

All-Big Ten: Todd Boeckman, QB; Chris Wells, RB; Kirk Barton, T; Vernon Gholston, DL; James Laurinaitis, LB; Malcolm Jenkins, DB.

Leaders: Rushing—Chris Wells (1,609 yards, 274 carries); Passing—Todd Boeckman (191 of 299, 2,379 yards); Receiving—Brian Robiskie (55 catches, 935 yards).

Ohio State was thought to be too young and inexperienced to challenge for the national championship, but went 11–1 to win the Big Ten title and reach the Bowl Championship Series game. For the second straight year though, the Buckeyes lost to an SEC opponent, 38–24 to LSU in New Orleans. LSU quarterback Matt Flynn had three of his four touchdown passes as the Tigers scored 31 unanswered

points. ... Junior James Laurinaitis, the Butkus
Award winner, was a finalist for five national
awards, and Big Ten defensive player of the year.
Vernon Gholston was Big Ten defensive lineman
of the year. ... Coach Jim Tressel won his 200th
career game.

**The 2007 loss against Illinois hurt the
Buckeyes in the polls, but the BCS standings kept OSU high enough that a win
against Michigan was all that was needed
to secure a berth in the BCS National
Championship Game.**

Future Schedules
2009

Sept. 5	Navy	Columbus
Sept. 12	Southern California	Columbus
Sept. 19	Toledo	Cleveland
Sept. 26	Illinois	Columbus
Oct. 3	Indiana	Bloomington
Oct. 10	Wisconsin	Columbus
Oct. 17	Purdue	West Lafayette
Oct. 24	Minnesota	Columbus
Oct. 31	New Mexico State	Columbus
Nov. 7	Penn State	University Park
Nov. 14	Iowa	Columbus
Nov. 21	Michigan	Ann Arbor

2010

Sept. 4	Marshall	Columbus
Sept. 11	Miami (Fla.)	Columbus
Sept. 18	Ohio	Columbus
Sept. 25	Eastern Michigan	Columbus
Oct. 2	Illinois	Champaign
Oct. 9	Indiana	Columbus
Oct. 16	Wisconsin	Madison
Oct. 23	Purdue	Columbus
Oct. 30	Minnesota	Minneapolis
Nov. 13	Penn State	Columbus
Nov. 20	Iowa	Iowa City
Nov. 27	Michigan	Columbus

2011

Sept. 3	Akron	Columbus
Sept. 10	Toledo	Columbus
Sept. 17	Miami (Fla.)	Miami
Oct. 1	Michigan State	Columbus
Oct. 8	Penn State	University Park
Oct. 15	TBA	TBA
Oct. 22	Minnesota	Columbus
Oct. 29	Indiana	Bloomington
Nov. 5	Northwestern	Columbus
Nov. 12	Purdue	West Lafayette
Nov. 19	Iowa	Columbus
Nov. 26	Michigan	Ann Arbor

2012

Sept. 1	Miami (Ohio)	Columbus
Sept. 8	Cincinnati	Columbus
Sept. 15	California	Columbus
Sept. 22	UAB	Columbus
Sept. 29	Michigan State	East Lansing
Oct. 6	Penn State	Columbus
Oct. 20	Minnesota	Minneapolis
Oct. 27	Indiana	Columbus
Nov. 3	Northwestern	Evanston
Nov. 10	Purdue	Columbus
Nov. 17	Iowa	Iowa City
Nov. 24	Michigan	Columbus

Through the Years

Ohio State Bowl Games

(Record 18–22)

Date	Bowl	Opponent	W/L	Score
Jan. 1, 1921	Rose	California	L	20–0
Jan. 2, 1950	Rose	California	W	17–14
Jan. 1, 1955	Rose	Southern California	W	20–7
Jan. 1, 1958	Rose	Oregon	W	10–7
Jan. 1, 1969	Rose	Southern California	W	27–16
Jan. 1, 1971	Rose	Stanford	L	27–17
Jan. 1, 1973	Rose	Southern California	L	42–17
Jan. 1, 1974	Rose	Southern California	W	42–21
Jan. 1, 1975	Rose	Southern California	L	18–17
Jan. 1, 1976	Rose	UCLA	L	23–10
Jan. 1, 1977	Orange	Colorado	W	27–10
Jan. 2, 1978	Sugar	Alabama	L	35–6
Dec. 29, 1978	Gator	Clemson	L	17–15
Jan. 1, 1980	Rose	Southern California	L	17–16
Dec. 26, 1980	Fiesta	Penn State	L	31–19
Dec. 30, 1981	Liberty	Navy	W	31–28
Dec. 17, 1982	Holiday	Brigham Young	W	47–17
Jan. 2, 1984	Fiesta	Pittsburgh	W	28–23
Jan. 1, 1985	Rose	Southern California	L	20–17
Dec. 28, 1985	Citrus	Brigham Young	W	10–7
Jan. 1, 1987	Cotton	Texas A&M	W	28–12
Jan. 1, 1990	Hall of Fame	Auburn	L	31–14
Dec, 27, 1990	Liberty	Air Force	L	23–11
Jan. 1, 1992	Hall of Fame	Syracuse	L	24–17
Jan. 1, 1993	Florida Citrus	Georgia	L	21–14
Dec. 30, 1993	Holiday	Brigham Young	W	28–21
Jan. 2, 1995	Florida Citrus	Alabama	L	24–17
Jan. 1, 1996	Florida Citrus	Tennessee	L	20–14
Jan. 1, 1997	Rose	Arizona State	W	20–17

Through the Years

Jan. 1, 1998	Sugar	Florida State	L	31–14
Jan. 1, 1999	Sugar	Texas A&M	W	24–14
Jan. 1, 2001	Outback	South Carolina	L	24–7
Jan. 1, 2002	Outback	South Carolina	L	31–28
Jan. 3, 2003	Fiesta	Miami	W 2OT	31–24
Jan. 1, 2004	Fiesta	Kansas State	W	35–28
Dec. 29, 2004	Alamo	Oklahoma State	W	33–7
Jan. 2, 2006	Fiesta	Notre Dame	W	34–20
Jan. 8, 2007	BCS	Florida	L	41–14
Jan. 7, 2008	BCS	LSU	L	38–24
Jan. 5, 2009	Fiesta	Texas	L	24–21

All-Time Records vs. Opponents

Team	W-L-T	First	Last
Air Force	0–1–0	1990	1990
Akron	6–1–0	1891	2007
Alabama	0–3–0	1978	1995
Antioch	1–0–0	1894	1894
Arizona	3–1–0	1967	2000
Arizona State	2–0–0	1980	1996
Auburn	0–1–1	1917	1990
Baylor	2–0–0	1978	1982
Boston College	3–0–0	1989	1995
Bowling Green	4–0–0	1992	2006
Brigham Young	3–0–0	1982	1993
California	5–1–0	1920	1972
Camp Sherman	1–0–0	1917	1917
Carlisle Indians	0–1–0	1904	1904
Case	11–10–2	1894	1918
Central Kentucky	0–1–0	1895	1895
Chicago	10–2–2	1920	1939
Cincinnati	13–2–0	1893	2006

Through the Years

Clemson	0–1–0	1978	1978
Colgate	1–0–1	1923	1934
Colorado	3–1–0	1971	1986
Columbia	2–0–0	1925	1926
Col. Barracks	2–1–0	1894	1897
Cornell	0–2–0	1939	1940
Dayton YMCA	1–0–0	1892	1892
Denison	14–1–2	1890	1927
DePauw	1–0–0	1905	1905
Drake	1–0–0	1935	1935
Duke	3–1–0	1955	1981
Florida	0–1–0	2006	2006
Florida State	0–3–0	1981	1997
Fort Knox	1–0–0	1942	1942
Fresno State	2–0–0	1994	2000
Georgia	0–1–0	1993	1993
Great Lakes	1–1–0	1943	1944
Heidelberg	3–0–0	1898	1907
Houston	1–0–0	1994	1994
Illinois	61–30–4	1902	2008
Indiana	65–12–5	1901	2006
Iowa	44–14–3	1922	2006
Iowa Seahawks	1–1–0	1942	1943
Kansas State	1–0–0	2003	2003
Kent State	2–0–0	2002	2007
Kentucky	3–0–0	1895	1935
Kenyon	17–6–0	1890	1929
LSU	1–1–1	1987	2008
Louisville	2–0–0	1991	1992
Marietta	6–2–0	1892	1902
Marshall	1–0–0	2004	2004
Miami (Fla.)	1–1–0	1977	1999
Miami (Ohio)	4–0–0	1904	2005

Maurice Clarett fends off a blocker against Indiana in 2002. The Hoosiers are one of many opponents that Ohio State has dominated over the years, with the Buckeyes posting a 65-12-2 record in the series.

Michigan	42–57–6	1897	2008
Michigan State	27–12–0	1912	2008
Minnesota	41–7–0	1921	2008
Missouri	10–1–1	1939	1998
Mount Union	1–0–0	1930	1930
Muskingum	7–0–0	1899	1928
Navy	3–0–0	1930	1981
Nebraska	2–0–0	1955	1956
New York University	2–0–0	1936	1938
North Carolina	3–1–0	1962	1975
North Carolina State	2–0–0	2003	2004
Northern Illinois	1–0–0	2006	2006
Northwestern	59–14–1	1913	2008
Notre Dame	3–2–0	1935	2005
Oberlin	13–10–3	1892	1922
Ohio Medical	5–2–1	1896	1906
Ohio	6–0–0	1899	2008
Ohio Wesleyan	26–2–1	1890	1932
Oklahoma	1–1–0	1977	1983
Oklahoma State	2–0–0	1989	2004
Oregon	7–0–0	1957	1987
Oregon State	2–0–0	1974	1984
Otterbein	13–2–3	1893	1912
Pennsylvania	3–0–0	1932	1953
Penn State	12–12–0	1912	2008
Pittsburgh	19–5–1	1929	1996
Princeton	0–1–1	1927	1928
Purdue	37–12–2	1919	2008
Rice	2–0–0	1993	1996
San Diego State	3–0–0	2001	2005
San Jose State	1–0–0	2002	2002
17th Regiment	1–0–0	1894	1894
South Carolina	0–2–0	2001	2002

Southern California	9–12–1	1937	2008
Southern Methodist	7–1–1	1950	1978
Stanford	2–3–0	1955	1982
Syracuse	4–2–0	1911	1992
Tennessee	0–1–0	1996	1996
Texas	1–2–0	2005	2008
Texas A&M	4–0–0	1963	1999
Texas Christian	4–1–1	1937	1973
Texas Tech	2–0–0	1990	2002
Toledo	1–0–0	1998	1998
Troy	1–0–0	2008	2008
UCLA	4–4–1	1961	2001
Utah	1–0–0	1986	1986
Vanderbilt	3–1–0	1908	1933
Virginia	1–0–0	1933	1933
Washington	8–3–0	1957	2007
Washington State	8–0–0	1952	2002
Western Reserve	5–6–1	1891	1934
West Virginia	5–1–0	1897	1998
Wilmington	1–0–0	1926	1926
Wisconsin	52–17–5	1913	2008
Wittenberg	12–3–0	1893	1929
Wooster	4–2–2	1890	1925
Wyoming	1–0–0	1997	1997
Youngstown State	2–0–0	2007	2008

7 The most wins by Ohio State over a school it has not lost to. The Buckeyes are 7–0 against both Muskigum and Oregon.

THE GREATEST PLAYERS

ARCHIE GRIFFIN
RUNNING BACK, 1972–1975
HEISMAN WINNER, 1974–1975

With any discussion about the greatest Buckeyes of all time, there's really only one place to start: Archie Griffin (1972–1975), the only player ever to win the Heisman Trophy twice. The heady, undersized tailback, who nearly bypassed Ohio State in favor of Navy or Northwestern, was voted college football's outstanding player in both 1974 and 1975, even though his totals of 1,450 yards and four touchdowns as a senior in 1975, while certainly not bad, were the worst since his freshman year.

As a four-year starter for the Buckeyes—his first season serendipitously coincided with the NCAA's decision to allow freshmen to play varsity football—he became the only player ever to start in four consecutive Rose Bowls. The 5-foot-9, 180-pounder played with more power than his size would indicate. He slashed past and ran over defenders for 5,589 yards in his career, averaging 6.0 yards per carry.

His career began inauspiciously with a fumble on his first carry as a freshman against Iowa. "After the fumble, I didn't think I would get the chance to carry the ball for the varsity again that year, because I continued to work on the scout squad the following week," Griffin said.

But in game No. 2, he ran for a then-school record 239 yards against North Carolina, jump-starting his record-shattering career. Ollie Cline's previous school record of 229 yards had stood since 1945.

In his last three seasons, after Coach Woody Hayes switched from a fullback-centric offense to one that featured Griffin, he gained 100 or more yards in 31 straight games—which still stands as the NCAA record. (As does his overall mark of 33 games with 100 rushing yards.) He remains Ohio State's career rushing yardage leader and is the only player ever to lead OSU in rushing four times.

His record-setting totals are even more impressive because of the fact that Hayes often took Griffin out of games at halftime, with the Buckeyes firmly in control.

The three-time first-team All-American graduated early with a degree in industrial relations and earned the highest honor the NCAA can bestow, the Top Five Award, for his excellence in athletics, academics, and leadership.

Griffin played eight years in the NFL, then went back to Columbus to work in the OSU athletics department. He's currently the president of the Ohio State Alumni Association.

"He's a better young man than he is a football player, and he's the best football player I've ever seen," Hayes gushed during Griffin's playing days.

LES HORVATH
QUARTERBACK/HALFBACK/SAFETY, 1940–1942, 1944
HEISMAN WINNER, 1944

The Buckeyes' first Heisman Trophy winner was Les Horvath in 1944. The two-way star (quarterback and halfback on offense, safety on defense) led OSU to a 9–0 record that year by leading the Big Ten in rushing (669 yards) and total offense (953 yards).

Strangely, Horvath (1940-42, 1944) almost didn't play that season. After helping Ohio State win its first national championship in 1942, the Parma native sat out the following year as he enrolled in dental school. But Coach Carroll Widdoes talked the 23-year-old Horvath into returning in 1944, utilizing a provision for an extra year of athletic eligibility because of World War II.

Horvath went on to become the only Heisman

The Greatest Players

Trophy winner who didn't play college football the previous season.

"At first, I wasn't sure I wanted to play," Horvath said years later. "Dental school was quite taxing. But Coach Widdoes said I wouldn't have to practice all the time and agreed to fly me to the games, both of which gave me more time to study."

Horvath played professionally for the Rams and Browns, then practiced dentistry in Los Angeles. He died in 1995 as a member of the National Football Foundation Hall of Fame.

VIC JANOWICZ
QUARTERBACK/HALFBACK/SAFETY/KICKER, 1949–1951
HEISMAN WINNER, 1950

Only six years after Les Horvath won the Heisman Trophy, Ohio State produced its second honoree: Vic Janowicz. In his junior year in 1950, Janowicz was among the best quarterbacks, halfbacks, and kickers in the country, and he played safety to boot. Considered by several historians to be the finest athlete ever to play football at Ohio State, Janowicz (1949–1951) accounted for 16 touchdowns and 875 total yards in his Heisman-winning season. He also kicked 10 extra points in a rout of Iowa, a Big Ten record.

But his most famous moments probably came in the infamous 1950 Snow Bowl against Michigan, during which visibility usually ranged from a few feet to a few inches. In that game, he made a 27-yard field goal for Ohio State's only points, called "one of the greatest individual accomplishments in Ohio State sports history" by the athletics department because the goal posts were barely visible. But also in that game, he had a punt blocked and recovered by Michigan for the 9–3 game's only touchdown. In the Snow Bowl, Janowicz punted 21 times for 685 yards, both school records.

After being asked to rejoin the Buckeyes while a dental student in 1944, Les Horvath took college football by storm and won Ohio State's first Heisman. Horvath to this day is the only Heisman winner to have not played college football the year before winning the award.

He played professional baseball for the Pirates and football for the Redskins before a car accident nearly killed him in 1956. He lived 40 more years, though, dying in 1996 as a member of the National Football Foundation Hall of Fame.

"Vic excelled in every phase of the game," former OSU Coach Wesley Fesler said. "He not only was a great runner, passer, and blocker, he also did all of our kicking. He was one of the finest, most versatile athletes I have ever seen."

HOWARD "HOPALONG" CASSADY
HALFBACK, 1952–1955
HEISMAN WINNER, 1955

Five years after Janowicz, Howard "Hopalong" Cassady became the school's third Heisman Trophy winner, in 1955. The slightly built halfback came off the bench to score three touchdowns against Indiana in his first college game, then was a mainstay in the OSU lineup for the rest of his career (1952–1955). He ran for 701 yards—an average of 5.7 per carry—in leading Ohio State to the national championship as a junior in 1954, then amassed 958 yards and 15 touchdowns as a senior.

The two-time first-team All-American from Columbus, who used to sneak into Ohio State football games as a child, was also an accomplished defensive back in addition to being the baseball team's starting shortstop for three seasons. He played professionally for the Lions, Browns, and Eagles. His nickname was borrowed from the Western movie character Hopalong Cassidy.

EDDIE GEORGE
TAILBACK, 1992–1995
HEISMAN WINNER, 1995

Tailback Eddie George won the Heisman Trophy in 1995. George (1992–1995) didn't have a ton of buzz coming into the season, but he wound up running away with the award with an Ohio State-record 1,927 rushing yards and 417 receiving yards during his senior season. He also piled up 24 touchdowns (an average of two per game) and three 200-yard efforts, including an OSU-record 314 yards against Illinois. His 47 receptions that season set a school record for a running back. He had 12 consecutive 100-yard games, including 207 yards in a highly anticipated showdown against Notre Dame.

A reserve his first two seasons in Columbus, George had a 1,442-yard season on the ground as a junior. His career total of 3,668 ranks behind only Archie Griffin on the school's all-time list.

George proceeded to have a remarkable career for the Oilers/Titans franchise. Since retirement, he has opened a couple of restaurants, including a popular hangout on High Street in Columbus.

OTHER BUCKEYE GREATS

The first five Heisman Trophy winners have had their jersey numbers retired by the school—22 for Horvath, 31 for Janowicz, 40 for Cassady, 45 for Griffin, and 27 for George. The only player to have his number retired without winning the Heisman is Chic Harley, who starred at OSU before the trophy even existed. His No. 47 came out of the cycle after linebacker A.J. Hawk's career ended with the 2005 season.

OSU's first superstar, Chic's real name was Charles, and he was an electrifying running back. In earning All-America honors three times (1916, 1917, and 1919), he became the first Buckeye to do it more than once. (Harley missed the 1918 season because of military obligations.) He was the driving force behind Ohio State's first two Big Ten championship teams—including the 1917 squad that outscored its opponents

The Greatest Players

292–6—and was posthumously inducted into the College Football Hall of Fame. Best known as a tailback, Harley also kicked, punted, and played defense.

Harley's most lasting legacy, however, is Ohio Stadium. The droves of fans he drew to old Ohio Field with his outstanding play were the impetus to construct a larger stadium. Three years after his playing career ended, the university opened the doors to a brand-new Ohio Stadium. Even to this day, it sometimes is referred to as "The House that Harley Built."

Of course, there are many notable former Buckeyes who never won the Heisman. Foremost among them might be left tackle Orlando Pace, the father of the "pancake block" and one of the best offensive linemen in football history. He started every game during his three-year Ohio State career (1994–1996) before passing up his final season to become a professional.

Pace did not allow a sack during his final two seasons as a Buckeye, earning the Lombardi Award in 1995 and 1996 and the Outland Trophy in 1996. After his junior season, he finished fourth in Heisman Trophy balloting, the highest for an offensive lineman since OSU's John Hicks finished second 23 years earlier. The Sandusky native was a two-time first-team All-American and was the Big Ten Offensive Player of the Year in 1996 after knocking his blocking assignment to the ground 80 times. That's 80 "pancakes."

He was picked No. 1 overall by the Rams in 1997 and spent the next 12 years with the franchise.

The aforementioned Hicks barely lost out to Penn State tailback John Cappelletti in Heisman Trophy voting in 1973, but he did take home the Lombardi Award and Outland Trophy. A Cleveland native, he won Big Ten titles in each of his three years as a starter (he missed 1971 because of a preseason knee injury), and twice was a first-team All-American.

Ever confident, Hicks (1970, 1972–1973) used to tell defensive players that a play was headed toward them as he lined up for the snap. "The way I looked at it, I didn't care if they knew or not, because even if they knew, they weren't going to stop us," he said.

Big No. 74 played briefly for the Giants before getting hurt and going into private business in Columbus. Hicks was elected to the College Football Hall of Fame in 2001.

"John and the other guys on the offensive line who blocked for me were the key to us having such great offenses," Archie Griffin said years later. "He was the leader of everything up front for us."

Continuing on the offensive lineman theme, Jim Parker was Ohio State's first truly special offensive lineman, from 1954 to 1956.

"Jim Parker was the greatest offensive lineman I ever coached," Woody Hayes said. "I'm not sure there has ever been a better offensive guard. He was everything an offensive lineman should be."

The three-year starter and two-time All-American was nimble for his immense size at the time (6'2", 200 pounds), allowing him to be a devastating pull blocker, as well as an agile pass blocker. He won the Outland Trophy in 1956. A native of Macon, Georgia, who moved to Toledo in high school, Parker was part of the 1954 national championship team and later went on to a splendid pro career with the Colts.

He's a member of the college and professional halls of fame. He died July 18, 2005, at age 71.

On the other side of the line of scrimmage, Jim Stillwagon was a destructive nose guard from 1968 to 1970. A key member of OSU's 1968 national championship team as a sophomore, Stillwagon went on to first-team All-America status as a junior and senior. He also won the Lombardi Award and Outland Trophy in 1970—the first time a player earned both in the same season.

With Stillwagon disrupting things in the middle, the 1969 Buckeyes allowed only 93 points all season. The next year, only two opponents scored more than 13 points, and five were held under 10. Drafted by the Green Bay Packers, Stillwagon instead played in the Canadian Football League. A member of the College Football Hall of Fame, Stillwagon is now in private business in Columbus.

LINEBACKER U

Over the past quarter-century Ohio State has become something of a "Linebacker U." Tom Cousineau, Randy Gradishar, and Pepper Johnson were among the best, but three names tend to stand out from the rest: Chris Spielman, Andy Katzenmoyer, and A.J. Hawk.

Spielman (1984–1987) won the Lombardi Award in 1987, even though his numbers were better as a junior (205 tackles, nine for a loss, two sacks, and six interceptions vs. 156 tackles, 10 for a loss, four sacks, and two interceptions). Maniacally intense, Spielman was the unquestioned leader of the Buckeyes as an upperclassman—and possibly even earlier.

He sprained his ankle twice during fall camp of his freshman year, costing him a starting spot in the season opener against Oregon State. But the ever-tough linebacker didn't believe that pain was enough to keep him out of any competition, so he stalked coach Earle Bruce along the sideline for the entire first quarter, yelling his demands to be put in the game. It was a gutsy display by a rookie.

"I never did know for sure if he heard me," Spielman said. "He had his headphones on."

But somebody heard Spielman, because he went into the game to start the second quarter. On his first play, Spielman made his first career tackle. By halftime,

Andy Katzenmoyer delivers a punishing hit in 1996. One of a long line of Ohio State star linebackers, Katzenmoyer is one of several players who have helped give OSU its reputation as a new "Linebacker U," with no apologies to Penn State.

he was the starter.

He finished his career as Ohio State's all-time leader with 283 solo tackles overall and 105 solo stops in a season (1986), and he also tied a school record with 29 tackles in the 1986 Michigan game. His 546 tackles overall rank third in school history behind Marcus Marek (572) and Tom Cousineau (569). A three-time All-Big Ten choice and two-time All-American, the Massillon native was known for threatening opposing ball carriers and giving wild pep talks in his own huddle—things that made him a cult hero in Ohio. His photo even graced the front of a local-edition Wheaties box—while he was still in high school. Spielman's No. 36 OSU jersey can be spotted in the stands at Ohio Stadium.

After college, Spielman went on to star for the Lions, then finish his career with the Bills and Browns. He now works for a sports talk radio station in Columbus and does color commentary for ESPN game broadcasts.

Though his NFL career fizzled in part because of a neck injury, Andy Katzenmoyer was among the most feared linebackers in the country during his three years at Ohio State (1996–1998). Wearing No. 45 with Archie Griffin's blessing, the 1997 Butkus Award winner started all 37 games of his career—along the way becoming the first OSU linebacker to start every game of his freshman season—and seemed to possess an innate ability to find the ball on running plays. He returned two interceptions for touchdowns during his career, tying a school record.

Katzenmoyer became only the second sophomore ever to win the Butkus Award as he compiled 97 tackles, 13 for a loss, two sacks, and two interceptions that season. A three-time All-Big Ten honoree, the Big Kat opted for the NFL after his junior season and was a first-round pick of the Patriots.

Next in the line of linebacker greats was the hard-nosed A.J. Hawk, who led the Buckeyes in tackles during his final three seasons in Columbus—the first player to do that since Steve Tovar (1990–1992). In the process, he twice earned first-team All-America honors and won the Lombardi Award in 2005. In his Lombardi-winning senior season, Hawk (2002–2005) paced the Buckeyes with 16.5 tackles for a loss and 9.5 sacks.

Fanatical about his workouts, Hawk posted 141 tackles as a junior, the most by a Buckeye since Spielman's 156 in 1986. Overall, he finished his career with 394 stops, ranking fifth on the school's all-time list. He was picked No. 5 overall in the 2006 NFL Draft by the Green Bay Packers.

THE SECONDARY: SECOND TO NONE

From Shawn Springs to Nate Clements to Ahmed Plummer to Chris Gamble, the Buckeyes have been well represented in NFL defensive backfields of late. But the first one of them who won the Thorpe Award as college football's best defensive back was Antoine Winfield in 1998. Among the firsts Winfield (1995–1998) accomplished in Ohio State history: winning the Thorpe, amassing 200 career solo tackles as a non-line-backer, being voted team MVP as a defensive back, and leading the team in tackles for a season as a cornerback (100 as a junior in 1997). His 82 solo tackles that year were the fifth-most ever at OSU.

At the other defensive backfield position—safety—two players stand out: Jack Tatum (1968–1970) and Mike Doss (1999–2002). Tatum, who went on to star for the Raiders, is one of the most feared hitters in football history. A key member of Ohio State's great teams from 1968 through 1970, Tatum twice was named an All-American and was the national Defensive Player of the Year as a senior. Perhaps more meaningful to him, however, was being voted one of four captains on Ohio State's All-Century Team in 2000. He is also a member of the College Football Hall of Fame.

Like Tatum, Doss was a ferocious hitter and a team leader. Many fans believe that OSU's run to the 2002 national championship began when Doss tearfully announced that he would return to school for his senior season instead of entering the NFL Draft. The three-time first-team All-American ranks in OSU's top 10 in career tackles with 331.

AWARD WINNERS

Two other individual award winners in Buckeye lore played for the offense: Terry Glenn (Biletnikoff) and LeCharles Bentley (Rimington). The flashy Glenn (1993–1995) came up with big play after big play during his junior season in 1995, leading the country in yards per catch as he finished with 64 catches for 1,411 yards and 17 touchdowns. Not bad for a guy who had 15 catches, 266 yards and no scores in his first two seasons combined. The single-season touchdown total remains a school record.

Glenn and Cris Carter (1984–1986) are the only OSU receivers to earn first-team All-America honors. Glenn, a Columbus native, left school a year early and has gone on to a long NFL career, most recently with the Cowboys. Carter, meanwhile, put up 164 career catches for 2,725 yards and 27 touchdowns during his three-year career. He went on to be a fantastic NFL receiver for the Minnesota Vikings.

TRULY SPECIAL TEAMS

In the early part of the new millennium, no school around the nation has been able to match the Buckeyes in terms of specialists. Punter Andy Groom (2000–2002) was an All-American during the 2002 national title season. Then his successor, punter B.J. Sander, won the Ray Guy Award in 2003. Sander (2000, 2003) punted 82 times that season, averaging 43.3 yards per kick. More impressive, however, were the 39 punts he downed inside the opponent's 20-yard line, versus only seven touchbacks. In a tight Purdue game, he kicked 10 times, downing seven of them inside the 20. The field position advantage helped the Buckeyes pull out a narrow victory.

The next season, it was a kicker who stole the show. Centerville native Mike Nugent—"Nuuuuuuuge," as he was known by fans—took home the Lou Groza Award as the nation's top kicker. He made 24 of 27 field goals, including five of six from 50 yards or longer. One of those massive boots was a 55-yarder to break a tie with Marshall as time expired. He also went 100 percent on extra points and smashed 40 of his 62 kickoffs for touchbacks.

Nugent (2001–2004) finished as Ohio State's all-time leading scorer with 356 points—eight more than former fullback Pete Johnson (1973–1976). In all, Nugent set or tied 22 Ohio State records during his four-year career, including field goals made (72), consecutive field goals made (24), and field-goal percentage (.857).

The Greatest Players

1 Kicker who has been named the Buckeyes' Most Valuable Player. It was Mike Nugent, recognized after his 2004 Lou Groza Award campaign.

THE HONORS

MAJOR AWARDS

Retired Jersey Numbers: 45 Archie Griffin, 31 Vic Janowicz, 40 Howard Cassady, 22 Les Horvath, 27 Eddie George, 47 "Chic" Harley, WH, Woody Hayes, 99 Bill Willis

Heisman Trophies (7): Les Horvath QB/HB 1944; Vic Janowicz HB 1950; Howard Cassady HB 1955; Archie Griffin RB 1974–75; Eddie George RB 1995; Troy Smith QB 2006.

Outland Trophy (interior lineman): Jim Parker G 1956; Jim Stillwagon MG 1970; John Hicks T 1973; Orlando Pace T 1996

Vince Lombardi Trophy (lineman): Jim Stillwagon MG 1970; John Hicks T 1973; Chris Spielman LB 1987; Orlando Pace T 1995–96; A.J. Hawk LB 2005

Walter Camp Award (outstanding player): Archie Griffin RB 1974–75; Eddie George RB 1995; Troy Smith QB 2006

Maxwell Award (offensive player): Howard Cassady HB 1955; Bob Ferguson RB 1961; Archie Griffin RB 1975; Eddie George RB 1995

Bronco Nagurski Award (defensive): James Laurinaitis LB 2006

Davey O'Brien Award (quarterback): Troy Smith 2006

Doak Walker Award (running back): Eddie George 1995

Dick Butkus Award (linebacker): Andy Katzenmoyer 1997; James Laurinaitis 2007

Jim Thorpe Award (defensive back): Antoine Winfield 1998; Malcolm Jenkins 2008

Fred Biletnikoff Award (receiver): Terry Glenn 1995

Dave Rimington Award (center): LeCharles Bentley 2001

Lou Groza Award (kicker): Mike Nugent 2004

Ray Guy Award (punter): B.J. Sander 2003

Draddy Trophy (academic Heisman): Bobby Hoying 1975; Craig Krenzel 2003

Chuck Bednarik Award (defensive player of the year): None

Johnny Unitas Golden Arm Award (outstanding senior quarterback): None

John Mackey Award (outstanding tight end): None

Ted Hendricks Award (defensive end): None.

OHIO STATE FOOTBALL

COLLEGE FOOTBALL HALL OF FAME

Warren Amling, 1944, guard/tackle, inducted 1984

Earle Bruce, 1972-92, coach, 2002

Hopalong Cassady, 1952-55, halfback, 1979

Jim Daniell, 1939-41, tackle, 1977

Bob Ferguson, 1959-61, fullback, 1996

Wes Fesler, 1928-30, end, 1954

Randy Gradishar, 1971-73, linebacker, 1998

Archie Griffin, 1972-75, halfback, 1986

Chic Harley, 1916-17, 1919, halfback, 1951

Woody Hayes, 1946-78, coach, 1983

John Hicks, 1970, 1972-73, tackle, 2001

Les Horvath, 1940-42, 1944, halfback/quarterback, 1969

Jim Houston, 1957-59, end, 2005

Vic Janowicz, 1949-51, halfback, 1976

Gomer Jones, 1933-35, center, 1978

Howard Jones, 1908-40, coach, 1951

Rex Kern, 1968-70, quarterback, 2007

Jim Parker, 1954-56, guard, 1974

Francis Schmidt, 1919-42, coach, 1971

Jim Stillwagon, 1968-70, middle guard, 1991

Gaylord Stinchcomb, 1917, 1919-20, halfback, 1973

Jack Tatum, 1968-70, safety, 2004

Aurealius Thomas, 1955-57, guard, 1989

John Wilce, 1913-28, coach, 1954

Bill Willis, 1942-44, tackle, 1971

Gust Zarnas, 1935-37, guard, 1975

FIRST-TEAM ALL-AMERICANS

(Source: NCAA. * consensus, # unanimous selection)

Robert Karch, T, 1916; Charles Harley, B, *1916, *1917, *1919; Charles Bolen, E, *1917; Lolas Huffman, G, *1920, T, *1921; Gaylord Stinchcomb, B, *1920; Ed Hess, G, *1925; Edwin Hayes, G, 1926; Marty Karow, B, 1926; Leo Raskowski, T, 1927; Wes Fesler, E, *1928, *1929, #*1930; Joe Gailus, G, 1932; Regis Monahan, G, 1934; Merle Wendt, E, 1934, 1935; Gomer Jones, C, 1935; Inwood Smith, G, 1935; Gus Zarnas, G, 1937; Esco Sarkkinen, E, *1939; Donald Scott, B, 1939; Charles Csuri, T, 1942 Bob Shaw, E, 1942; Lindell Houston, G, 1942;

Jack Dugger, E, *1944; Bill Hackett, G, *1944; Les Horvath, QB, #*1944; Bill Willis, T, 1944; Warren Amling, G, #*1945, T, *1946; Vic Janowicz, HB, #*1950; Bob McCullough, C, 1950; Bob Momsen, G, 1950; Mike Takacs, G, 1952; Howard Cassady, HB, #*1954, #*1955; Dean Dugger, E, 1954; Jim Parker, G, 1955, #*1956; Aurelius Thomas, G, 1957; Jim Houston, E, 1958; Jim Marshall, T, 1958; Bob White, B, *1958; Bob Ferguson, FB, #*1960, #*1961; Dwight Kelley, LB, 1964, Kelly1965; Arnold Chonko, DB, 1964; Jim Davidson, T, 1964; Doug Van Horn, OT, 1965; Ray Pryor, C, 1966; Dave Foley, OT, #*1968; Jim Otis, FB, *1969; Kern Jim Stillwagon, MG, *1969, #*1970; Jack Tatum, DB, *1969, #*1970; Rex Kern, QB, 1969; John Brockington, FB, 1970; Mike Sensibaugh, DB, 1970; Jan White, TE, 1970; Tom DeLeone, C, 1971; Gradishar John Hicks, OT, 1972, #*1973; Randy Gradishar, LB, *1972, #*1973; Griffin Van DeCree, DE, 1973, 1974; Archie Griffin, TB 1973, #*1974, #*1975; Kurt Schumacher, OT, *1974; Steve Myers, C, *1974; Neal Colzie, DB, 1974; Tom Skladany, P, 1974, 1975; Ted Smith, OG, *1975; Tim Fox, DB, *1975; Chris Ward, OT, *1976, #*1977; Bob Brudzinski, DE, *1976; Tom Cousineau, LB, *1977, *1978; Aaron Brown, MG, 1977; Ken Fritz, OG, *1979; Marcus Marek, LB, *1982; Jim Lachey, OG, *1984; Keith Byars, TB, #*1984; Pepper Johnson, LB, 1985; Cris Carter, SE, *1986; Chris Spielman, LB, *1986, #*1987; Tom Tupa, P (QB), #*1987; Steve Tovar, LB, 1991, 1992; Dan Wilkinson, DL, *1993; Korey Stringer, OL, 1993, *1994; Eddie George, RB, #*1995; Terry Glenn, WR, *1995; Orlando Pace, OL, #*1995, #*1996; Mike Vrabel, DL, 1995, *1996; Shawn Springs, DB, *1996; Andy Katzenmoyer, LB, *1997; Rob Murphy, OL, 1997; Antoine Winfield, DB, 1997; Rob Murphy, OL, *1998; Antoine Winfield, DB, #*1998; David Boston, WR, 1998; Damon Moore, DB, 1998; Na'il Diggs, LB, 1999; Mike Doss, DB, 2000, 2001; LeCharles Bentley, C, *2001; Mike Nugent, PK, *2002, #*2004; Matt Wilhelm, LB, *2002; Mike Doss, DB, #*2002; Andy Groom, P, 2002; Will Allen, DB, *2003, Will Smith, DL, 2003; A.J. Hawk, LB, *2004, #*2005; Troy Smith, QB, #*2006; Quinn Pitcock, DL, 2006; James Laurinaitis, LB, 2006, *#2007, *2008; Kirk Barton, T, 2007; Malcolm Jenkins, DB, *2008.

ACADEMIC ALL-AMERICANS

1952 John Borton QB; 1954 Dick Hilinski T; 1958 Bob White FB; 1961 Tom Perdue E; 1965 Bill Ridder MG; 1966-68 Dave Foley T; 1968 Mark Stier LB; 1969 Bill Urbanik DT; 1971 Rick Simon T; 1973 Randy Gradishar LB; 1974-75 Brian Baschnagel RB; 1976 Pete Johnson FB; 1976 Bill Lukens OG; 1977 Jeff Logan RB; 1980 Marcus Marek LB; 1982-83 Joe Smith OT; 1982 John Frank TE; 1984 Dave Crecelius DT; 1984-85 Mike Lanese FL; 1989 Joe Staysniak T; 1992 Len Hartman G; 1992 Greg Smith NG; 1995-96 Greg Bellisari LB; 1999 Ahmed Plummer CB; 2003 Craig Krenzel QB; 2006 Anthony Gonzalez SE; 2006 Stan White Jr. FB; 2007-08 Brian Robiskie WR.

The Greatest Players

2 **Ohio State players who have won the Draddy Trophy, considered the "academic Heisman." Bobby Hoying won the award in 1995 and Craig Krenzel was recognized in 2003.**

Big Ten Awards

PLAYER OF THE YEAR (SELECTED BY MEDIA)

1984: Keith Byars

OFFENSIVE PLAYER OF THE YEAR (SELECTED BY COACHES AND MEDIA)

1995: Eddie George (coaches and media)

1996: Orlando Pace (coaches and media)

1998: Joe Germaine (coaches)

2006: Troy Smith (coaches and media)

OFFENSIVE LINEMAN OF THE YEAR (SELECTED BY BIG TEN RADIO BROADCASTERS UNTIL 1991; COACHES SINCE)

1993: Korey Stringer

1994: Korey Stringer

1995: Orlando Pace

1996: Orlando Pace

2001: LeCharles Bentley

DEFENSIVE PLAYER OF THE YEAR (SELECTED BY COACHES AND MEDIA)

1992: Steve Tovar (coaches)

1993: Dan Wilkinson (media)

1996: Shawn Springs (coaches)

2002: Mike Doss (coaches)

2003: Will Smith (coaches and media)

2005: A.J. Hawk (coaches and media)

2007: James Laurinaitis (coaches and media)

2008: James Laurinaitis (coaches and media)

DEFENSIVE LINEMAN OF THE YEAR (SELECTED BY RADIO BROADCASTERS UNTIL 1991; COACHES SINCE)

1986: Eric Kumerow

1993: Dan Wilkinson

1995: Mike Vrabel

1996: Mike Vrabel

2003: Will Smith

2007: Vernon Gholston

FRESHMAN OF THE YEAR (SELECTED BY COACHES AND MEDIA)

1990: Robert Smith (coaches and media)

1992: Korey Stringer (coaches)

1994: Orlando Pace (coaches and media)

1996: Andy Katzenmoyer (coaches and media)

2002: Maurice Clarett (coaches and media)

2008: Terrelle Pryor (coaches and media)

DAVE MCCLAIN COACH OF THE YEAR (SELECTED BY MEDIA)

1973: Woody Hayes

1975: Woody Hayes

1979: Earle Bruce

OHIO STATE TEAM MVP
VOTED BY PLAYERS AT THE END OF THE SEASON.

1930: Wes Fesler, end

1931: Robert Haubrich, tackle

1932: Lew Hinchman, halfback

1933: Mickey Vuchinich, fullback

1934: Gomer Jones, center

1935: Gomer Jones, center

1936: Ralph Wolf, center

1937: Ralph Wolf, center

1938: Jim Langhurst, fullback

1939: Steve Andrako, center

1940: Claude White, center

1941: Jack Graf, fullback

1942: Chuck Csuri, tackle

1943: Gordon Appleby, center

1944: Les Horvath, quarterback

1945: Ollie Cline, fullback

1946: Cecil Souders, end

1947: Dave Templeton, guard

1948: Joe Whisler, fullback

1949: Jack Lininger, center

1950: Vic Janowicz, halfback

1951: Vic Janowicz, halfback

The Greatest Players

1952: Fred Bruney, halfback

1953: George Jacoby, tackle

1954: Howard "Hopalong" Cassady, halfback

1955: Howard "Hopalong" Cassady, halfback

1956: Jim Parker, guard

1957: Bill Jobko, guard

1958: Jim Houston, end

1959: Jim Houston, end

1960: Tom Matte, quarterback

1961: Bob Ferguson, fullback

1962: Billy Armstrong, center

1963: Matt Snell, fullback

1964: Ed Orazen, defensive lineman

1965: Doug Van Horn, offensive guard

1966: Ray Pryor, center

1967: Dirk Worden, linebacker

1968: Mark Stier, linebacker

1969: Jim Otis, fullback

1970: Jim Stillwagon, defensive lineman

1971: Tom DeLeone, center

1972: George Hasenohrl, defensive lineman

1973: Archie Griffin, running back

1974: Archie Griffin, tailback

1975: Cornelius Greene, quarterback

1976: Bob Brudzinski, defensive end

1977: Dave Adkins, linebacker

1978: Tom Cousineau, linebacker

1979: Jim Laughlin, linebacker

1980: Calvin Murray, tailback

1981: Art Schlichter, quarterback

1982: Tim Spencer, running back

1983: John Frank, tight end

1984: Keith Byars, running back

1985: Jim Karsatos, quarterback

1986: Cris Carter, wide receiver

1987: Chris Spielman, linebacker

1988: Jeff Uhlenhake, center

1989: Derek Isaman, linebacker

1990: Jeff Graham, wide receiver

A two-time team MVP, Howard "Hopalong" Cassady was one of football's biggest stars of the 1950s. The Heisman Trophy winner in 1955, he held a number of Ohio State rushing records for decades.

1991: Carlos Snow, tailback

1992: Kirk Herbstreit, quarterback

1993: Raymont Harris, tailback

1994: Korey Stringer, offensive tackle

1995: Eddie George, tailback

1996: Orlando Pace, offensive tackle

1997: Antoine Winfield, defensive back

1998: Joe Germaine, quarterback

1999: Ahmed Plummer, defensive back

2000: Derek Combs, tailback

2001: Jonathan Wells, tailback

2002: Craig Krenzel, quarterback; Chris Gamble, wide receiver/ defensive back

2003: Michael Jenkins, wide receiver

2004: Mike Nugent, placekicker

2005: A.J. Hawk, linebacker

2006: Troy Smith, quarterback

2007: Chris "Beanie" Wells, tailback

2008: Chris "Beanie" Wells, tailback

NFL Draft Picks

Year, Round, Name (Position), Team

1936: 8, Dick Heekin (B) New York Giants

1937: 6, Merle Wendt (E) Green Bay Packers

1938: 1, James McDonald (HB) Philadelphia Eagles; 3, Gust Zarnas (G) Chicago Bears

1939: None

1940: 3, Esco Sarkkinen (E) Green Bay Packers; 15, Steve Andrako (C) Washington Redskins

1941: 3, Don Scott (B) Chicago Bears; 20, Jim Strasbaugh (B) Green Bay Packers

1942: 10, Jim Daniell (T) Chicago Bears; 14, Tom Kinkade (B) Green Bay Packers

1943: 11, Don McCafferty (T) New York Giants

1944: 9, Lin Houston (G) Chicago Bears

1945: 2, Gordon Appleby (C) New York Giants; 2, Jack Dugger (E) Pittsburgh Steelers; 11, Bill Hackett (B) Green Bay Packers;

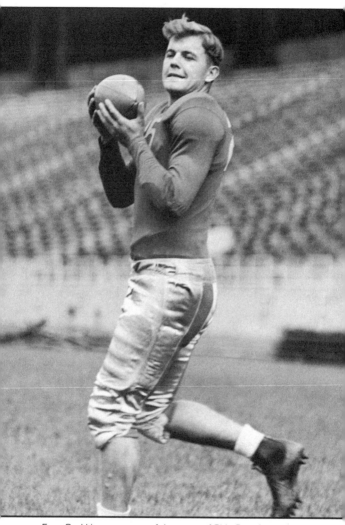

Esco Sarkkinen was one of the stars of Ohio State's prewar teams, and he was drafted to the NFL by the Green Bay Packers. His brother Eino also played for the Buckeyes, contributing at running back.

15, Bob Jabbusch (G) New York Giants; 23, Cy Souders (E) Washington Redskins; 29, John Friday (B) Green Bay Packers

1946: 6, Joe Waisler (B) Los Angeles Rams; 9, Tom Phillips (B) Los Angeles Rams; 11, Warren Amling (G) New York Giants

1947: 10, Tony Adamle (C) Chicago Bears; 10, Dante Lavelli (E) Los Angeles Rams; 28, Dean Hall (G) Los Angeles Rams

1948: 4, Bob Brugge (B) Chicago Bears; 8, Dick Flanagan (E) Chicago Bears; 8, Dick Flanagan (E) Chicago Bears

1949: 6, Jerry Krall (B) Chicago Bears

1950: 1, Fred Morrison (B) Chicago Bears; 11, Jack Wilson (T) Detroit Lions; 14, Bill Trautwein (T) Los Angeles Rams; 23, George Mattey (G) Green Bay Packers

1951: 7, Bob Monsen (T) Detroit Lions; 26, Bill Miller (T) Green Bay Packers

1952: 7, Vic Janowicz (B) Washington Redskins; 9, Sherwin Gandee (E) Detroit Lions; 15, Julius Wittman (T) Washington Redskins

1953: 11, Jim Ruehl (C) New York Giants; 16, John Hlay (FB) Green Bay Packers

1954: 6, George Jacoby (T) New York Giants; 13, Mike Takacs (G) Green Bay Packers; 22, Robert Meyer (T) Baltimore Colts; 25, George Rosso (G) Washington Redskins

1955: 2, Bobby Watkins (HB) Chicago Bears; 28, James Hoffman (B) Los Angeles Rams; 28, Robert Myers (T) Baltimore Colts; 28, Dave Williams (G) Pittsburgh Steelers

1956: 1, Howard Cassady (B) Detroit Lions; 4, Fran Machinsky (T) Washington Redskins; 9, Ken Vargo (C) Chicago Bears; 22, Jerry Harkrader (B) New York Giants

1957: 1, Jim Parker (T) Baltimore Colts; 2, Bill Michael (T) Pittsburgh Steelers; 11, Jim Roseboro (HB) Green Bay Packers; 16, Joe Cannavino (HB) Baltimore Colts; 18, Richard Guy (G) San Francisco 49ers; 22, Aurelius Thomas (G) Pittsburgh Steelers; 27, Don Vicic (FB) San Francisco 49ers; 30, Lee Williams (B) Los Angeles Rams

1958: 7, Bill Jobko (G) Los Angeles Rams; 8, Don Sutherin (B) New York Giants

1959: 1, Don Clark (B) Chicago Bears; 1, Dan James (C) San Francisco 49ers; 23, Frank Kremblas (QB) New York Giants; 26, John Scott (T) Pittsburgh Steelers

1960: AFL: 1, Birtho Arnold (OL) Buffalo Bills; 1, James Houston (E) Buffalo Bills; 1, Bob White (FB) Houston Oilers; 2, Jim Marshall (DT) Houston Oilers

1961: 1, Tom Matte (HB) Baltimore Colts; 14, Jim Tyrer (T) Chicago Bears; 15, Jerry Fields (HB) New York Giants; 15, Ernie Wright (T) Los Angeles Rams; 18, George Tolford (T) Washington Redskins; 20, Mike Ingram (G) Washington Redskins; 21, Bob Brooks (FB) New York Jets, AFL: 3, Jim Tyrer (T) Kansas City Chiefs; 5, Tom Matte (HB) New York Jets

1962: 1, Bob Ferguson (FB) Pittsburgh Steelers; 20, Jack Roberts (T) Chicago Bears, AFL: 1, Bob Ferguson (FB) San Diego Chargers; 13, Charles Bryant (E) San Diego Chargers; 20, Sam Tidmore (E) Buffalo Bills

1963: 1, Daryl Sanders (T) Detroit Lions; 1, Bob Vogel (T) Baltimore Colts; 5, Gary Moeller (LB) San Francisco 49ers; 7, Dave Francis (B) Washington Redskins; 13, Dave Katterhenrich (B) Cleveland Browns; 10, Rod Foster (G) Washington Redskins, AFL: 3, Bob Vogel (T) Boston Patriots; 4, Daryl Sanders (G) Kansas City Chiefs; 8, Rod Foster (G) Boston Patriots; 23, Bob Middleton (E) Buffalo Bills

1964: 4, Matt Snell (FB) New York Giants; 14, Tom Jenkins (G) Pittsburgh Steelers, AFL 1, Matt Snell (FB) New York Jets; 4, Paul Warfield (WR) Buffalo Bills

1965: AFL: 1, Jim Davidson (T) Buffalo Bills

1966: 3, Tom Barrington (FB) Washington Redskins; 4, Doug Van Horn (G) Detroit Lions, AFL: 5, Doug Van Horn (G) Kansas City Chiefs; 16, Tom Barington (RB) Kansas City Chiefs; 18, Greg Lashutka (E) Buffalo Bills

1967: 7, Bo Rein (FL) Baltimore Colts; 12, Ron Sepic (E) Washington Redskins, AFL: 3, Mike Current (T) Denver Broncos

1968: 3, Dick Himes (T) Green Bay Packers

1969: 1, Rufus Mayes (T) Chicago Bears, AFL: 1, Dave Foley (T) New York Jets; 10, Steve Howell (TE) Cincinnati Bengals

1970: 7, Ted Provost (DB) Los Angeles Rams; 9, Jim Otis (RB) New Orleans Saints

1971: 1, Tim Anderson (CB) San Francisco 49ers; 1, John Brockington (RB) Green Bay Packers; 1, Leo Hayden (RB) Minnesota Vikings; 1, Jack Tatum (DB) Oakland Raiders; 2, Jan White (TE) Buffalo Bills; 5, Jim Stillwagon (LB) Green Bay Packers; 7, Doug Adams (CB) Denver Broncos; 8, Mike

Sensibaugh (S) Kansas City Chiefs; 10, Bruce Jankowski (WR) Kansas City Chiefs; 10, Rex Kern (QB) Baltimore Colts; 15, Ron Maciejowski (QB) Chicago Bears; 16, Mark Debevc (LB) Cincinnati Bengals

1972: 5, Tom DeLeone (C) Cincinnati Bengals; 9, Harry Howard (DB) Los Angeles Rams; 12, Jimmy Harris (WR) Dallas Cowboys; 17, Stan White (LB) Baltimore Colts

1973: 8, John Bledsoe (RB) Detroit Lions; 8, George Hasenhohrl (DT) New York Giants; 8, Rich Seifert (S) New York Jets; 9, Rich Galbos (RB) Washington Redskins; 17, Earl Belgrave (T) Detroit Lions

1974: 1, Randy Gradishar (LB) Denver Broncos; 1, John Hicks (G) New York Giants; 1, Rick Middleton (LB) New Orleans Saints; 4, Morris Bradshaw (WR) Oakland Raiders; 8, Gregg Hare (QB) Buffalo Bills; 10, Jim Kregel (G) Pittsburgh Steelers; 12, Vic Koegel (LB) Atlanta Falcons

1975: 1, Neal Colzie (DB) Oakland Raiders; 1, Doug France (T) Los Angeles Rams; 1, Kurt Schumacher (G) New Orleans Saints; 3, Pete Cusick (DT) New England Patriots; 4, Bruce Elia (LB) Miami Dolphins; 4, Harold Henson (RB) Minnesota Vikings; 4, Steve Luke (S) Green Bay Packers; 11, Dave Hazel (WR) Baltimore Colts; 11, Steve Myers (G) Detroit Lions; 12, Doug Plank (DB) Chicago Bears; 14, Larry O'Rourke (DT) Philadelphia Eagles; 17, Mike Bartoszek (TE) New York Jets

1976: 1, Tim Fox (DB) New England Patriots; 1, Archie Griffin (RB) Cincinnati Bengals; 3, Brian Baschnagel (WR) Chicago Bears; 4, Leonard Willis (WR) Minnesota Vikings; 7, Ken Kuhn (LB) Cincinnati Bengals; 8, Craig Cassady (S) New Orleans Saints; 10, Tom Klaban (K) Cincinnati Bengals; 11, Cornelius Green (QB) Dallas Cowboys; 13, Larry Kain (LB) Pittsburgh Steelers; 16, Pat Curto (LB) Atlanta Falcons;17, Scott Dannelley (OG) Cincinnati Bengals

1977: 1, Bob Brudzinski (LB) Los Angeles Rams; 2, Pete Johnson (FB) Cincinnati Bengals; 8, Ed Thompson (LB) New York Jets; 9, Nick Buonamici (DT) Chicago Bears

1978: 1, Chris Ward (T) New York Jets; 2, Ray Griffin (CB) Cincinnati Bengals; 7, Herman Jones (WR) Chicago Bears; 7, Jeff Logan (RB) Baltimore Colts; 8, David Adkins (LB) Atlanta Falcons; 10, Aaron Brown (LB) Tampa Bay Buccaneers

1979: 1, Tom Cousineau (LB) Buffalo Bills; 5, Ron Springs (RB)

Vic Janowicz won the Heisman Trophy in 1950 and was drafted by the Washington Redskins in 1952, but passed on the NFL to play pro baseball. Janowicz eventually returned to the gridiron, and started for the Redskins before an automobile accident ended his career.

Dallas Cowboys; 6, Jim Moore (OT) Baltimore Colts; 9, Joe Robinson (T) Kansas City Chiefs

1980: 4, Jim Laughlin (LB) Atlanta Falcons; 6, Mike Guess (DB) Chicago Bears; 10, Ken Fritz (G) Pittsburgh Steelers

1981: 2, Doug Donley (WR) Dallas Cowboys; 4, Todd Bell (DB) Chicago Bears; 4, Calvin Murray (RB) Philadelphia Eagles; 4, Al Washington (LB) New York Jets; 5, Keith Ferguson (LB) San Diego Chargers; 6, Vince Skillings (DB) Dallas Cowboys; 10, Robert Murphy (DS) Atlanta Falcons; 12, Ray Ellis (SS) Philadelphia Eagles

1982: 1, Art Schlichter (QB) Baltimore Colts; 4, Anthony Griggs (LB) Philadelphia Eagles; 12, Bob Atha (K) St. Louis Cardinals

1983: 5, Jerome Foster (DE) Houston Oilers; 11, Joe Lukens (G) Miami Dolphins; 11, Tim Spencer (RB) San Diego Chargers; 11, Gary Williams (WR) Cincinnati Bengals

1984: 1, William Roberts (T) New York Giants; 2, John Frank (TE) San Francisco 49ers; 6, Rowland Tatum (LB) Miami Dolphins; 10, Joe Dooley (C) Los Angeles Rams; 10, Shaun Gayle (DB) Chicago Bears; 12, Thad Jemison (WR) Tampa Bay Buccaneers

1985: 1, Jim Lachey (T) San Diego Chargers; 3, Kirk Lowdermilk (C) Minnesota Vikings

1986: 1, Keith Byars (RB) Philadelphia Eagles; 2, Thomas Johnson (LB) New York Giants; 7, Larry Kolic (LB) Miami Dolphins; 7, Byron Lee (LB) Philadelphia Eagles

1987: 6, Sonny Gordon (FS) Cincinnati Bengals; 7, Jamie Holland (WR) San Diego Chargers; 9, Scott Leach (LB) New Orleans Saints; 12, Jim Karsatos (QB) Miami Dolphins, Supplemental: 4, Cris Carter (WR) Philadelphia Eagles

1988: 1, Eric Kumerow (DE) Miami Dolphins; 2, Chris Spielman (LB) Detroit Lions; 3, Alex Higdon (TE) Atlanta Falcons; 4, William White (CB) Detroit Lions; 6, George Cooper (FB) Miami Dolphins; 7, Ray Jackson (CB) Seattle Seahawks; 10, Henry Brown (T) Washington Redskins

1989: 5, Jeff Uhlenhake (C) Miami Dolphins; 5, Vince Workman (RB) Green Bay Packers; 9, Derek MacCready (DE) Detroit Lions; 12, Everett Ross (WR) Minnesota Vikings

1990: 5, Jeff Davidson (G) Denver Broncos; 7, Joe Staysniak (T) San Diego Chargers; 9, Tim Moxley (G) Washington Redskins

Chris Spielman poses with the Lombardi Award in 1987. The two-time All-American had a fantastic career in the NFL, leading the Detroit Lions in tackles for eight straight years and making four Pro Bowls.

Eddie George sprinted away from the competition to win the Heisman in 1995, then went on to a sensational NFL career after being drafted by the Houston Oilers in 1996. George went on to make four Pro Bowls and played in a Super Bowl.

1991: 1, Vinnie Clark (CB) Green Bay Packers; 2, Jeff Graham (WR) Pittsburgh Steelers; 11, Bobby Olive (WR) Kansas City Chiefs

1992: 1, Alonzo Spellman (DT) Chicago Bears; 7, Scottie Graham (FB) Pittsburgh Steelers; 8, Kent Graham (QB) New York Giants

1993: 1, Robert Smith (RB) Minnesota Vikings; 2, Roger Harper (S) Atlanta Falcons; 3, Steve Tovar (LB) Cincinnati Bengals; 8, Brian Stablein (WR) Denver Broncos

1994: 1, Dan Wilkinson (DL) Cincinnati Bengals; 3, Jeff Cothran (RB) Cincinnati Bengals; 4, Raymont Harris (RB) Chicago Bears; 6, Jason Winrow (G) New York Giants; 7, Butler By'not'e (RB) Denver Broncos

1995: 1, Joey Galloway (WR) Seattle Seahawks; 1, Korey Stringer (T) Minnesota Vikings; 1, Craig Powell (LB) Cleveland Browns; 3, Preston Harrison (LB) San Diego Chargers; 3, Marlon Kerner (CB) Buffalo Bills; 3, Chris Sanders (WR) Houston Oilers; 3, Lorenzo Styles (LB) Atlanta Falcons

1996: 1, Rickey Dudley (TE) Oakland Raiders; 1, Eddie George (RB) Houston Oilers; 1, Terry Glenn (WR) New England Patriots; 3, Bobby Hoying (QB) Philadelphia Eagles

1997: 1, Orlando Pace (T) St. Louis Rams; 1, Shawn Springs (CB) Seattle Seahawks; 2, Rob Kelly (S) New Orleans Saints; 3, Mike Vrabel (DE) Pittsburgh Steelers; 3, Ty Howard (CB) Arizona Cardinals; 4, Nicky Sualua (FB) Dallas Cowboys; 6, Matt Finkes (DL) Carolina Panthers

1998: None

1999: 1, David Boston (SE) Arizona Cardinals; 1, Antoine Winfield (CB) Buffalo Bills; 1, Andy Katzenmoyer (LB) New England Patriots; 2, Joe Montgomery (TB) New York Giants; 4, Joe Germaine (QB) St. Louis Rams; 4, Damon Moore (SS) Philadelphia Eagles; 6, Brent Bartholomew (P) Miami Dolphins; 6, Dee Miller (FL) Green Bay Packers

2000: 1, Ahmed Plummer (CB) San Francisco 49ers; 4, Na'il Diggs (LB) Green Bay Packers; 4, Gary Berry (FS) Green Bay Packers; 5, Michael Wiley (RB) Dallas Cowboys; 7, James Cotton (LB) Chicago Bears; 7, Kevin Houser (ST) New Orleans Saints

2001: 1, Nate Clements (CB) Buffalo Bills; 1, Ryan Pickett

[DT] St. Louis Rams; 6, Rodney Bailey [DE] Pittsburgh Steelers; 7, Reggie Germany [WR] Buffalo Bills; 7, Derek Combs [RB] Oakland Raiders; 7, Ken-Yon Rambo [WR] Oakland Raiders

2002: 2, LeCharles Bentley [C] New Orleans Saints; 3, Derek Ross [CB] Dallas Cowboys; 4, Jonathan Wells [RB] Houston Texans; 4, Darnell Sanders [TE] Cleveland Browns; 4, Jamar Martin [FB] Dallas Cowboys; 5, Courtland Bullard [OLB] St. Louis Rams; 6, Tyson Walter [OT] Dallas Cowboys; 6, Steve Bellisari [QB] St. Louis Rams

2003: 2, Mike Doss [SS] Indianapolis Colts; 3, Kenny Peterson [DE] Green Bay Packers; 3, Cie Grant [OLB] New Orleans Saints; 4, Matt Wilhelm [MLB] San Diego Chargers; 5, Donnie Nickey [FS] Tennessee Titans

2004: 1, Chris Gamble [CB] Carolina Panthers; 1, Michael Jenkins [WR] Atlanta Falcons; 1, Will Smith [DE] New Orleans Saints; 3, Tim Anderson [DT] Buffalo Bills; 3, Ben Hartsock [TE] Indianapolis Colts; 3, B.J. Sander [P] Green Bay Packers; 3, Darrion Scott [DE] Minnesota Vikings; 4, Will Allen [FS] Tampa Bay Buccaneers; 4, Alex Stepanovich [C] Arizona Cardinals; 5, Drew Carter [WR] Carolina Panthers; 5, Craig Krenzel [QB] Chicago Bears; 5, Robert Reynolds [LB] Tennessee Titans; 7, Adrien Clarke [OG] Philadelphia Eagles; 7, Shane Olivea [OT] San Diego Chargers

2005: 2, Mike Nugent [K] New York Jets; 3, Dustin Fox [CB] Minnesota Vikings; 3, Maurice Clarett [RB] Denver Broncos

2006: 1, A.J. Hawk [LB] Green Bay Packers; 1, Donte Whitner [DB] Buffalo Bills; 1, Bobby Carpenter [LB] Dallas Cowboys; 1, Santonio Holmes [WR] Pittsburgh Steelers; 1, Nick Mangold [C] New York Jets; 3, Ashton Youboty [CB] Buffalo Bills; 3, Anthony Schlegel [ILB] New York Jets; 4, Nate Salley [DB] Carolina Panthers; 4, Rob Sims [OL] Seattle Seahawks

2007: 1, Ted Ginn Jr. [WR] Miami Dolphins; 1, Anthony Gonzalez [WR] Indianapolis Colts; 3, Quinn Pitcock [DT] Indianapolis Colts; 4, Antonio Pittman [RB] New Orleans Saints; 5, Jay Richardson [DE] Oakland Raiders; 5, Roy Hall [WR] Indianapolis Colts; 5, Troy Smith [QB] Baltimore Ravens; 6, Doug Datish [C] Atlanta Falcons

2008:1, Vernon Gholston [DL] New York Jets; 7, Larry Grant [LB] San Francisco 49ers; 7, Kirk Barton [OL] Chicago Bears

All-Century Team

Selected by the Columbus Touchdown Club, 2000 (80 man roster, names listed alphabetically)

QB: Joe Germaine 1996–98; Bobby Hoying 1993–95; Rex Kern 1968–70; Art Schlichter 1978–81; Don Scott 1938–40

FB: John Brockington 1968–70; Ollie Cline 1944–46; Bob Ferguson 1959–61; Pete Johnson 1973–76; Jim Otis 1967–69

HB: Keith Byars 1982–85; Howard "Hopalong" Cassady 1952–55; Eddie George 1992–95; Archie Griffin 1972–75; Chic Harley 1916–17, 1919; Les Horvath 1940–42, 1944; Vic Janowicz 1949–51; Gaylord Stinchcomb 1917–19, 1920

WR: David Boston 1996–98; Cris Carter 1984–86; Doug Donley 1977–80; Joey Galloway 1991, 1993–94; Terry Glenn 1993–95; Paul Warfield 1961–63

TE: Wed Fesler 1928–30; John Fran 1980–83; Esco Sarkkinen 1937–39; Bob Shaw 1941–42; Merle Wendt 1935–36; Jan White 1968–70

C: Tom DeLeone 1969–71; Gomer Jones 1933–35; Steve Myers 1972–74

G: Warren Amling, Lindell Houston, Iolas Huffman 1918–21; Jim Lachey 1981–84; Jim Parker 1954–56; Gust Zarnas 1935–37

T: John Hicks 1970–73; Jim Marshall 1956–57; Orlando Pace 1994–96; Kurt Schumacher 1972–74; Korey Stringer 1992–94; Chris Ward 1974–77

DE: Bob Brudzinsku 1973–76; Van Ness DeCree 1972–74; Dean Dugger 1952–54; Jim Houston 1957–59; Matt Snell 1961–63; Muke Vrabel 1993–96

DL: Aaron Brown 1974–77; Chuch Csuri 1941–42, 1946; Pete Cusick 1972–74; Jerome Fister 1979–82; Jim Stillwagon 1968–70; Dan Wilkinson 1992–93; Bill Willis 1942–44

LB: Tom Cousineau 1975–78; Randy Gradishar 1971–73; Pepper Johnson 1982–85; Andy Katzenmoyer 1996–98; Ike Kelley 1963–65; Marcus Marek 1979–82; Chris Spielman 1984–87; Steve Tovar 1989–92

DB: Arnie Chonko 1962–64; Neal Colzie 1972–75; Tim Fox 1972–75; Ray Griffin 1974–77; Mike Sensibaugh 1968–70; Shawn Springs 1994–96; Jack Tatum 1968–70; Antoine Winfield 1995–98

P: Brent Bartholomew 1995-98; Tom Skladany 1973-76; Tom Tupa 1984-87

K: Vlade Janakievski, Rich Spangler 1982-85; Tim Williams 1990-93

Coaches: Paul Brown 1941-43; Earle Bruce 1979-87; Woody Hayes 1951-78; John Wilce 1913-28

Captains: Archie Griffin, Rex Kern, Chris Spielman, Jack Tatum

MVP: Archie Griffin

"He's a better young man than he is a football player, and he's the best football player I've ever seen." – Woody Hayes on All-Century Ohio State MVP Archie Griffin

The MVP of Ohio State's All-Century team is Archie Griffin the best college football player to ever lace up the pads. Many have tried but none have managed to duplicate his two Heisman Trophies.

RECORDS/LEADERS
Rushing

Game

Yards	Name	Carries	Opponent	Year
1. 314	Eddie George	36	Illinois	1995
2. 274	Keith Byars	39	Illinois	1984
3. 246	Archie Griffin	30	Iowa	1973
4. 239	Archie Griffin	27	North Carolina	1972
5. 235	Raymont Harris	39	vs. BYU	1993
6. 230	Maurice Clarett	31	Washington State	2002
7. 229	Ollie Cline	32	Pitt	1945
8. 224	Calvin Murray	35	Indiana	1980
9. 222	Chris Wells	39	Michigan	2007
10. 221	Chris Wells	31	at Michigan State	2007

Season

Yards	Name	Carries	Year
1. 1,927	Eddie George	328	1995
2. 1,764	Keith Byars	336	1984
3. 1,695	Archie Griffin	256	1974
4. 1,609	Chris Wells	274	2007
5. 1,577	Archie Griffin	247	1973
6. 1,538	Tim Spencer	273	1982
7. 1,484	Pepe Pearson	299	1996
8. 1,450	Archie Griffin	262	1975
9. 1,442	Eddie George	276	1994
10. 1,344	Raymont Harris	273	1993

Career

Yards	Name	Carries	Years
1. 5,589	Archie Griffin	924	1972–75
2. 3,768	Eddie George	683	1992–95
3. 3,553	Tim Spencer	644	1979–82
4. 3,382	Chris Wells	585	2006–08
5. 3,200	Keith Byars	619	1982–85

6. 3,121	Pepe Pearson	659	1994–97
7. 2,974	Carlos Snow	610	1987–89, '91
8. 2,951	Michael Wiley	509	1996–99
9. 2,945	Antonio Pittman	557	2004–06
10. 2,649	Raymont Harris	574	1990–93

Passing

Game

Yards	Name	Comp-Att	Opponent	Year
1. 458	Art Schlichter	31–52	Florida State	1981
2. 378	Joe Germaine	29–43	at Penn State	1997
3. 362	Greg Frey	20–31	at Minnesota	1989
4. 354	Bobby Hoying	24–35	at Penn State	1995
5. 351	Joe Germaine	31–45	at Indiana	1998
6. 342	Troy Smith	19–28	vs. Notre Dame	2005
(tie) 342	Joe Germaine	19–35	at Northwestern	1998
8. 339	Joe Germaine	27–39	Minnesota	1998
9. 336	Art Schlichter	19–33	at Purdue	1981
10. 330	Joe Germaine	16–28	Michigan	1998

Season

Yards	Name	Comp-Att	Year
1. 3,330	Joe Germaine	230–384	1998
2. 3,269	Bobby Hoying	211–341	1995
3. 2,551	Art Schlichter	183–350	1981
4. 2,542	Troy Smith	203–311	2006
5. 2,379	Todd Boeckman	191–299	2007
6. 2,335	Bobby Hoying	170–301	1994
7. 2,319	Steve Bellisari	163–310	2000
8. 2,311	Jim Karsatos	177–289	1985
9. 2,282	Troy Smith	149–237	2005
10. 2,132	Greg Frey	144–246	1989

The Greatest Players

Art Schlichter and Gary Williams celebrate a touchdown run against Michigan in 1981. Though personal demons haunted Schlichter in later years, his prodigious performances as a Buckeye still keep him on top of OSU's career passing list.

Career

Yards	Name	Comp-Att	Years
1. 7,547	Art Schlichter	497–951	1978–81
2. 7,232	Bobby Hoying	498–858	1992–95
3. 6,370	Joe Germaine	439–741	1996–98
4. 6,316	Greg Frey	443–835	1987–90
5. 5,878	Steve Bellisari	386–759	1998–01
6. 5,720	Troy Smith	420–670	2003–06
7. 5,569	Mike Tomczak	376–675	1981–84
8. 5,089	Jim Karsatos	359–629	1984–86
9. 4,493	Craig Krenzel	329–579	2000–03
10. 2,660	Stanley Jackson	194–353	1994–97

Receiving

Game

Yards	Name	Catches	Opponent	Year
1. 253	Terry Glenn	9	at Pitt	1995
2. 224	Santonio Holmes	10	Marshall	2004
3. 220	Gary Williams	13	Florida State	1981
4. 217	David Boston	10	Michigan	1998
5. 199	Dimitrious Stanley	10	Wisconsin	1996
6. 191	David Boston	10	Minnesota	1998
7. 187	Robert Grimes	9	Washington State	1952
8. 186	Joey Galloway	9	Michigan State	1993
9. 181	Ken-Yon Rambo	7	Ohio	1999
10. 179	Ken-Yon Rambo	7	Iowa	1999

The Greatest Players

Season

Yards	Name	Catches	Year
1. 1,435	David Boston	85	1998
2. 1,411	Terry Glenn	64	1995
3. 1,127	Cris Carter	69	1986
4. 1,076	Michael Jenkins	61	2002
5. 981	Dee Miller	58	1997
6. 977	Santonio Holmes	53	2005
7. 970	David Boston	73	1997
8. 950	Cris Carter	58	1985
9. 946	Joey Galloway	47	1993
10. 941	Gary Williams	50	1981

Career

Yards	Name	Catches	Years
1. 2,898	Michael Jenkins	165	2000–03
2. 2,855	David Boston	191	1996–98
3. 2,792	Gary Williams	154	1979–82
4. 2,725	Cris Carter	168	1984–86
5. 2,295	Santonio Holmes	140	2003–05
6. 2,252	Doug Donley	106	1977–80
7. 2,090	Dee Miller	132	1995–98
8. 1,943	Ted Ginn Jr.	135	2004–06
9. 1,894	Joey Galloway	108	1991–94
10. 1,866	Brian Robiskie	127	2005–08

Other Records

Points, game: 30 Keith Byars vs. Illinois 1984; Pete Johnson vs. North Carolina 1975

Points, season: 156 Pete Johnson, 1975

Points, career: 356 Mike Nugent, 2001–04

All-purpose yards, game: 354 Keith Byars at Purdue, 1984

All-purpose yards, season: 2,441 Keith Byars, 1984 (12 games)

All-purpose yards, career: 6,559 Archie Griffin (45 games) 1972–75

Interceptions, game: 3, nine players (Fred Bruney, Fred Bruney, Arnie Chonko, Ted Provost, Bruce Ruhl, Craig Cassady, Mike Guess, William White, Damon Moore)

Interceptions, season: 9, Mike Sensibaugh, 1969

Interceptions, career: 22, Mike Sensibaugh, 1968–70

Tackles, game: 29, Chris Spielman vs. Michigan 1986; Tom Cousineau vs. Penn State, 1978

Tackles, season: 211, Tom Cousineau, 1978

Tackles, career: 572 Marcus Marek, 1979–82

Sacks, game: 4.0 Vernon Gholston vs. Wisconsin 2007; Bobby Carpenter vs. Michigan State 2005; Jason Simmons vs. Washington State 1991

Sacks, season: 14.0 Vernon Gholston 2007

Sacks, career: 36.0 Mike Vrabel 1993–96

The Greatest Players

THE COACHES

Name	Years	W-L-T
Alexander S. Lilley	1890–91	3–5–0
Jack Ryder	1892–95, 1898	22–22–2
Charles A. Hickey	1896	5–5–1
David F. Edwards	1897	1–7–1
John B. Eckstorm	1899–1901	22–4–3
Perry Hale	1902–03	14–5–2
E.R. Sweetland	1904–05	14–7–2
A.E. Herrnstein	1906–09	28–10–1
Howard Jones	1910	6–1–3
Harry Vaughn	1911	5–3–2
John R. Richards	1912	6–3–0
John W. Wilce	1913–28	78–33–9
Sam S. Willaman	1929–33	26–10–5
Francis A. Schmidt	1934–40	39–16–1
Paul E. Brown	1941–43	18–8–1
Carroll C. Widdoes	1944–45	16–2–0
Paul O. Bixler	1946	4–3–2
Wesley E. Fesler	1947–50	21–13–3
W.W. "Woody" Hayes	1951–78	205–61–10
Earle Bruce	1979–87	81–26–1
John Cooper	1988–2000	111–43–4
Jim Tressel	2001–	83–19–0

COACHES' AWARDS

Paul "Bear" Bryant Award: Jim Tressel 2002.
Eddie Robinson Coach of the Year Award: Woody Hayes 1957, 1968, 1975;
Earle Bruce 1979; Jim Tressel 2002.
Bobby Dodd Coach of the Year Award: Jim Tressel 2002.
Walter Camp Coach of the Year Award: Woody Hayes 1968.
AFCA Coach of the Year Award: Carroll Widdoes 1944; Woody Hayes 1957; Earle Bruce 1980; Jim Tressel 2002.

Broyles Award (Assistant Coach of the Year): Jim Heacock, 2007

2009 COACHING STAFF

Jim Tressel	Head Coach
Jim Bollman	Offensive Coordinator and Offensive Line
Jim Heacock	Defensive Coodinator
Joe Daniels	Passing Game Coordinator/Quarterbacks
Luke Fickell	Co-Defensive Coordinator/Linebackers Coach
Paul Haynes	Safeties
Darrell Hazell	Assistant Head Coach and Wide Receivers
Taver Johnson	Cornerbacks
John Peterson	Tight Ends and Recruiting Coordinator
Dick Tressel	Running Backs
Bob Tucker	Director of Football Operations

Woody Hayes

Discuss great college football coaches with an Ohioan, and the conversation probably won't deviate from one name: Woody.

Wayne Woodrow Hayes led the Buckeyes to five national championships (and nearly four more), 13 Big Ten titles, and 205 victories during his tenure from 1951 to 1978. Ohio State twice won a conference-record 17-straight Big Ten games under his guidance and became the only Big Ten school ever to qualify for four straight Rose Bowls (1973–1976). Overall, he coached in eight Rose Bowls and freed OSU from its nickname, "the graveyard of coaches."

Hayes' fiery demeanor and unbridled intensity endeared him to fans. Among his too-many-to-count blowups, he destroyed his own hat, watch, and glasses (the latter until his hands bled) at various times and threw water coolers, hats, wallets, down markers, coffee, and telephones in fits of rage. He once even punched himself in the face with both fists—cutting

The Coaches

his cheek with his 1968 national championship ring—simply because a player was injured in practice. Hayes detested injuries. During his tenure, the Buckeyes led the nation in attendance in 21 seasons and finished second in the other seven.

He coached three Heisman Trophy winners and 56 first-team All-Americans. Four times he went undefeated, and in five more seasons he suffered only one loss. His two best stretches were from 1968 to 1970, when he went 27–2 with two national championships and three Big Ten titles, and from 1972 to 1977, when he won six straight league championships and went 58–10–2.

The creator of the "three yards and a cloud of dust" power rushing philosophy, Hayes won national titles in 1954, 1957, 1961, 1968, and 1970.

Woody was born on Valentine's Day in 1913 in Clifton, Ohio, grew up in Newcomerstown and graduated from Denison University, where he coached the first three years of his career. He then moved on to the "cradle of coaches" at Miami (Ohio) for two seasons before landing the Ohio State job. His career record was 238–72–10, which puts him ninth on the all-time Division I-A wins list, four ahead of his old protégé and rival, Bo Schembechler. Hayes twice won National Coach of the Year honors while at OSU. Among his notable assistant coaches through the years were Earle Bruce, Joe Bugel, Lou Holtz, Bill Mallory, Glen Mason, Gary Moeller, and Schembechler.

Off the field, Hayes was passionate about military history and taught at OSU as an associate professor during the offseason. He was fired by the university after punching Clemson defensive lineman Charlie Bauman following an interception return along the Ohio State sideline during the 1978 Gator Bowl, but he still kept a fondness for the Buckeyes. He delivered a commencement speech after the university's winter quarter in 1986.

The Coaches

Woody Hayes caught during a quiet moment in 1951. This was his first season in Columbus after a successful run at Miami, a 4–3–2 campaign that sent Hayes on his way to 205 wins at OSU.

He died on March 12, 1987. Many thousands came out for his memorial service.

"For thirty years, I was privileged to know the real Woody Hayes, the man behind the media myth," President Richard Nixon said in eulogizing Hayes in Marble Cliff, Ohio, five days after his death.

"Instead of a know-nothing Neanderthal, I found a renaissance man with a consuming interest in history and a profound understanding of the forces that move the world. Instead of a cold, ruthless tyrant on the football field, I found a warmhearted softie—very appropriately born on Valentine's Day—who spoke of his affection for his boys and for his family."

The street on which Ohio Stadium sits has since been renamed Woody Hayes Drive, and a sign commemorating his achievements was unveiled inside the stadium during the 2005 season.

Woody Hayes is carried off the field following the Buck-eyes' trouncing of Illinois in 1974. Big wins were a staple of Hayes' tenure, and he never tired of tipping his cap to the fans while being carried off the field—a sure sign that his team had come out victorious.

Hayes at Ohio State

Year	Record	Big Ten	Bowl
1951	4–3–2	2–3–2	
1952	6–3	5–2	
1953	6–3	4–3	
1954	10–0*	7–0	Rose
1955	7–2	6–0	
1956	6–3	4–2	
1957	9–1*	7–0	Rose
1958	6–1–2	4–1–2	
1959	3–5–1	2–4–1	
1960	7–2	5–2	
1961	8–0–1*	6–0	
1962	6–3	4–2	
1963	5–3–1	4–1–1	
1964	7–2	5–1	
1965	7–2	6–1	
1966	4–5	3–4	
1967	6–3	5–2	
1968	10–0*	7–0	Rose
1969	8–1	6–1	
1970	9–1*	7–0	Rose
1971	6–4	5–3	
1972	9–2	7–1	Rose
1973	10–0–1	7–0–1	Rose
1974	10–2	7–1	Rose
1975	11–1	8–0	Rose
1976	9–2–1	7–1	Orange
1977	9–3	7–1	Sugar
1978	7–4–1	6–2	Gator
Total	205–61–10		

Claimed National Championship

Jim Tressel

Though he's not close to matching the longevity of Hayes, current Ohio State Coach Jim Tressel is inching toward Woody in terms of popularity. Winning a school's first national title in more than three decades will do that.

Tressel led the Buckeyes to the 2002 national championship with the first 14–0 season in the history of college football, capped by a dramatic, double-overtime win over Miami (Florida) in the Fiesta Bowl. In so doing, he was named the National Coach of the Year by the American Football Coaches Association, Football Writers Association of America, the Touchdown Club of Columbus, and the Pigskin Club of Washington, D.C. He also won the Bobby Dodd and Paul "Bear" Bryant awards as national coach of the year.

Such honors were not new territory for Tressel. He earned three national coach of the year honors from the AFCA during his 15 years at Division I-AA Youngstown State, making him the first coach honored by the organization at two different schools.

The son of the late Lee Tressel, the longtime head coach at Division III Baldwin Wallace, Jim Tressel was born December 5, 1952, and grew up in northeastern Ohio. He played quarterback for his father for four years before going to Akron for graduate school. His coaching career included stops as an assistant at Akron, Miami (Ohio), Syracuse, and Ohio State before landing his first head coaching gig at Youngstown State in 1986. He won four national titles with the Penguins, making him OSU's choice to replace the fired John Cooper after the 2000 season.

His calm, calculating demeanor, both on the sideline and in conversation, have earned Tressel the nickname "Senator." In that way, he couldn't be more different from Hayes. But both have won their share of football games.

The Coaches

Tressel at Ohio State (through 2008)

Year	Record	Big Ten	Bowl
2001	7–5	5–3	Outback
2002	14–0*	8–0	Fiesta
2003	11–2	6–2	Fiesta
2004	8–4	4–4	Alamo
2005	10–2	7–1	Fiesta
2006	12-1	8-0	BCS Championship
2007	11-2	7-1	BCS Championship
2008	10-3	7-1	Fiesta

Claimed National Championship

The Coaches

Other Buckeyes Coaches

The first coach to spend a significant amount of time at OSU was John W. Wilce from 1913 to 1928. He went 78–33–9 in 16 seasons and led the Buckeyes into their first league affiliation, in the Western Conference. The Wisconsin alumnus and College Football Hall of Fame member also was the first at OSU to coach an All-American (Boyd Cherry in 1914) and to beat Michigan (13–3 in 1919). Ohio Stadium opened under Wilce's watch, and the fight song "Across the Field" was introduced and dedicated to him in 1915. He also initiated the Senior Tackle tradition, which still takes place today.

Francis Schmidt, who coached the Buckeyes from 1934 to 1940, was the first OSU head coach signed to a multiyear contract. The southerner inspired the Gold Pants tradition for beating Michigan, which he did by shutout four straight years (1934–1937). Schmidt also was the first coach to lead Ohio State to a top-10 national ranking.

Though he later gained more fame with the Browns and Bengals in the NFL, Paul Brown took over from Schmidt and led the Buckeyes from 1941 to 1943. A member of the Pro Football Hall of Fame, Brown went 18–8–1 and led OSU to its first national championship in 1942. The "father" of the West Coast offense was the first coach to use playbooks, study his players on film, and use the 40-yard dash as a measuring stick for speed. He also instituted the facemask, full-time coaching staff, and calling plays from the sideline through a messenger.

Joining Hayes and Tressel on OUS's all-time wins list are Earle Bruce and John Cooper. Bruce replaced his former coach and boss Hayes in 1979 and guided the Buckeyes to 81 wins, 26 losses and one tie in the next nine years. He was the national coach of the year

The Coaches

after the 1979 season, when his No. 1–ranked team lost, 17–16, to USC in the Rose Bowl. He earned four Big Ten titles, went 5–4 against Michigan, and remained an ardent supporter of Ohio State football while in retirement.

Cooper came from Arizona State to replace the fired Bruce, starting with the 1988 season, and spent 13 seasons building a powerhouse program that never quite got over the hump under his watch. A master recruiter, Cooper had three teams finish the season in the top five in the country but never won a national title. His teams often were derailed by late-season losses to Michigan, against whom he was only 2–10–1. That mark was a major cause of his dismissal after the 2000 season, despite an overall record of 111–43–4 in Columbus. The native Tennessean did breathe new life into the program, especially during the mid-1990s. His 1995 squad—led by Heisman Trophy winner Eddie George—rolled up 475 points on the season, a school record.

THE BIG TEN CONFERENCE

ILLINOIS

Location: Urbana-Champaign, Illinois

Founded: 1867

Enrollment: 27,770

Nickname: Fighting Illini

Colors: Orange and blue

Mascot: Chief Illiniwek

Stadium: Memorial Stadium (69,249 capacity)

Coach: Ron Zook

Consensus National Championships: None

Other National Championship (4): 1914, 1919, 1923, 1927

Big Ten Championships (15): 1910, 1914, 1915, 1918, 1919, 1923, 1927, 1928, 1946, 1951, 1953, 1963, 1983, 1990, 2001

First season: 1890

Heisman Winners: None

Retired Jerseys: 50 Dick Butkus, 77 Red Grange

INDIANA

Location: Bloomington, Ind.

Founded: 1820

Enrollment: 38,903

Nickname: Hoosiers

Colors: Cream and crimson

Mascot: None

Stadium: Memorial Stadium (52,354 capacity)

Coach: Bill Lynch

Consensus National Championships: None

Big Ten Championships (2): 1945, 1967

First season: 1887

Heisman Winners: None

Retired Jerseys: 32 Anthony Thompson

IOWA

Location: Iowa City

Founded: 1847

Enrollment: 29,979

Nickname: Hawkeyes

Colors: Old gold and black

Mascot: Herky the Hawk

Stadium: Kinnick Stadium (70,397 capacity)

Coach: Kirk Ferentz

Consensus National Championships: None

Other National Championships (1): 1958

Big Ten Championships (11): 1900, 1921, 1922, 1956, 1958, 1960, 1981, 1985, 1990, 2002, 2004

First season: 1889

Heisman Winners (1): Nile Kinnick, 1939

Retired Jerseys: 24 Nile Kinnick, 62 Cal Jones

MICHIGAN

Location: Ann Arbor

Founded: 1817

Enrollment: 38,006

Nickname: Wolverines

Colors: Maize and blue

Mascot: None. The original live wolverine was named "Biff."

Stadium: Michigan Stadium (107,501 capacity, with ongoing renovations scheduled to be completed in 2010), nicknamed the "Big House."

Coach: Rich Rodriguez

Consensus National Championships (3): 1947, 1948, 1997

Other National Championships (8): 1901, 1902, 1903, 1904, 1918, 1923, 1932, 1933

Big Ten Championships (42): 1898, 1901, 1902, 1903, 1904, 1906, 1918, 1922, 1923, 1925, 1926, 1930, 1931, 1932, 1933, 1943, 1947, 1948, 1949, 1950, 1964, 1969, 1971, 1972, 1973, 1974,

The Big Ten

1976, 1977, 1978, 1980, 1982, 1986, 1988, 1989, 1990, 1991, 1992, 1997, 1998, 2000, 2003, 2004

First season: 1879

Heisman Winners (3): Tom Harmon, 1940; Desmond Howard, 1991; Charles Woodson, 1997

Retired Jerseys: 11 Francis Wistert, Albert Wistert, and Alvin Wistert; 47 Bennie Oosterbaan; 48 Gerald Ford; 87 Ron Kramer; 98 Tom Harmon

MICHIGAN STATE

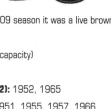

Location: East Lansing

Founded: 1855

Enrollment: 45,520

Nickname: Spartans

Colors: Green and white

Mascot: Sparty (although for the 1909 season it was a live brown bear named Brewer's Bruin).

Stadium: Spartan Stadium (75,005 capacity)

Coach: Mark Dantonio

Consensus National Championships (2): 1952, 1965

Other National Championships (4): 1951, 1955, 1957, 1966

Big Ten Championships (6): 1953, 1965, 1966, 1978, 1987, 1990

First season: 1896

Heisman Winners: None

Retired Jerseys: 46 John Hannah, 78 Don Coleman, 90 George Webster, 95 Charles "Bubba" Smith

MINNESOTA

Location: Minneapolis

Founded: 1851

Enrollment: 46,618

Nickname: Golden Gophers

Colors: Maron and gold

Mascot: Goldy the Gopher

Stadium: TCF Bank Stadium (50,300 capacity)

Coach: Tim Brewster

Consensus National Championships (4): 1936, 1940, 1941, 1960

Other National Championships (2): 1934, 1935

Big Ten Championships (18): 1900, 1903, 1904, 1906, 1909, 1910, 1911, 1915, 1927, 1933, 1934, 1935, 1937, 1938, 1940, 1941, 1960, 1967

First season: 1882

Heisman Winners (1): Bruce Smith, 1941

Retired Jerseys: 10 Paul Giel, 15 Sandy Stephens, 54 Bruce Smith, 79 Bronko Nagurski

NORTHWESTERN

Location: Evanston, Illinois

Founded: 1851

Enrollment: 7,840

Nickname: Wildcats

Colors: Purple and white

Mascot: Willie the Wildcat

Stadium: Ryan Field (47,130 capacity)

Coach: Pat Fitzgerald

Consensus National Championships: None

Big Ten Championships (8): 1903, 1926, 1930, 1931, 1936, 1995, 1996, 2000

First season: 1876

Heisman Winners: None

Retired Jerseys: None

PENN STATE

Location: University Park, Pennsylvania

Founded: 1855

Enrollment: 42,000

Nickname: Nittany Lions

Colors: Blue and white

Mascot: The Nittany Lion

Stadium: Beaver Stadium (107,782 capacity)

Coach: Joe Paterno

Consensus National Championships (2): 1982, 1986

Big Ten Championships (3): 1994, 2005, 2007

First season: 1887

Heisman Winners (1): John Cappelletti, 1973

Retired Jerseys: None

PURDUE

Location: West Lafayette, Indiana

Founded: 1869

Enrollment: 39,228

Nickname: Boilermakers

Colors: Old gold and black

Mascot: Purdue Pete; special mascot train

Stadium: Ross-Ade Stadium (62,500 capacity)

Coach: Joe Tiller

Consensus National Championships: None

Big Ten Championships (8): 1918, 1929, 1931, 1932, 1943, 1952, 1967, 2000

First season: 1887

Heisman Winners: None

Retired Jerseys: None

WISCONSIN

Location: Madison, Wisconsin

Founded: 1848

Enrollment: 41,169

Nickname: Badgers

Colors: Cardinal and white

Mascot: Bucky Badger

Stadium: Camp Randall Stadium (80,321 capacity)

Coach: Bret Bielema

The Big Ten

Consensus National Championships: None

Big Ten Championships (11): 1896, 1897, 1901, 1906, 1912, 1952, 1959, 1962, 1993, 1998, 1999

First season: 1889

Heisman Winners (2): Alan Ameche, 1954; Ron Dayne, 1999

Retired Jerseys: 33 Ron Dayne, 35 Alan Ameche, 40 Elroy "Crazylegs" Hirsch, 80 Dave Schreiner, 83 Allan Shafer, 88 Pat Richter.

BIG TEN TROPHY GAMES

Trophy	Teams	First Year
Little Brown Jug	Michigan-Minnesota	1909
Old Oaken Bucket	Purdue-Indiana	1925
Illibuck	Ohio State-Illinois	1925
Floyd of Rosedale	Minnesota-Iowa	1935
Purdue Cannon	Purdue-Illinois	1943
Sweet Sioux Tomahawk	Illinois-Northwestern	1945
Paul Bunyan's Axe	Wisconsin-Minnesota	1948
Megaphone	Michigan State-Notre Dame	1949
Old Brass Spittoon	Michigan State-Indiana	1950
Paul Bunyan-Governor of Michigan	Michigan-Michigan State	1953
Shillelagh	Purdue-Notre Dame	1958
Cy-Hawk	Iowa-Iowa State	1977
Governor's Victory Bell	Penn State-Minnesota	1993
Land Grant Trophy	Penn State-Michigan State	1993
The Heartland Trophy	Iowa-Wisconsin	2004

BIG TEN CHAMPIONS

Year	Team(s)	Record
1896	Wisconsin	2-0-1
1897	Wisconsin	3-0-0
1898	Michigan	3-0-0
1899	Chicago	4-0-0
1900	Iowa	2-0-1
	Minnesota	3-0-1

Craig Krenzel eludes a sack attempt in Ohio State's 2002 game at Illinois. The two teams play for the Illibuck, the only travelling trophy that the Buckeyes compete for.

1901	Michigan	4-0-0
	Wisconsin	2-0-0
1902	Michigan	5-0-0
1903	Michigan	3-0-1
	Minnesota	3-0-1
	Northwestern	1-0-2
1904	Michigan	2-0-0
	Minnesota	3-0-0
1905	Chicago	7-0-0
1906	Michigan	1-0-0
	Minnesota	2-0-0
	Wisconsin	3-0-0
1907	Chicago	4-0-0
1908	Chicago	5-0-0
1909	Minnesota	3-0-0
1910	Illinois	4-0-0
	Minnesota	2-0-0
1911	Minnesota	3-0-1
1912	Wisconsin	5-0-0
1913	Chicago	7-0-0
1914	Illinois	6-0-0
1915	Illinois	3-0-2
	Minnesota	3-0-1
1916	Ohio State	4-0-0
1917	Ohio State	4-0-0
1918	Illinois	4-0-0
	Michigan	2-0-0
	Purdue	1-0-0
1919	Illinois	6-1-0
1920	Ohio State	5-0-0
1921	Iowa	5-0-0
1922	Iowa	5-0-0
	Michigan	4-0-0

The Big Ten

1923	Illinois	5-0-0
	Michigan	4-0-0
1924	Chicago	3-0-3
1925	Michigan	5-1-0
1926	Michigan	5-0-0
	Northwestern	5-0-0
1927	Illinois	5-0-0
1928	Illinois	4-1-0
1929	Purdue	5-0-0
1930	Michigan	5-0-0
	Northwestern	5-0-0
1931	Michigan	5-1-0
	Northwestern	5-1-0
	Purdue	5-1-0
1932	Michigan	6-0-0
1933	Michigan	5-0-1
1934	Minnesota	5-0-0
1935	Minnesota	5-0-0
	Ohio State	5-0-0
1936	Northwestern	6-0-0
1937	Minnesota	5-0-0
1938	Minnesota	4-1-0
1939	Ohio State	5-1-0
1940	Minnesota	6-0-0
1941	Minnesota	5-0-0
1942	Ohio State	5-1-0
1943	Michigan	6-0-0
	Purdue	6-0-0
1944	Ohio State	6-0-0
1945	Indiana	5-0-1
1946	Illinois	6-1-0
1947	Michigan	6-0-0
1948	Michigan	6-0-0

The Big Ten

1949	Michigan	4-1-1
	Ohio State	4-1-1
1950	Michigan	4-1-1
1951	Illinois	5-0-1
1952	Purdue	4-1-1
	Wisconsin	4-1-1
1953	Illinois	5-1-0
	Michigan State	5-1-0
1954	Ohio State	7-0-0
1955	Ohio State	6-0-0
1956	Iowa	5-1-0
1957	Ohio State	7-0-0
1958	Iowa	5-1-0
1959	Wisconsin	5-2-0
1960	Iowa	5-1-0
	Minnesota	5-1-0
1961	Ohio State	6-0-0
1962	Wisconsin	6-1-0
1963	Illinois	5-1-1
1964	Michigan	6-1-0
1965	Michigan State	7-0-0
1966	Michigan State	7-0-0
1967	Indiana	6-1-0
	Minnesota	6-1-0
	Purdue	6-1-0
1968	Ohio State	7-0-0
1969	Michigan	6-1-0
	Ohio State	6-1-0
1970	Ohio State	7-0-0
1971	Michigan	8-0-0
1972	Michigan	7-1-0
	Ohio State	7-1-0
1973	Michigan	7-0-1

	Ohio State	7-0-1
1974	Michigan	7-1-0
	Ohio State	7-1-0
1975	Ohio State	8-0-0
1976	Michigan	7-1-0
	Ohio State	7-1-0
1977	Michigan	7-1-0
	Ohio State	7-1-0
1978	Michigan	7-1-0
	Michigan State	7-1-0
1979	Ohio State	8-0-0
1980	Michigan	8-0-0
1981	Iowa	6-2-0
	Ohio State	6-2-0
1982	Michigan	8-1-0
1983	Illinois	9-0-0
1984	Ohio State	7-2-0
1985	Iowa	7-1-0
1986	Michigan	7-1-0
	Ohio State	7-1-0
1987	Michigan State	7-0-1
1988	Michigan	7-0-1
1989	Michigan	8-0-0
1990	Illinois	6-2-0
	Iowa	6-2-0
	Michigan	6-2-0
	Michigan State	6-2-0
1991	Michigan	8-0-0
1992	Michigan	6-0-2
1993	Ohio State	6-1-1
	Wisconsin	6-1-1
1994	Penn State	8-0-0
1995	Northwestern	8-0-0

1996	Northwestern	7-1
	Ohio State	7-1
1997	Michigan	8-0
1998	Michigan	7-1
	Ohio State	7-1
	Wisconsin	7-1
1999	Wisconsin	7-1
2000	Michigan	6-2
	Northwestern	6-2
	Purdue	6-2
2001	Illinois	7-1
2002	Iowa	8-0
	Ohio State	8-0
2003	Michigan	7-1
2004	Iowa	7-1
	Michigan	7-1
2005	Penn State	7-1
	Ohio State	7-1
2006	Ohio State	8-0
2007	Ohio State	7-1
2008	Penn State	7-1
	Ohio State	7-1

The Big Ten

2

Times the Buckeyes have gone undefeated in Big Ten play in the 2000s.
Iowa's 2002 squad is the only other
Big Ten team to have an undefeated
conference record this decade. The
two teams split the conference title.

The Buckeyes sing "Carmen Ohio" after the 2008 Michigan game. The win sealed a share of the Buckeyes' 33rd Big Ten championship.

0

THE RIVALRIES

Ohio State vs. Michigan

In Columbus, there's a 365-day-a-year preoccupation with beating Michigan, particularly in football. Ask an Ohio State grad what time it is, and you very often will hear, "It's 3 o'clock...and Michigan still sucks." The same epithet ensues when the Value City Arena announcer tells a hockey crowd that there is a minute left in the period—regardless of whether OSU is actually playing Michigan. "We Don't Give a Damn for the Whole State of Michigan" echoes around the city with vigor, sung heartily by complete strangers decked out in scarlet and gray.

Coach Jim Tressel knows how many days there are until the next Michigan game at all times. Ask him in April; he knows. Ask him in July; he knows. It's one of his only quirks that belies the one-game-at-a-time mantra coaches so love, and for the most part his teams have dominated the series.

With so much history and so much usually at stake, few were surprised that ESPN named the Ohio State vs. Michigan football series as the No. 1 rivalry in all of sports in 1999.

To this day, Ohio State players who beat Michigan are rewarded with "Gold Pants"—a trinket based on Francis Schmidt's 1934 declaration that the big, bad Wolverines put on their pants one leg at a time, just like everybody else. "Gold Pants," given by the Gold Pants Club, are among the most treasured possessions of most former Buckeyes. They include the player's initials, the date of the game, and the final score.

Why the rivalry has reached such grand proportions is up for debate, but its earliest incarnation probably stems from the Toledo War in the early 1800s. The "war" was over whether Michigan or Ohio right-

The Rivalries

fully owned a few hundred square miles of land in which the city of Toledo lies. Ohio claimed it under the Northwest Ordinance. Michigan reasoned that the Northwest Ordinance's representation of the southern edge of Lake Michigan was inaccurate, and thus, the land should belong to it. After each state amassed troops along the border—not much more than threat and bluster—President Jackson stepped in and awarded the land to Ohio.

Michigan and Ohio State first met in football in 1897. At the time, touchdowns and field goals were worth four points apiece, and "extra points" were worth two. Roster sizes were about 20 per side. You had three plays to pick up a first down, rather than four. The Wolverines had been playing football for more than a quarter-century; the Buckeyes less than a decade. It showed. The game ended 34–0, and intense dislike for Michigan sprouted along the OSU sideline.

Michigan dominated the early chapters of the rivalry, including an 86–0 pounding in 1902. The first Ohio State victory didn't come for another 19 years. (The teams didn't play from 1913 to 1917.) Chic Harley scored on a 42-yard run, intercepted four passes, kicked an extra point, and punted 11 times in OSU's 13–3 win on October 25, 1919, in Ann Arbor. The subsequent Ohio State University Monthly described it as "perhaps the biggest game of all Ohio State athletics to date" and said it led to "the biggest night's celebration Columbus had ever seen."

There would be no such celebrating in 1922, however, as Michigan ruined the dedication of 65,000-seat Ohio Stadium with a 19–0 victory.

After the 1934 victory, the OSU student body rushed the field afterward and tore down the south goal posts. The next season, OSU whipped UM again, 38–0 in Ann Arbor. The 20,000 or so Ohioans who made the trip tried to recreate the 1934 scene by tearing down the goal posts. An hourlong fight ensued, stretching from one end zone to the other as the scarlet and gray marauders first made a run at the north goal posts, then the south. One man reportedly was knocked unconscious while another had six teeth kicked in.

Probably no single person did more to make the game The Game than Woody Hayes.

"[Hayes] spoke of how terrible Michigan was and how bad they were and how they'd do things to try to get an advantage, and the whole works," Archie Griffin said. "He had us believing that Michigan was the worst team that you could possibly ever want to play against, and he had you feeling like you wanted to kill them.

"I remember, at the end of his talk, as I looked around that room, I saw tears coming out of my teammates' eyes. He said, you know, 'This is not a game, this is war.'"

The high point of the Michigan vs. Ohio State series undoubtedly was from 1969 to 1978, commonly referred to as the "Ten-Year War." That was the decade when Hayes squared off against Michigan's Bo Schembechler, a former player under Hayes at Miami (Ohio) and assistant coach under Woody at Ohio State.

It started during Schembechler's rookie year, with one of the greatest upsets in college football history. Embarrassed by a 50–14 thrashing the previous season, the Wolverines were 17-point underdogs to the undefeated defending national champions, with the No. 1 Buckeyes riding a 22-game winning streak and averaging 46 points per game.

Thanks to Barry Pierson's 60-yard punt return to the Ohio State 3-yard line, the Wolverines ran up a 24–12 halftime lead. Pierson, a defensive back, then picked off three Buckeye passes in the second half as neither team could score. Schembechler, said Pierson had "one of the greatest performances I have ever seen in a single game."

The Rivalries

It cost the greatest team Hayes ever coached (his words) a chance at a repeat national title. "We'll start preparing for those guys on the way home," he muttered. Even more than a decade later, Hayes still stewed about it. At a post-retirement banquet, he told Schembechler, "Damn you, Bo. You will never win a bigger game than that."

During the "Ten-Year War," the Big Ten championship was decided by the game nine times. Hayes' obsession with the rivalry grew, as did that of both schools' fan bases.

The undefeated rivals tied in 1973, which meant that the league's Rose Bowl representative would be chosen by a vote of Big Ten athletics directors. No. 4 Michigan was better statistically, leading many to believe that it would be the choice. But Wolverine quarterback Dennis Franklin broke his collarbone against OSU, so the 6-4 vote sent the No. 1 Buckeyes to Pasadena.

Woody—who always whispered in the locker room at Michigan Stadium for fear of it being bugged—went 4–5–1 during the "Ten-year war" and 16–11–1 overall against Michigan before his firing after the 1978 season.

"No game meant more to me (than Michigan)," OSU linebacker Chris Spielman once said. "I pride myself on being ready to play every game, but when it came to playing Michigan, I was ready on Monday. When you grow up in Ohio, it is kind of in your blood. It's a game that means so much. When you lose, it's devastating and stays with you all year. When you win, there is no feeling like it. You are on air until you play them again. Winning that game my senior year was the best win I ever experienced at Ohio State."

Buckeye quarterback Art Schlichter is lifted in the air by teammates after Ohio State's thrilling 18–15 win over Michigan in 1979. The Buckeyes came from behind to win after blocking a punt in the fourth quarter.

Ohio State vs. Michigan
(Michigan leads series 57–42–6)

Year	Winner	Score	Site
1897	Michigan	34–0	Ann Arbor
1900	Tie	0–0	Ann Arbor
1901	Michigan	21–0	Columbus
1902	Michigan	86–0	Ann Arbor
1903	Michigan	36–0	Ann Arbor
1904	Michigan	31–6	Columbus
1905	Michigan	40–0	Ann Arbor
1906	Michigan	6–0	Columbus
1907	Michigan	22–0	Ann Arbor
1908	Michigan	10–6	Columbus
1909	Michigan	33–6	Ann Arbor
1910	Tie	3–3	Columbus
1911	Michigan	19–0	Ann Arbor
1912	Michigan	14–0	Columbus
1918	Michigan	14–0	Columbus
1919	Ohio State	13–3	Ann Arbor
1920	Ohio State	14–7	Columbus
1921	Ohio State	14–0	Ann Arbor
1922	Michigan	19–0	Columbus
1923	Michigan	23–0	Ann Arbor
1924	Michigan	16–6	Columbus
1925	Michigan	10–0	Ann Arbor
1926	Michigan	17–16	Columbus
1927	Michigan	21–0	Ann Arbor
1928	Ohio State	19–7	Columbus
1929	Ohio State	7–0	Ann Arbor
1930	Michigan	13–0	Columbus
1931	Ohio State	20–7	Ann Arbor
1932	Michigan	14–0	Columbus
1933	Michigan	13–0	Ann Arbor
1934	Ohio State	34–0	Columbus
1935	Ohio State	38–0	Ann Arbor

1936	Ohio State	21–0	Columbus
1937	Ohio State	21–0	Ann Arbor
1938	Michigan	18–0	Columbus
1939	Michigan	21–14	Ann Arbor
1940	Michigan	40–0	Columbus
1941	Tie	20–20	Ann Arbor
1942	Ohio State	21–7	Columbus
1943	Michigan	45–7	Ann Arbor
1944	Ohio State	18–14	Columbus
1945	Michigan	7–3	Ann Arbor
1946	Michigan	58–6	Columbus
1947	Michigan	21–0	Ann Arbor
1948	Michigan	13–3	Columbus
1949	Tie	7–7	Ann Arbor
1950	Michigan	9–3	Columbus
1951	Michigan	7–0	Ann Arbor
1952	Ohio State	27–7	Columbus
1953	Michigan	20–0	Ann Arbor
1954	Ohio State	21–7	Columbus
1955	Ohio State	17–0	Ann Arbor
1956	Michigan	19–0	Columbus
1957	Ohio State	31–14	Ann Arbor
1958	Ohio State	20–14	Columbus
1959	Michigan	23–14	Ann Arbor
1960	Ohio State	7–0	Columbus
1961	Ohio State	50–20	Ann Arbor
1962	Ohio State	28–0	Columbus
1963	Ohio State	14–10	Ann Arbor
1964	Michigan	10–0	Columbus
1965	Ohio State	9–7	Ann Arbor
1966	Michigan	17–3	Columbus
1967	Ohio State	24–14	Ann Arbor
1968	Ohio State	50–14	Columbus
1969	Michigan	24–12	Ann Arbor
1970	Ohio State	20–9	Columbus

The Rivalries

1971	Michigan	10–7	Ann Arbor
1972	Ohio State	14–11	Columbus
1973	Tie	10–10	Ann Arbor
1974	Ohio State	12–10	Columbus
1975	Ohio State	21–14	Ann Arbor
1976	Michigan	22–0	Columbus
1977	Michigan	14–6	Ann Arbor
1978	Michigan	14–3	Columbus
1979	Ohio State	18–15	Ann Arbor
1980	Michigan	9–3	Columbus
1981	Ohio State	14–9	Ann Arbor
1982	Ohio State	24–14	Columbus
1983	Michigan	24–21	Ann Arbor
1984	Ohio State	21–6	Columbus
1985	Michigan	27–17	Ann Arbor
1986	Michigan	26–24	Columbus
1987	Ohio State	23–20	Ann Arbor
1988	Michigan	34–31	Columbus
1989	Michigan	28–18	Ann Arbor
1990	Michigan	16–13	Columbus
1991	Michigan	31–3	Ann Arbor
1992	Tied	13–13	Columbus
1993	Michigan	28–0	Ann Arbor
1994	Ohio State	22–6	Columbus
1995	Michigan	31–23	Ann Arbor
1996	Michigan	13–9	Columbus
1997	Michigan	20–14	Ann Arbor
1998	Ohio State	31–16	Columbus
1999	Michigan	24–17	Ann Arbor
2000	Michigan	38–26	Columbus
2001	Ohio State	26–20	Ann Arbor
2002	Ohio State	14–9	Columbus
2003	Michigan	35–21	Ann Arbor
2004	Ohio State	37–21	Columbus

The Rivalries

2005	Ohio State	25–21	Ann Arbor
2006	Ohio State	42–39	Columbus
2007	Ohio State	14–3	Ann Arbor
2008	Ohio State	42–7	Columbus

Ohio State vs. Illinois

Illinois vs. Ohio State is an old-time rivalry that has faded a bit in the past few decades. The teams still play for the Illibuck trophy, which is the only traveling trophy in Ohio State lore. The Illibuck was a live turtle when the tradition began in 1925, but after it met its demise upon escaping from a fraternity-house bathtub in Champaign, it was replaced by a wooden replica turtle in 1927. The scores of each game are painted on its shell. Unlike most traveling trophies, however, the Illibuck doesn't get claimed at the end of the game. Instead, it's presented during halftime to the winner of the teams' previous meeting, which delays the gratification by about a year. Honorary societies from each school—Bucket and Dipper of Ohio State and Sachem of Illinois—handle the presentation and also smoke a peace pipe in a show of halftime unity.

The Rivalries

Ohio State vs Illinois
Illibuck Trophy
[Ohio State leads the series 61–34–4]

Year	Winner	Score	Site
1902	Tie	0–0	Columbus
1904	Illinois	46–0	Columbus
1914	Illinois	37–0	Champaign
1915	Tie	3–3	Columbus
1916	Ohio State	7–6	Champaign
1917	Ohio State	13–0	Columbus
1918	Illinois	13–0	Champaign
1919	Illinois	9–7	Columbus
1920	Ohio State	7–0	Champaign
1921	Illinois	7–0	Columbus
1922	Ohio State	6–3	Champaign
1923	Illinois	9–0	Columbus
1924	Illinois	7–0	Champaign
1925	Illinois	14–9	Columbus
1926	Ohio State	7–6	Champaign
1927	Illinois	13–0	Columbus
1928	Illinois	8–0	Champaign
1929	Illinois	27–0	Columbus
1930	Ohio State	12–9	Champaign
1931	Ohio State	40–0	Columbus
1932	Ohio State	3–0	Champaign
1933	Ohio State	7–6	Columbus
1934	Illinois	14–13	Champaign
1935	Ohio State	6–0	Columbus
1936	Ohio State	13–0	Champaign
1937	Ohio State	19–0	Columbus
1938	Ohio State	32–14	Champaign
1939	Ohio State	21–0	Columbus
1940	Ohio State	14–6	Champaign
1941	Ohio State	12–7	Columbus
1942	Ohio State	44–20	Cleveland

1943	Ohio State	29–26	Columbus
1944	Ohio State	26–12	Cleveland
1945	Ohio State	27–2	Columbus
1946	Illinois	16–7	Champaign
1947	Illinois	28–7	Columbus
1948	Ohio State	34–7	Champaign
1949	Ohio State	30–17	Columbus
1950	Illinois	14–7	Champaign
1951	Tie	0–0	Columbus
1952	Ohio State	27–7	Champaign
1953	Illinois	41–20	Columbus
1954	Ohio State	40–7	Champaign
1955	Ohio State	27–12	Columbus
1956	Ohio State	26–6	Champaign
1957	Ohio State	21–7	Columbus
1958	Ohio State	19–13	Champaign
1959	Illinois	9–0	Columbus
1960	Ohio State	34–7	Champaign
1961	Ohio State	44–0	Columbus
1962	Ohio State	51–15	Champaign
1963	Tie	20–20	Columbus
1964	Ohio State	26–0	Champaign
1965	Ohio State	28–14	Columbus
1966	Illinois	10–9	Champaign
1967	Illinois	17–13	Columbus
1968	Ohio State	31–24	Champaign
1969	Ohio State	41–0	Columbus
1970	Ohio State	48–29	Champaign
1971	Ohio State	24–10	Champaign
1972	Ohio State	26–7	Columbus
1973	Ohio State	30–0	Champaign
1974	Ohio State	49–7	Columbus
1975	Ohio State	40–3	Champaign

The Rivalries

Donald Washington crushes Illinois quarterback Juice Williams in 2008. Although the rivalry has cooled in recent decades, the resurgence of the Illini with Williams at quarterback has brought some heated and memorable games the last few meetings.

1976	Ohio State	42–10	Columbus
1977	Ohio State	35–0	Champaign
1978	Ohio State	45–7	Columbus
1979	Ohio State	44–7	Champaign
1980	Ohio State	49–42	Columbus
1981	Ohio State	34–27	Columbus
1982	Ohio State	26–21	Champaign
1983	Illinois	17–13	Champaign
1984	Ohio State	45–38	Columbus
1985	Illinois	31–28	Champaign
1986	Ohio State	14–0	Champaign
1987	Ohio State	10–6	Columbus
1988	Illinois	31–12	Columbus
1989	Illinois	34–14	Champaign
1990	Illinois	31–20	Columbus
1991	Illinois	10–7	Champaign
1992	Illinois	18–16	Columbus
1993	Ohio State	20–12	Champaign
1994	Illinois	24–10	Columbus
1995	Ohio State	41–3	Columbus
1996	Ohio State	48–0	Champaign
1997	Ohio State	41–6	Columbus
1998	Ohio State	41–0	Champaign
1999	Illinois	46–20	Columbus
2000	Ohio State	24–21	Champaign
2001	Illinois	34–22	Columbus
2002	Ohio State	23–16 OT	Champaign
2005	Ohio State	40–2	Columbus
2006	Ohio State	17–10	Champaign
2007	Illinois	28–21	Columbus
2008	Ohio State	30–20	Champaign

The Rivalries

Ohio State vs. Penn State

Aside from Michigan, the only school OSU is guaranteed to play every season is Penn State. Both series are protected in scheduling under the Big Ten's rivalry pairings, and with the two teams frequently at least near the top of the standings the intensity quickly grew. The Buckeyes are 12–11 against PSU, dating to the teams' first meeting in 1912. They didn't meet again until 1956, then played a handful more times before the Nittany Lions joined the Big Ten in 1993.

Ohio State vs Penn State
[Penn State leads the series 12–11]

Year	Winner	Score	Site
1912	Penn State	37–0	Columbus
1956	Penn State	7–6	Columbus
1963	Penn State	10–7	Columbus
1964	Penn State	27–0	Columbus
1975	Ohio State	17–9	Columbus
1976	Ohio State	12–7	University Park
1978	Penn State	19–0	Columbus
1980	Penn State	31–19	Fiesta Bowl
1993	Ohio State	24–6	Columbus
1994	Penn State	63–14	University Park
1995	Ohio State	28–25	University Park
1996	Ohio State	38–7	Columbus
1997	Penn State	31–27	University Park
1998	Ohio State	28–9	Columbus
1999	Penn State	23–10	University Park
2000	Ohio State	45–6	Columbus
2001	Penn State	29–27	University Park
2002	Ohio State	13–7	Columbus
2003	Ohio State	21–20	University Park
2004	Ohio State	21–10	Columbus
2005	Penn State	17–10	University Park
2006	Ohio State	28–6	Columbus
2007	Ohio State	37–17	University Park
2008	Penn State	13–6	Columbus

Brian Robiskie skies high to make a catch against Penn State in 2008. Though the rivalry has only seen 21 match-ups over nearly a century of play, the hatred between the Buckeyes and Nitanny Lions has grown to great proportions in recent years.

TRADITIONS

SCRIPT OHIO

The Ohio State marching band—marketed by the school and known around the state as The Best Damn Band in the Land—has given college football its signature formation, Script Ohio, which it performs before each football game to the march "Le Regiment." Starting from a writhing mass of black-clad bodies at the 25-yard line, the drum major leads the single-file troupe into a cursive spelling of "Ohio" across some 50 yards of the field. Trombonists and other musicians with long instruments must take care not to gore their bandmates as they cross paths.

Script Ohio was first performed during the Pittsburgh game on October 10, 1936. If the formation gets any TV time, it invariably will be for the dotting of the "i" at the end. At 16 measures from the end of "Le Regiment," with all four letters spelled out, the drum major high-steps out to the top of the "i," followed closely by a fourth- or fifth-year sousaphone (think tuba) player. The drum major dramatically points out the mark to the sousaphone player, who stops on the spot to complete the picture, then takes deep bows to each side of the roaring stadium. No sousaphone player does it more than once in his or her career. Being chosen to dot the "i" is a high honor indeed, particularly for the Michigan game. Among the few non-band members who have had the privilege are former OSU coach Woody Hayes (after retirement, of course) and entertainer Bob Hope.

SKULL SESSION

Another band-related Ohio State tradition is the pregame skull session at St. John Arena, the former home of Buckeye basketball. This band warmup takes place about 90 minutes before home kickoffs and usually draws a capacity crowd of more than 13,000 fans. Since coach Jim Tressel arrived in 2001, the football team has attended the skull session to soak in some of the energy before walking to the stadium. Tressel often gives a brief address to the crowd.

THE SONGS

Ohio State boasts two fight songs, "The Buckeye Battle Cry" and "Across the Field," and an alma mater, "Carmen Ohio," which was composed by football player Fred Cornell in 1902. During the train ride back to Columbus after an 86–0 loss to Michigan, Cornell wrote the song's phrases on the back of an envelope. The glee club members' hymn was published in OSU's student newspaper, The Lantern, on October 10, 1906, and was included in the program for the Michigan game 10 days later. The word "carmen" means "song" in Latin. The music for the alma mater was taken from an ancient tune entitled "Spanish Chant."

The other song that will resonate with Buckeye fans—and might even be played on the radio—is "Hang On Sloopy," by the McCoys. It was a commercial hit for the Ohio-based band in the 1960s and eventually became the state's official rock song. The OSU band debuted it in the rain during the 1965 Illinois game, and the fans enjoyed its return even more during the fair weather of the following home date. Nowadays, fans shout "O-H-I-O" while making the letters with their arms—YMCA-style—on the four beats between repetitions of the refrain.

One more tune known by most Columbus natives—but not officially recognized by the school—is "We Don't Give a Damn for the Whole State of Michigan." This derisive fan-favorite dates to the 1920s and is most often heard a capella in the weeks leading up to a game against Michigan or Michigan State.

Traditions

THE COLORS

Aside from music, the "look" of the Buckeyes is another point of pride for OSU faithful. Scarlet and gray have been the school's colors since a trio of students chose them during an 1878 meeting in University Hall. The reasoning, according to committee member Alice Townshend Wing: "It was a pleasing combination...and had not been adopted by any other college."

THE HELMET

The Buckeyes' silver helmets are plain, save for a red stripe and smaller black and white stripes down the center. Through the course of a season, however, that headgear gets covered by Buckeye leaves, easily the most famous helmet decals in football. The white stickers are a bit bigger than a quarter and feature a branch of five Buckeye leaves. Coaches award these decals to players each week of the season for exceptional plays made during the previous game. Coach Woody Hayes started the tradition upon changing the team's uniforms prior to the national championship season of 1968.

THE NICKNAME

Ohio State athletes officially became known as "Buckeyes" in 1950, though they were called such long before that. Buckeyes are the nuts produced by the Buckeye tree, the state tree of Ohio. Small, shiny, and two-toned brown, the nuts resemble the eye of a deer. Folk wisdom holds that carrying one in your pocket brings good luck.

HOMECOMING

A few other OSU traditions are designed to lure far-flung former players and alumni back to Columbus a couple of times each year. Homecoming is a big deal at

Traditions

Quarterback Todd Boeckman signs a helmet for a fan in 2007. The Buckeye helmet is world famous, and is one of the many traditions that make Ohio State's culture some of the deepest in college football.

Ohio State, as it is at most schools, with expanded pre-game revelry and an annual parade entering its fifth decade. The most notable Homecoming-related story dates all the way back to 1926, when a group of student pranksters campaigned for Maudine Ormsby to be Homecoming queen. Their pitch to the student body was so convincing that Maudine was elected handily, even though she was a cow. Literally.

The football-related constant regarding Homecoming is the Captains Breakfast. Each year since 1934, past football captains have been invited back to Columbus for breakfast the Sunday after the game to meet Ohio State's new captains (and catch up with each other, of course).

TUNNEL OF PRIDE

A newer tradition is the Tunnel of Pride, which was the brainchild of former OSU quarterback Rex Kern and former OSU athletics director Andy Geiger. At the Notre Dame game in 1995, Kern and Geiger invited former Buckeye players to form a human tunnel onto the field for the current players. The Tunnel of Pride is now conducted when Michigan visits every other year.

BLOCK "O"

Ohio State also boasts one of the oldest organized student cheering sections in America, Block "O." Started in 1938, Block "O" was inspired by a similar group at the University of Southern California. It since has become the largest student organization on campus. Situated in the south end zone of Ohio Stadium, Block "O" is the driving force behind many chants and cheers, most notably the around-the-stadium spelling of "O-H-I-O," which it initiates with a yell of "Hey, stadium...'O!'"

BRUTUS BUCKEYE

Also in charge of riling up the spectators is Brutus

Traditions

Buckeye, the school's nut-headed mascot. Decked out in a scarlet-and-gray horizontally striped shirt, scarlet pants, and a Buckeye hat, Brutus has been entertaining fans and antagonizing opponents since 1965, when student Ray Bourhis convinced the school's athletic council to adopt a mascot. He originally was designed by an art student and named "Brutus" following a vote of the student body, then was redesigned to his current look in the mid-1970s.

VICTORY BELL

If Block "O" and Brutus do their jobs and urge the Buckeyes to a win, the Victory Bell will proclaim the good news across campus. Located 150 feet up in the southeast tower of Ohio Stadium, the bell has rung after every Ohio State victory since a win over California on October 2, 1954. Members of Alpha Phi Omega have the honor of ringing the bell, which weighs 2,420 pounds. It was a gift from the classes of 1943, 1944, and 1945.

SENIOR TACKLE

One tradition that has fallen out of the public's eye is the annual Senior Tackle. It started in 1913 and consists of the symbolic hitting of a practice sled one last time for each senior on the team. Beginning in 1935, it took place during the last practice before the Michigan game, but it sometimes is held during the last workout before departing for the bowl game. Whereas the Senior Tackle used to be held in front of fans, Jim Tressel has made it into a closed-door ceremony with the team.

BUCKEYE GROVE

Should a Buckeye player be fortunate enough to be named an All-American, he is honored with the planting

Traditions

of a buckeye tree in the Buckeye Grove just southwest of the stadium. The planting usually takes place during a ceremony just before the annual spring game.

OHIO STADIUM

Ohio Stadium itself—known as The Horseshoe to folks around the country, or just The Shoe to locals—is in the National Registry of Historic Places. Designed by architect Howard Dwight Smith and opened in 1922 as a 66,210-seat arena along the banks of the Olentangy River, The Shoe is now among the biggest facilities in the country, comfortably seating 101,568. It underwent a $194 million renovation at the turn of the millennium, including the addition of permanent south stands, closing off the horseshoe shape. The whole thing only cost $1.3 million to build in the first place.

105,711

The record for largest crowd at Ohio Stadium, set during the 2008 matchup against #9 Penn State.

Since opening its gates to the Buckeye faithful in 1922, Ohio Stadium has seen its share of memorable moments. One of the largest and most famous stadiums in the world, The Horseshoe is instantly recognizable to any fan of the game.

THE GREAT TEAMS

2002

The second edition of Coach Jim Tressel's Buckeyes sure seemed charmed. In going 14–0 and winning the school's first national championship in three and a half decades, Ohio State survived close shave after close shave to remain unscathed. In all, OSU won seven games by seven or fewer points.

Buoyed by a rare win in Ann Arbor and a spirited rally from 28 points down in the Outback Bowl the previous season, the Buckeyes entered 2002 with a healthy amount of confidence. "I thought we had the makings of something special, and I wanted to be part of it," said safety Mike Doss, who put the NFL on hold for a year to play his senior season. "We believed in ourselves, we believed in Coach Tressel, and we believed, with hard work, we could be national champions."

Most of the players who contributed to the team that season—including Doss and first-year starting quarterback Craig Krenzel—had been brought to campus by former Coach John Cooper. Star tailback Maurice Clarett was an exception. The true freshman was signed by Tressel, enrolled at OSU early, and earned a starting backfield spot during spring practice. In his college debut in the season-opening 45–21 romp over Texas Tech, he ran for 175 yards, including a memorable touchdown during which he ran over two Red Raider defenders before turning up the sideline for a score.

After that, the Buckeyes rolled over Kent State and stymied No. 10 Washington State before traveling to Paul Brown Stadium in Cincinnati for their first in-state road game since 1934. The UC Bearcats were no pushovers. With Clarett missing the game because of minor knee surgery, Krenzel had to scramble for a go-

With Maurice Clarett on the shelf following minor knee surgery, Craig Krenzel threw the Buckeyes on his back against Cincinnati, rushing for the game-winning touchdown in the fourth quarter.

ahead touchdown with 3:44 left, and OSU's defense survived four Cincinnati passes into the end zone in the waning seconds of a 23–19 victory. Two of the late throws hit Bearcat receivers in the hands.

"We got a little lucky," Doss admitted.

The Buckeyes didn't need much luck in dismantling Indiana, Northwestern, and San Jose State in the following weeks—although Clarett did fumble three times during the 27–16 win in Evanston—but a trip to Wisconsin on October 19 raised another stiff challenge to the perfect season. Down 14–13 in the fourth quarter and facing a third-and-6 at his own 16, Krenzel heaved a 45-yard pass that receiver Michael Jenkins grabbed in heavy traffic just past midfield. The semimiraculous play set up the winning touchdown pass to tight end Ben Hartsock for a 19–14 victory in enemy territory.

The Buckeyes beat No. 18 Penn State 13–7 the following week without the aide of an offensive touchdown, thanks mostly to Chris Gamble's interception return for a score in the second half. Gamble, a cornerback/receiver, had become Ohio State's first two-way starter since Paul Warfield in 1963.

After smoking Minnesota, Ohio State went back on the road to Purdue, and the inconsistent Buckeye offense was floundering once again. It could only manage one Mike Nugent field goal during the first 96 percent of the game and trailed, 6–3, with less than two minutes remaining. Facing fourth-and-1 from the Purdue 37-yard line, Tressel called the play named King Right 64 Y Shallow. But upon diagnosing the coverage, Jenkins broke off his short post route and headed to the end zone. Krenzel heaved a pass into the stiff wind at Ross-Ade Stadium, and it fluttered down just past the outstretched arm of Purdue cornerback Antwaun Rogers right to Jenkins with 1:36 on the clock. "Touchdown! Touchdown! Michael Jenkins!... Holy Buckeye!" shouted ABC broadcaster Brent

Musberger in a line that seemed to sum up Ohio State's season.

But there was still much work to be done after the dramatic 10–6 win over the Boilermakers. The next weekend, Illinois made a field goal as the fourth-quarter clock expired to force overtime against the visiting Buckeyes—the first overtime in OSU football history. Tailback Maurice Hall, playing for the again-injured Clarett, scored on an eight-yard touchdown run to put the Buckeyes up, then the defense stopped the Illini to seal a 23–16 victory and keep hopes of perfection alive.

Ohio State was 12–0 and ranked No. 2 in the country heading into a nerve-racking Michigan game. Scores of fans privately and publicly worried that Michigan was about to ruin another glorious OSU season. Through three and a half quarters of the game, their fears were realized. Behind three field goals and a stingy defense, the Wolverines led 9–7 with less than seven minutes to play. The sense of dread at edgy Ohio Stadium was palpable. But on fourth-and-one at the Michigan 34 with 6:25 left, Krenzel ran the ball for a first down. Then Clarett—playing through a shoulder injury—slipped out on a wheel route, and Krenzel found the wide-open back with a 26-yard pass to the UM 6. Hall finished the drive by taking an option pitch—the first time OSU had run such a play all season—for a three-yard touchdown and a 14–9 lead.

The Buckeyes squelched Michigan's first comeback attempt with a fumble, but still had to sweat out a last-minute gasp by the Wolverines. On fourth down at the OSU 24-yard line with one second remaining, UM quarterback John Navarre was picked off by OSU safety Will Allen at the goal line, luring masses of fans onto the field and clinching a trip to the Fiesta Bowl for the BCS national title game.

The Great Teams

FIESTA FOR THE AGES

In Tempe, Arizona, the Buckeyes would meet heavily favored Miami (Florida), the defending national champion riding a 34-game winning streak. More than a few national pundits predicted that the Hurricanes would win in a rout. Ohio State was thought to be too slow to keep up with the fleet 'Canes, who seemed to have a potential first-round NFL draft pick at every position.

But after a quick, easy Miami touchdown to take a 7-0 lead, OSU's stingy defense was shockingly effective at bottling up the Hurricanes. The Buckeyes forced five first-half turnovers and converted two of them into touchdown runs (by Krenzel and Clarett) for a 14-7 lead at halftime.

Clarett, who finished with only 47 rushing yards on 23 carries, made up for his so-so statistics with one play in particular. After Miami's Sean Taylor intercepted Krenzel in the end zone, Clarett chased him down and took the ball right out of his arms as Taylor was tackled. The fresh possession led to a Mike Nugent field goal and a 17-7 lead.

But after a late touchdown—and a gruesome knee injury to star Miami tailback Willis McGahee—the Hurricanes sent the game to overtime with a 40-yard Todd Sievers field goal as time expired. Miami got the ball first in OT and scored a touchdown on Ken Dorsey's seven-yard pass to Kellen Winslow Jr. to take a 24-17 lead. On its ensuing possession, Ohio State faced a daunting fourth-and-14 situation with its season on the line. Krenzel found Jenkins open just past the first-down marker to keep alive the drive.

On fourth-and-3 from the Miami 5, official Terry Porter made one of the most famous calls in college football history when he flagged Miami's Glenn Sharpe for pass interference on Gamble in the end zone. The flag, which came a few agonizing seconds after the pass

Miami's Glenn Sharpe interfered with Chris Gamble in the end zone on this famous play, allowing the Buckeyes to stay alive in their bid for a national championship.

fell incomplete—after fireworks had sounded to signal the Hurricanes' national championship—gave OSU new life. Krenzel took advantage, sneaking in from the 1 to force double OT.

Ohio State got the ball first, and it put pressure on Miami with Clarett's 5-yard touchdown run. Needing a touchdown to tie, Miami drove inside OSU's 5, but was stopped cold. On fourth-and-goal from the 1, OSU linebacker Cie Grant came unmolested on a weakside blitz, got to Dorsey and forced a desperation pass. Linebacker Matt Wilhelm batted it down, and OSU had won its first national championship in a generation.

"We always had the best damn band in the land," Tressel told the crowd from the midfield podium. "Now we've got the best damn team in the land."

1968

The most revered class in Ohio State football history led the squad to perhaps its most cherished national championship as sophomores. The "Super Sophs" of quarterback Rex Kern, nose guard Jim Stillwagon, safety Jack Tatum, fullback John Brockington, tight end Jan White, and others were the heroes of Columbus during the late 1960s. In their first season of eligibility (freshmen weren't allowed to play at the time), the Super Sophs led OSU to a perfect 10–0 season.

Preseason practices were intense as the veteran players fought to hold onto their jobs and younger guys smelled opportunity. Despite summer back surgery, Kern quickly established himself atop the depth chart at QB. Coach Woody Hayes, who was largely skeptical of passing the ball, felt an unusual degree of trust in young Kern's decision making.

The 1968 season opened against Southern Methodist and Coach Hayden Fry's radical passing attack. Mustangs quarterback Chuck Hixson threw 69 times, completing 37 for 417 yards, but he was picked off five times by OSU. Kern, meanwhile, was 8-for-14 for 227 yards in the 35-14 win, leading Hayes to deadpan, "We're becoming quite a passing team."

Oregon was the next victim, and then came No. 1 Purdue. Hayes had quite a distaste for the Boilermakers after they dismantled Ohio State, 41-6, the previous season—all while Purdue Coach Jack Mollenkopf appeared to take a nap on the bench. Some say that, given his choice, Woody would have rather beaten Purdue than Michigan in 1968.

In the game, Hayes employed a rare no-huddle offense to stun Purdue at the beginning, then let his athletic defense beat up on the Boilers. Ted Provost returned an interception for a touchdown as the Buckeyes throttled their opponent, 13-0. (Legend has it that clairvoyant Lou Holtz, then OSU's defensive backs coach, bet another assistant $100 before the game that the Buckeyes would shut out the mighty Boilermakers.)

A rout of Northwestern was followed by a near-disaster at Illinois. OSU blew a 24-0 lead and allowed the Fighting Illini to tie it up before backup quarterback Ron Maciejowski (another Super Soph) subbed for the injury-prone Kern and led the Buckeyes on the game-winning drive.

A similar situation presented itself the following week, as Michigan State nearly came back from a 19-7 deficit before losing, 25-20. Wisconsin was no match, but Iowa shaved a 19-0 deficit to 33-27 in the waning seconds. Of course, Ohio State held on and was 8-0 and ranked No. 2 in the nation heading into the Michigan game.

The fourth-ranked Wolverines were no slouches themselves, and the Big Ten title was on the line at Ohio Stadium. Now starting 13 sophomores, the Buckeyes rolled over Michigan. Fullback Jim Otis

The Great Teams

picked up 143 rushing yards and four touchdowns. After the final one, which made it 48–14 in OSU's favor, Hayes called for a two-point conversion. Asked why he went for two, Hayes famously growled, "Because I couldn't go for three." And that was that.

The only remaining obstacle impeding a national title was Southern California in the Rose Bowl. Led by Heisman Trophy–winning tailback O.J. Simpson, the Trojans were ranked No. 2 in the country—right behind OSU. Hayes made sure his players were all business heading into the game, steering them away from much of the pageantry associated with the Rose Bowl. "They're trying to fatten us up," he told his players in explaining why he declined to have them participate in the traditional Lawry's Beef Bowl eating contest.

Once the game started, Simpson busted an 80-yard touchdown run to help USC take an early 10–0 lead, but Ohio State rallied to tie it by halftime. In the second half, Hayes assigned linebacker Mark Stier to shadow Simpson wherever the back went. The Juice still got his yards (171 rushing, 85 receiving), but Stier forced two second-half fumbles that OSU turned into touchdowns. Kern was the MVP, completing 9 of 15 passes for 101 yards and two touchdowns in the 27–16, championship-clinching victory.

Simpson visited the OSU locker room after the game and lauded the Buckeyes as "the best ball team in the country." Certainly, nobody could argue with that.

1954

Future Heisman Trophy winner Hopalong Cassady carried the Buckeyes to their first 10-win season in 1954—and the first national title for Hayes. In only his fourth season in Columbus, Hayes assembled a team that outscored its opponents 249–75 in going 10–0.

Cassady was a first-team All-American who rushed for 701 yards and caught a team-high 13 passes, and end Dean Dugger also was named an All-American.

Fullback Jim Otis holds a hand to his head in disbelief after his performance against Michigan. Otis carried the Buckeyes into the Rose Bowl with 143 rushing yards and four touchdowns.

The Buckeye defense, which also featured two-way lineman Jim Parker, forced 35 turnovers during the season and never allowed more than two touchdowns in a game.

OSU opened the year with a shutout of Indiana, then took care of powerhouse California, 21–13, in Columbus. The third game was a rout of Illinois, followed by a convincing 31–14 win over No. 2-ranked Wisconsin. Northwestern, Pittsburgh, and Purdue fell next, leading to the big Michigan game in Columbus.

The Buckeyes and Wolverines were deadlocked at 7–7 through three quarters, but Cassady (94 rushing yards, one TD) and quarterback Will Leggett (100 total yards, two touchdown passes) produced 14 fourth-quarter points to clinch a 21–7 victory and a trip to the Rose Bowl to face USC. The Trojans were expected to be tough, but they simply weren't in the same class as the Buckeyes, who forced seven fumbles and only allowed six first downs in a 20–7 win.

1942

Ohio State claimed its first national championship with this dominant squad coached by Hall of Famer Paul Brown. The Buckeyes averaged 33.7 points per game while only giving up 11.4 in going 9–1 overall. The lone blemish was a 17–7 loss at Wisconsin at midseason—and that was largely because several Buckeyes picked up a debilitating sickness from a water fountain on the train ride from Chicago to Madison.

As would be expected for the era, OSU did most of its damage on the ground, amassing 281.2 rushing yards per game on an average of 5.2 yards per carry. Fullbacks Gene Fekete and Paul Sarringhaus were among the conference rushing leaders with 916 and 672 yards, respectively, and led the league in scoring with 92 and 72 points. In the same backfield was quarterback Les Horvath, who would go on to win the

Heisman Trophy two years later. That trio ran behind a line that featured two All-Americans, tackle Chuck Csuri and guard Lindell Houston, in 1942.

Another All-American, end Robert Shaw, lurked on defense. In the defensive backfield, George James and Tom Lynn picked off five passes apiece during the season.

Ohio State opened the championship season with a 59–0 rout of Fort Knox, outrushing the service academy 440 to -14. Next was a too-close-for-comfort, come-from-behind 32–21 home win over Indiana, then relatively easy victories over USC, Purdue, and Northwestern. After losing to Wisconsin, Ohio State rolled over Pittsburgh and Illinois to set up a showdown against Michigan.

The Wolverines were substantially favored, but the Buckeyes passed for three touchdowns—one by Horvath, two by Sarringhaus—in the rain-soaked 21–7 victory. Jubilant OSU players carried Brown off the field, and the Buckeyes whipped the Iowa Seahawks the following week to clinch the Associated Press national championship.

5 **Losses by Iowa Pre-Flight during its three seasons of collegiate play. Located on the campus of the University of Iowa, the Seahawks were service academy national champions in 1943 and finished 10–1 in 1944.**

THE GREAT GAMES

THE SNOW BOWL

One of the few times an Ohio State vs. Michigan game earned fame for something other than its result was 1950's infamous Snow Bowl.

The night before the game, the biggest blizzard to hit the Midwest in nearly four decades blanketed Columbus in snow. And it was still falling.

The morning temperature on November 25 was in the neighborhood of 5 degrees Fahrenheit, and the wind whipped at about 40 miles per hour. Cars trying to get to the game were at a standstill in all corners of the state, and trains had been delayed up to two hours. Even the teams faced transportation nightmares. Michigan stayed the night in Toledo, meaning it still had a good two hours to travel on game day.

The schools' athletics directors faced an agonizing decision. Should they postpone the game? What about all of the fans who had risked life and limb to make it to the stadium? How would they refund the tickets to the rest? Michigan AD Fritz Crisler reportedly was pushing to play, perhaps because he thought the apocalyptic conditions would level the playing field for his underdog Wolverines. Both teams still had a shot at the Big Ten title, although OSU was out of consideration for the Rose Bowl because of the conference's no-repeat rule of the time. Without being able to reach the conference commissioner, OSUs Dick Larkins acceded to Crisler's wishes.

So it was on. The game would be played. Just not on time.

It took almost two and a half hours after the

scheduled kickoff time to prepare the field for some semblance of football. A makeshift, volunteer grounds crew that included local Boy Scout troops literally peeled the shredding tarp off the field as snow continued to fall. After a couple of hours of clearing snow, the teams squeezed in some quick warmups, then got ready for some craziness.

"Having the ball today is a liability," Michigan Coach Bennie Oosterbaan said. No kidding. Anything other than straight-ahead running was almost pointless on the slushy turf. The field markings were mostly obscured. Volunteers with brooms had to be summoned whenever the officials needed to measure for a first down.

The longest play from scrimmage of the entire day turned out to be Buckeye Heisman Trophy winner Vic Janowicz's 13-yard pass to Tom Watson a few plays after a blocked punt in the first quarter. It set up a third-and-goal at the Michigan 21-yard line. Deciding that running another play had as good of a shot of going backward as going forward, OSU Coach Wes Fesler called for a field goal on third down. Janowicz—who did everything for the Buckeyes at season—lined up for the kick with the goal posts barely visible.

"When he kicked the ball, it went up in a cloud of snow," former OSU sports information director Marv Homan said. "It just disappeared."

It also made its way through the uprights for a 3-0 Ohio State lead. The kick later was called one of the "greatest feats in American sports" by a panel of sportswriters. But it didn't hold up. Later in the first quarter, Fesler called for a Janowicz punt on first down, but Michigan's Allen Wahl blocked it out of the end zone for a safety.

Michigan took the lead at the end of the first

half on one of the most controversial calls in Ohio State history. On third down on his own 13-yard line with 47 seconds until halftime, Fesler ordered Janowicz to punt again. It was only one of an astounding 45 punts on the day, easily a conference record, but this one was doomed. Michigan's Tony Momsen, an Ohio native, crashed through the line of scrimmage, blocked the punt off his chest, and fell on it in the end zone for the only touchdown of the game. Well, he actually fell on it twice, as it squirted away from him the first time.

Critics howled that Fesler should have tried to run out the first-half clock instead of risking a punt so deep in his own territory. The backlash he felt was a major reason Fesler tendered his resignation at the end of the season, citing the "immense" pressure fans put on him to win football games.

The weather at the Snow Bowl got even worse after halftime, so much so that the players on the field were often invisible from the upper reaches of the grandstands. With punts and turnovers galore, neither team came close to scoring in the second half, and Michigan won, 9–3—without picking up a single first down the entire game.

Overall, the Snow Bowl saw 10 fumbles. Michigan didn't complete any of its nine passes and gained only 27 yards on the ground. OSU went 3-for-18 passing for 25 yards and rushed for 16 more.

Some fans in attendance—the announced crowd of 50,503 was grossly exaggerated—cut holes in cardboard boxes and put them over their heads to protect their faces from the cold. Alcohol was applied to band members' instruments to keep the valves from freezing in place. The city mostly shut down after the game, and restaurants began run-

The 1950 "Snow Bowl" was a true test of coaching wits for Ohio State's Wes Fesler (left) and Michigan's Bennie Oosterbaan. Both coaches had to strive to find a strategy that would work in the appalling game conditions.

ning out of food. The university didn't resume classes until the next Thursday.

THE GREATEST GAME

Coincidentally, Ohio State also lost another famous game more than a half-century ago. In the first college football game dubbed the "Game of the Century," the Buckeyes welcomed undefeated Notre Dame to Ohio Stadium for a midseason contest. The game attracted national media coverage and was broadcast nationwide by CBS Radio.

Ohio State was considered to be the best team in the land that season, and Francis Schmidt's Buckeyes sure looked like it in the first half.

"I had never seen a Notre Dame offense so completely stopped," football historian Francis Wallace wrote. "When the Irish passed, the ball was intercepted and converted into a touchdown. It was difficult to get a running play started against the hard-charging Ohio State line. It was even hard to get a punt away."

The Buckeyes scored first as Frank Antenucci intercepted Mike Layden's pass and lateraled to Arthur Boucher for a 70-yard touchdown return. Later in the first quarter, OSU's Stanley Pincura picked off a pass near the 50-yard line to set up another touchdown drive. Joe Williams scored on a 15-yard run to give OSU a 13–0 lead after the extra point failed.

At halftime, Notre Dame Coach Elmer Layden—Mike's brother—implored his charges to "win this half for themselves." The speech apparently worked, as the Fighting Irish played with renewed vigor after the break. Notre Damze kept OSU's offense off the board—and started moving the ball a bit too—but couldn't break through in the third quarter. It was still 13–0 in Ohio State's favor heading into the fourth.

That's when Notre Dame halfback Andy Pilney rose

In the nearly-undisputed best game of the first 50 years of the 20th century, Notre Dame and Ohio State fought tooth and nail until the final gun. Here, the Notre Dame defense leaps to block a Buckeyes kick.

to the occasion. On the last play of the third quarter, he returned a short punt to the OSU 12-yard line. On the first play of the fourth, he completed a pass to Frank Gaul down to the 1. Steve Miller took it in from there, cutting ND's disadvantage to 13–6.

With about three minutes to play, the slashing Pilney led a drive down to the Buckeyes' 33-yard line, then hit a wide-open Mike Layden with a pass in the end zone with 1:40 left. But the extra point missed again, making it appear that Ohio State would escape with a victory and keep alive its national title hopes. Notre Dame tried an onside kick, but the Buckeyes recovered, to the delight of the 81,018 spectators at Ohio Stadium. All they had to do was run out the clock.

On first down, tailback Dick Beltz fumbled the ball on a hit by Pilney, and it was recovered by ND's Henry Pojman. On the first irish offensive play, Pilney scampered 30 yards to the 19—tearing the meniscus in his knee in the process. All-American Bill Shakespeare took over for Pilney as Notre Dame's quarterback and nearly gave Beltz a dose of redemption by throwing at him on his first pass.

But it just wasn't Beltz's day. He dropped the interception in the final minute, and Shakespeare took advantage of his second chance by finding Wayne Millner in the end zone for the game-winning touchdown. It was Ohio State's only loss in a, Big Ten championship-winning season.

When a panel of sportswriters voted on the best games of the first half of the 20th century, Notre Dame's 18–13 triumph over Ohio State was the landslide winner.

The Great Games